Confronting

JIHAD

Israel and the World After 9/11

Columns & Editorials by *The Jerusalem Post's*
Saul Singer

"With succinct commonsensical wisdom, historical penetration, inescapable logic, and scrupulous commentary, Saul Singer demonstrates the record, almost blow by blow, of the Palestinian Arab war against Israel from 1997 to the present hour. Generations from now, historians will turn to these level-headed essays for an understanding of how a beleaguered nation retained its ethical vitality, its dignity, and its sense of civilization's imperatives. And readers who may require a Guide for the Perplexed concerning the current travail of the Jewish state will be illumined by necessary insights not often found in the American press. *Confronting Jihad* carries the indispensable freight of political and moral truth-telling." – *Cynthia Ozick*

Confronting JIHAD

Israel and the World After 9/11

Saul Singer

Cold Spring Press

Cold Spring Press

P.O. Box 284
Cold Spring Harbor, NY 11724
E-mail: Jopenroad@aol.com

Copyright©2003 by Saul Singer
– All Rights Reserved –
ISBN: 1-59360-001-1
Library of Congress Control No. 2003110556

Front cover photo©Ariel Jerozolimski

To my brother Alex Singer, whose life, words, and art continue to inspire me and countless others who only came to know him after his death, and to Jeanne Singer, our grandmother, a writer and Alex's drawing partner, a colleague of Eleanor Roosevelt's, who moved to Israel at the age of 82, and who loves everything that I write.

Contents

Foreword

by William Kristol
Editor, *The Weekly Standard*

It is an honor to be associated, if only by virtue of this brief foreword, with this book of essays by Saul Singer. Why? Singer isn't the only fine editorialist writing on Israel and the Middle East. He's not the only commentator who presciently criticized the Oslo "peace process." He's not the only analyst who has patiently tried to keep the Bush and Sharon governments on track in the past couple of years. But no one else, in my judgment, has written regularly about Israel in recent years with more unapologetic honesty, and with more unself-conscious moral clarity, than Singer. His character, as well as his mind, are visible in these essays, and that's why it's an honor to present them, and him, to American readers.

The essays are short, easy to read, and well-organized, so I won't here slow down the reader from getting to the book itself. I will simply call attention to the fact, alluded to at times by Singer, that there is much to be learned from these essays not just about Israel but about America.

There's much to be learned about the similarities (and differences) between Israel's and America's wars on terror (or is it one war on terror?). But there's also much to be learned from these essays about America, because America, like Israel, is a democracy. And America, like Israel, is a democracy committed to certain high principles, seeking, like Israel, to make a distinctive contribution to the family of nations. In considering Singer's thoughtful treatment of Israel's challenges, we learn to think about our own. In considering how Israel has borne her burdens, we learn to think about how to bear our own. In learning about Israel's lessons, we learn to think about lessons for us, as Americans.

We also learn from these essays how to think about politics. Reading these editorials and columns produced on deadline, in the heat of events, one sees a fine political mind at work, making judgments, considering distinctions, coming to conclusions. History and hindsight have their place. But there is nothing more educational than seeing real, informed, intelligent political thinking taking place in real time. That is what we have here.

One example only. In Singer's first column after September 11, on September 14, he wrote: "There are 189 members of the United Nations. Roughly five of them use terrorism as an instrument of national policy. America's goal should be to reduce the number of governments that support terrorism to zero by the time the new soaring, wispy, inspiring World Trade Center is rebuilt. This goal may sound utopian, but it is both realistic and necessary." Has anyone captured the aim of our war on terror more succinctly and more eloquently in the two years since Singer wrote these words?

Acknowledgments

About half of the pieces in this collection are editorials, which means they were published unsigned, representing the voice of the *Jerusalem Post*. The process of deciding what to write about and what position to take usual fell to me and the editor-in-chief. Though the editor-in-chief would bear ultimate responsibility for what I wrote, I have always been given much flexibility, and have never, to my memory, had to write something I really disagreed with.

I am therefore indebted to David Bar-Illan, the outgoing editor who recommended me as an editorial writer to his successor, Jeff Barak, and to David Makovsky, Carl Shrag, and our current editor-in-chief, Bret Stephens. If I have been on the right track, all of them deserve much credit for either indulging or steering me there.

In January 2001 I began writing a weekly column under my own byline called "Interesting Times." It was with some trepidation that I broke out of the comfortable anonymity of editorial writing, but it was about time that I take credit or blame for my opinions rather than hide behind the good name of the *Jerusalem Post*. My thanks to Jeff Barak, during his second stint as editor, for giving me this opportunity. In addition, my colleagues Amotz Asa-El, Calev Ben-David, Elliot Jager, Ruthie Blum, and Judy Montagu have been invaluable sounding boards at all stages, but particularly in deciding which ideas are worth expressing on paper.

I am grateful to Bret Stephens for appointing me editor of the opinion pages, for bringing his own rich experience from one of the world's greatest newspapers, the *Wall Street Journal*, for indulging my making time for this project, and for his friendship and guidance as writer and colleague. He has been, for me and the *Jerusalem Post*, a tide that raises all boats.

I want to thank my family: my father, Max Singer, for being my intellectual mentor and model for fearless and creative thinking, my mother, Suzanne Singer, for contributing considerable time and her own professional skills gleaned from over 25 years of editorial work, and our children Noa, Tamar, and Yarden for helping to keep me grounded in some semblance of a more innocent reality.

Speaking of reality, I cannot fully convey the contribution of my wife Wendy, my first editor and reality check. It is not pleasant to imagine how my writings would have turned out absent her sharp editorial eye, and as head of the American Israel Public Affairs Committee's office in Jerusalem, her counsel based on knowledge of the inner workings of both the American and Israeli systems at the highest levels. Without her personal and professional help, carving this book out of our lives would have been impossible.

Introduction

In the summer of 2002, on my first visit to the United States since September 11, I remember being struck by the crowds of people at outdoor cafés or in malls without any security guard checking people as they came in. It took a few days to shed my Israeli sense that every public place – from kindergartens to banks – needed someone at the entrance to check pocketbooks and pat people down looking for suicide bomb belts. In Israel such security measures had become an almost unnoticed part of our lives, like metal detectors in airports, only everywhere. I did not feel oppressed by this. Yet spending some time in a place where such precautions were not taken seemed like a strange, almost reckless, form of freedom.

After 9/11, many commented that America had become like Israel. But less than a year after that event, Israel and America felt like they were different worlds. Life in America was not quite the same as before but, compared to Israel, had gone more or less back to normal. By contrast, the attacks against Israelis that had begun a year before 9/11 were still continuing almost three years later.

If there is a thread running through the essays of this book, it is that there is less separating these two worlds than meets the eye. The war is the same war, the enemy is the same enemy, and the strategy for victory is the same strategy.

Until a short time ago, almost no one appreciated this, including Israelis and Americans. Israel's struggle for survival and America's security were seen to be completely separate. Since Israel's lightning victory in the 1967 Six Day War, in which it captured the West Bank, Gaza Strip, the Golan Heights, and the Sinai, the Arab-Israeli conflict has been understood as one between Israeli security and Palestinian rights. This struggle seemed to have had as much to do with Western

11

security as other local disputes, such as Northern Ireland or Cyprus – that is to say, nothing.

On September 11, 2001, however, three hijacked aircraft were steered into the World Trade Center towers and the Pentagon, and a fourth was brought down by its passengers before it could reach its target, perhaps the Capitol or the White House. The hijackers, 15 Saudis and 4 Egyptians, did not act as part of the Arab-Israeli conflict, but rather aimed to open a much broader front: pitting militant Islam versus the leader of the free world, the United States.

To the hijackers, destroying Israel would be, of course, desirable, but the real target was American civilization. It is America that ultimately stands in the way of the spread of fundamentalist Islamic regimes, such as the Taliban in Afghanistan and the mullahs in Iran. America embodies the very freedom and modernity that the Islamists reject and oppose, first for their own people, then the world.

But even after 9/11, the connection between the two conflicts has been unclear. Was not American support for Israel a reason that al-Qaida attacked? If Israel could be compelled to give the Palestinians what they want, would not a major cause of Arab enmity for America be removed? Luckily, most Americans do not think this way and support Israel despite the knowledge that it makes America's enemies angrier. They instinctively understand that doing what terrorists want does not make them stop, but makes them want more.

On the human level, the intersection between the two conflicts was most sharpened just before the war in Iraq. Israel was at that time still contending with the usual spate of terrorist attacks, but in addition had to prepare for a possible missile attack from Iraq, as occurred in 1991 during the first Gulf War.

Our daughter's nursery school, at Jerusalem's Kol Haneshama Synagogue, was confronted with a concrete problem: how to explain to four-year-old children why they were being asked to try on gas masks designed to protect against chemical or biological attack?

In our case, the teacher, Anat, called the children into the building's bomb shelter (almost all Israeli public buildings are so equipped), took out a mask and told them that there is a war with Iraq, and that Iraq is far away from Israel. She then told the kids that if the war should come even close to Israel, she would make sure that they are all safe. In order for the children to stay healthy and safe, they would each need to wear a gas mask. Anat added gently but firmly that these masks are not like those they just wore for the Jewish holiday of Purim, where the children can say "yes" or "no" depending on their mood. With these masks, they were not allowed to say no. With this, she gave them snacks in the shelter, and managed to ensure a positive, educational, but still serious encounter with the current reality of living in this region.

The people of Israel have shown remarkable resilience in the face of overlapping threats and a war that seems to have no fronts or boundaries. On the human level, we have adapted – sometimes, it seems, too much so.

The process, however, of integrating the two conflicts has, in both American and Israeli minds, been a long one and is not yet complete. The challenge of the Arab-Israeli conflict is still mainly seen as one of inducing Israel to fulfill Palestinian needs rather than of compelling the Arab world to end its jihad against Israel.

Israelis have been debating for years whether a Palestinian state is necessary to ensure that their country remains Jewish and democratic or, alternatively, a Trojan horse threatening Israel's existence. Ariel Sharon's joining the former camp indicates that this debate has been resolved in favor of statehood. But the emphasis on creating a Palestinian state tends to distract from the fact that Israel and America are both at the receiving ends of what is essentially the same jihad: an expansionist war by militant Islamists who cannot tolerate any form of non-Islamic power.

When the Palestinians not only turned down the state that Israeli Prime Minister Ehud Barak offered them at Camp David in the summer of 2000, but launched a wave of terrorism a few months later, it became clear to Israelis that they wanted a state instead of Israel, not beside Israel.

The corollary of this realization, that the desire to destroy Israel is a branch of the desire to destroy America, has not completely sunk in. The unity of the conflicts and the implications for both countries is one thread running through this collection of editorials and columns written over six years for the *Jerusalem Post*. Another is the journey Israelis have taken from the euphoria of the Oslo period, to holding together as a society under a threat of terror perhaps more ubiquitous and pervasive than any people has ever known.

Part of the journey has been continuing to contend with the many challenges and dilemmas that have percolated in the background, under the shadow of the debate over peace and security. While under attack, Israel has held two elections in which the religious-secular divide also featured prominently. The economy, though oddly absent from the political debate, is high on the minds of most Israelis, who are suffering under one of the longest and deepest downturns in years. Lastly, there is the demographic crisis facing the Jewish people which should be of greatest concern in North America and in Israel, its two largest communities.

In all, I have never found the title of my column, "Interesting Times" – based on the alleged Chinese curse "may you live in interesting times" – to be overtaken by events, as much as I might wish it would be. Israel, more than anything, aspires to be a "normal" country with less weighty things to worry about. Even then, however, there will be people like me who want even more than normalcy, who believe that Israel can make a contribution to the family of nations beyond its diminutive size.

Saul Singer
Jerusalem, Israel
September 2003

1. Ephemeral Peace

From early 1997 up to the beginning of the fighting in Israel in September 2000.

I hope this editorial gets points for prescience, since it named as "flies in the ointment" all three countries that five years later President George W. Bush would label the "axis of evil." On the other hand, it did not foresee that militant Islam would rise up to become a global threat to the free world, along the lines of Nazism and Communism.

Bush, by declaring that the US would not tolerate rogue nations developing weapons of mass destruction, and by ousting Saddam Hussein according to this doctrine, has taken great strides toward closing the "window of vulnerability" discussed here.

1997: A Year for Action
January 1, 1997

In a provocative book of the same title, Francis Fukuyama predicted that mankind had reached the "end of history." If history is marked by great upheavals and conflicts, then the year 1996 does indeed seem to mark a hiatus in history, at least in part of the world. In the Middle East, of course, history continues apace.

The collapse of the Soviet Union and the end of the Cold War left the Western model of democratic politics and free market economics as the basic paradigm aspired to by nations the world over. In those regions where democracy prevails, there is peace and prosperity. Western Europe is moving towards deeper integration, including the adoption of a single European currency. Conflicts continue among some democratic countries, but the closest thing most democracies have to war is a trade dispute.

In the rest of the world – including central Europe, the nations of the former Soviet Union, the Middle East, parts of Asia, and most of Africa – old-fashioned history continues. This other world still lives with dictatorship, disease, poverty, and war.

Israel, in effect, straddles the two worlds. It is a thriving democracy stuck in the middle of a neighborhood in which military power remains critical to survival, and modernity is still considered a threat rather than an aspiration.

The primary thrust of history is now towards the expansion of the areas of peace and democracy, and the shrinking of the areas of turmoil, poverty, and dictatorship. The good news is that the democratic revolution today has no long-term, worldwide competition. Communism retains its grip on a few countries, but it has collapsed as an ideological alternative.

Nationalism and fundamentalism remain powerful forces in some places, but they are unlikely to resist the human yearning for freedom.

Right now, for example, the people of Serbia are using peaceful mass protests to reverse the stealing of local elections by President Slobodan Milosevic. In the end, as in the rest of central Europe, nationalism will prove to be a weak reed on which to sustain legitimacy, and the dictator will back down.

Closer to home, Islamic fundamentalism may temporarily gain momentum in some economically struggling quasi-dictatorships, but in the meantime it is collapsing from sheer exhaustion at its center of power, Iran.

The regimes of Iran, Iraq, North Korea, Syria and Libya remain the most troublesome flies in the ointment of democratic progress in the world today. The question facing the West is whether it will allow them to win the race between decreasing political legitimacy and increasing military power.

During the Cold War, aggressive dictatorships were protected from any serious challenges by the patronage of the Soviet Union. Since then, as the Gulf war illustrated, they remain vulnerable to the West's concerted effort to defend itself. The problem is that it is becoming easier for rogue nations to build or obtain weapons of mass destruction that not only threaten other nations, but limit the West's ability to respond.

If Saddam Hussein had waited until he had built nuclear weapons before invading Kuwait (a few years by many estimates), the United States might not have gone to war against Iraq [in 1991]. To borrow a Cold War term, the rogue states are now within a window of vulnerability between the collapse of the Soviet Union and their acquisition of weapons of mass destruction. That window is rapidly closing. In the end, the technology of destruction will not protect them from the technology of communications, which is rendering closed regimes porous to the infectious will to freedom. But even dying regimes can cause tremendous damage and, to a small country like Israel, pose an existential threat.

The West's record to date of responding to this threat is neither encouraging nor adequate. The United States has failed to convince Europe and Japan to economically isolate anti-Western regimes, and is under pressure to weaken its own 'containment' policy.

The European claim that its 'critical dialogue' is somehow more effective at moderating Iran's behavior is embarrassingly hollow. It is nothing more than a thinly disguised form of appeasement that prolongs the life of the regime which takes advantage of the time to enhance its ability to blackmail the West.

Evidence is mounting that the bomb which killed 19 American servicemen in Saudi Arabia last year was planted by Iranian-trained operatives. The US should respond to this attack by stepping up pressure on Iran on a multilateral basis through a combination of military and diplomatic actions.

With a secretary of state-designee fresh out of the United Nations [Madeleine Albright], it makes sense to finally employ Chapter 7 of the UN Charter, which provides for a series of economic and military sanctions against nations that threaten international peace. In the past, these provisions were a dead letter because of the Soviet Union's inevitable veto. It still would take some doing to convince the Security Council to take serious action, but a US determined to breathe meaning into the principle of collective security could carry the day.

As 1997 begins, history may be taking a break, but it is not over. It is too soon for the US to hang up its gloves and declare victory. The time for concerted action against growing threats to the international order is now, not when the countries posing those threats become better-armed and more desperate.

◆ ◆ ◆

The debate over peace and security has dominated Israeli politics since before the founding of the state. This is a country full of unfinished business that has been set aside for a day in which existential issues have finally been resolved. When this was written, that day seemed to be coming in the near future.

The Year Ahead
April 20, 1999

The first thing to celebrate about Israel's 51st birthday is that the jubilee year is over. Israel's jubilee year came at an awkward time, a time of transition during which it was difficult to celebrate and think expansively of the nation's past and future. This awkwardness continues into the anniversary beginning tonight, but the number 51 is not so portentous, so we can relax in our awkwardness.

In the past year, Israel's population topped the six million mark. Though the population growth rate is down a bit due to a decline in immigration, the 1998 growth rate of 2.3 percent is still higher than most Western countries.

Like an adolescent, Israel is growing and changing at the same time, and perspective is in particularly short supply.

By most measures, Israel is a phenomenal success story and, as Prime Minister Binyamin Netanyahu crows in his Independence Day message to Diaspora Jews, "better prepared than ever to meet the challenges of our time." What began as an ancient dream has become a thriving reality. A nation whose survival was in question since the day of its birth is now militarily and economically a regional power.

Even the social splits that rightly concern most Israelis tend to obscure what should not be taken for granted: an incredibly diverse population, most of whom grew up in the authoritarian cultures of the Soviet bloc and Arab world, has created a working democracy.

If anything, many of the problems facing Israel arise from the very normalcy to which the nation has strived so successfully. The loss of identity stemming from absorption into a global, modern, information age society tends to increase with Israel's success.

While the IDF is reporting that the number of soldiers requesting combat units is up substantially over the past two years, the connection of these same youth to Israel may be weakening. As one teenager told *Ma'ariv*, "I [plan] to go to a combat unit, to go into Lebanon. But I will live wherever I can find the best conditions. In general, I wouldn't mind living in New York."

As Diaspora Jewry struggles with a crisis of continuity, Israelis are only slowly awakening to a similar challenge. Just as American Jews, in particular, are having trouble maintaining their identity in the attractive, open society around them, Israel is increasingly drawn to assimilate into the international community from which it has been excluded for so long.

The halls of the United Nations may still be hostile territory, but Israelis Dana International and Linor Abergil won the Eurovision and Miss World contests. Israelis probably travel more per capita than any other nation. Israeli companies have gravitated towards the internet, the ultimate global homogenizer.

Some of Israel's desire to become one with the world is probably a temporary attraction to what was forbidden fruit. The countries that Israelis are now barred from, or cannot easily fly to, are few and far between. But freedom to travel does not change Israel's diminutive size, which will always engender in its inhabitants a cultural and physical wanderlust.

'The land is very small,' wrote poet Yehuda Amichai, 'and I can contain it inside me. The erosion of the land erodes my rest, and the level of the Kinneret is always on my mind.' As only a poet can do, Amichai captured both the Israeli sense of confinement and what is attractive about it – the sense of a personal, graspable neighborhood within the global village.

It is not too soon, however, to ask how Israel will nurture its unique identity once the edge is taken off the burning issues of the peace process and the religious secular rift. As intractable as these issues may seem at the moment, they are probably not the challenges that will dominate the coming century, perhaps not even beyond the next decade.

For all of its history, Israel has busied itself with the challenges of survival - both physically in the region and living together as a society. As we look ahead in the final year of the millennium, the longer term challenges facing Israel arise from the successful conquest of these historic threats. Do we want Israel to be so 'normal' as to be indistinguishable from other nations, or does the 'Jewish state' proclaimed in the Declaration of Independence have meaning beyond being a state in which Jews live?

The almost issue-free election campaign does not bode well for addressing even the more immediate problems in sight. But the general ideological confusion has perhaps created an opportunity to place new items on the national agenda. The election of 1999, for all its unprecedented aspects, is firmly ensconced in the politics of the past. A modest goal for the year ahead would be to begin to grapple with the challenges of national identity, not just those of national survival.

◆ ◆ ◆

When Ehud Barak ousted Binyamin Netanyahu in the 1999 elections, there was a huge sigh of relief on both sides of the ocean. The Netanyahu period seemed dominated by strife, between Arabs and Israelis, between Israelis, and between Jerusalem and Washington. Barak seemed to be the perfect antidote: supportive of the peace process, but with the security credentials of a former Israeli Defense Forces Chief of Staff.

Here we see Barak's caution toward the interim phase of the process, which later made his sweeping concessions a year later at Camp David all the more surprising.

Peace is No Simple Game
July 16, 1999

The two strikingly different tones struck by US President Bill Clinton and Prime Minister Ehud Barak on the eve of their first tete-a-tete in Washington provide the clearest signal yet that, despite Barak's election victory over Binyamin Netanyahu, there is no guarantee Israel and the United States are fully in tune on how to restore the peace process's rhythm and momentum.

Clinton, drumming the beat of excited impatience, talked of 'energizing' the peace process and, in a revealing self-description, said: "I'm as eager as a kid with a new toy." As every parent knows, such eagerness often ends in tears as the new toy fails to match the excited child's expectations or over-eager handling.

Barak has tried to muffle in advance the chorus proclaiming that peace is at hand. In interviews with both the *New York Times* and the *Washington Post*, Barak deliberately stressed his aim of renegotiating parts of the Wye agreement and of transposing American involvement in the peace process from a major to a minor key.

While it is more than likely that both leaders will portray their first meeting last night as a great success it would be a mistake to assume that, now Netanyahu is no longer conducting Israel's foreign policy, Washington and Jerusalem have no differences as to how the process should proceed.

Of course, on the issue of direct American involvement in the minutia of the peace process, both sides will probably agree that now is the time for the US to stand back. One of the major failings of the Wye agreement, as negotiated by Netanyahu, was the umpire role it granted Washington. Instead of Israeli security officials deciding whether the Palestinians were meeting their commitment to fight terror effectively, the Central Intelligence Agency became the final arbiter of disputes between Israel and the Palestinian Authority.

In his interviews, Barak talked about the inappropriateness of this CIA involvement, saying the Americans should return to their traditional role of facilitators, and stop acting as "arbitrator, policeman, and judge." This has already met with a prompt, positive American response, with State Department spokesman James Rubin pointing out that the Americans only became involved due to the breakdown of trust between Israel and the Palestinians. The US, said Rubin, would be happy for Israel and the PA to resume settling these disputes bilaterally, without outside intervention.

Whether the Americans will be just as happy with Barak's desire to reopen the Wye package, to which Clinton devoted so much time and energy, is another matter. Barak, correctly, is arguing that it makes no sense – if Israel and the Palestinians are nearing a final agreement – to waste valuable political capital on small-scale pullbacks in the West Bank. Barak has described a troop withdrawal in terms of giving birth – it's painful, but gives happiness later. As he told the *Washington Post*, "You will never ask a woman to give birth in three different stages. We have to give birth to one peace agreement, and we should be careful not to limit or to reduce the chances of achieving it by cutting it into too many painful steps."

Barak's point here of "one peace agreement" is crucial. If Israel is to hand over significant amounts of territory and acquiesce to Palestinian statehood, then the agreement under which it does so has to guarantee Israel a full peace in return.

There is no point in Israel agreeing to give up all its bargaining chips if the really troublesome issues of the peace process with the Palestinians – Jerusalem and the refugees – are left unresolved, to be settled at some later date. Even Israel's greatest friend, Clinton himself, has recently disappointed on both these issues, introducing a jarring note with his refusal to move the US Embassy to Jerusalem and his remarks on the Palestinian right of return.

For Barak truly to succeed in his first visit to Washington as premier, he must convince Clinton not only of his sincere desire for peace, but also of the difficulties that lie ahead. Middle East diplomacy is no simple game or toy to be played with in haste.

◆ ◆ ◆

The year 1999, with Ehud Barak in office and before the Camp David summit, is remembered as a hopeful time, a time when Israelis and Palestinians seemed headed smoothly toward a peace agreement. Those who raised the issue of Palestinian incitement at this time, as we did here, were largely dismissed as worry-warts and trouble-makers who threatened the broadly positive flow of events.

Looking back, what is striking is how openly vicious the Palestinians were toward Israel, even under a Labor government, and even in front of the American first lady. If this had been an isolated incident, it would perhaps have been properly ignored. But at this juncture, incitement against Israel had become systemic, and fatal to the prospects for peace.

Poisonous Palestinian Rhetoric
November 15, 1999

In a prepared speech with the visiting Hillary Clinton at her side, Suha Arafat last Thursday unexpectedly launched into a primitive diatribe against Israel that smacked of classic antisemitic blood libels. Accusations so fantastic and vicious might have turned heads even between peoples at war; at the current juncture they bring into question the nature of the Palestinian conception of peace.

According to Yasser Arafat's wife, "For years, our people have been subjected to a daily, intensive use of poison gas by the Israeli forces, which has led to an increase in cancer and other horrible diseases among women and children ... Israel has [also] chemically contaminated about 80 percent of water sources used by Palestinians."

It is hard to understand how someone could believe such baseless fabrications, let alone disseminate them at such a high-profile public event. Indeed, these comments are clearly cut from the cloth of centuries – old antisemitic fantasies in which Jews are accused of poisoning children and other unspeakable acts. Perhaps inadvertently, Suha managed to combine a medieval-style blood libel, a Nazi-era reference to poison gas, and modernist concern for the environment all in the same repulsive brew.

One can only hope, for her sake, that Hillary Clinton's failure to immediately protest Suha Arafat's remarks was related to an incomplete simultaneous translation. Yet this does not explain why her eventual response was of the tepid "not helpful to the peace process" variety. For his part, President Bill Clinton strongly protested the remarks directly to Yasser Arafat. In response, Palestinian negotiator Saeb Erekat expressed regret for any embarrassment caused to Hillary Clinton, and claimed Suha Arafat's mention of poison gas was a "confused" reference to tear gas used by Israeli security forces.

This is, of course, a wholly unsatisfactory response given the magnitude of the charges leveled at Israel. Prime Minister Ehud Barak, rather than being satisfied by an apology elicited by and directed toward the United States, should take the opportunity to demand that the Palestinians finally implement their commitment to ending virulent incitement against Israel.

Though it is important to distinguish between obnoxious speech and incitement to violence, Suha Arafat's diatribe was correctly deemed by the Israeli members of the joint Israeli-American-Palestinian anti-incitement committee as falling in the latter category. Since the assassination of Yitzhak Rabin, calling a political leader a 'traitor' or 'murderer,' though not a direct call to violence, is correctly seen as incitement to violence. By the same token, charging that Israel is poisoning women and children clearly risks provoking violence.

Anti-incitement committee chairman Ya'akov Erez did lodge a formal complaint regarding Suha Arafat's remarks, but the matter should not end there. Incitement is not only inconsistent with the peace process, it is the antithesis of building peace. Yet the Palestinians regard incitement as a nuisance at best and a right at worst.

As recently as March 1, 1999, Palestinian Authority official Othman Abu Gharbiya explained the tenets of the right-to-incite school: "They [the Israelis] talk about [our] incitement and want to kill our people's spirit and erase our heritage, our truths, our history, and our people. [But] the spirit of our people lies in those national inciters and in our hate of the invaders and the invasion [of our land.] We understand incitement as meaning a call to violence against innocents, but not against others [who are not innocent.] We are right to believe,' Abu Gharbiya continued, 'that the rifle is a means of life and not death..." (Al-Hayat al-Jadida, as translated by the Middle East Media and Research Institute).

These remarks, made at a ceremony to award Palestinian poets, novelists, and painters, can be regarded as not only justifying but encouraging incitement. One might argue that years of indoctrination in the ideology of "armed struggle" cannot be erased over night. The problem, however, is not that the Palestinians have failed to eradicate incitement, but they have barely begun to try. The poison of incitement continues to be spread in mosques, by PA officials, on Palestinian television, and in Palestinian textbooks.

If Israel and the Palestinians are truly partners in the peace process, the problem of incitement should be tackled in a partner-like way. A first step might be for Suha Arafat to accept Environment Minister Dalia Itzik's invitation to jointly examine environmental threats to Israelis and Palestinians. If she did, Suha Arafat would learn that raw sewage from Kalkilya and Nablus is today polluting Israeli rivers, and that illegal Palestinian garbage dumps are polluting ground water used by Israelis and Palestinians.

For years, the Palestinians have refused to cooperate with Israel in building sewage treatment plants and proper garbage disposal sites. Given a cooperative spirit, Israeli environmental awareness would no doubt improve as well. But by making such environmental cooperation further away than ever, Suha Arafat is not only perpetuating the pollution she derides, but polluting the atmosphere of peace with poisonous rhetoric.

◆ ◆ ◆

Immediately after the failure of the July 2000 Camp David summit, President Bill Clinton made it fairly clear that Ehud Barak had made extraordinary concessions, while Yasser Arafat had not made similar efforts. This was an understatement, since Arafat had not even begun to negotiate, but at least there was no attempt to spread blame equally.

By the time Barak went to Camp David, his government had fallen apart and his electoral prospects seemed slim. Understanding the need to support Barak, and to pressure the Palestinians to reengage, Clinton raised the ideas of moving the US embassy to Jerusalem and downgrading the US relationship with the Palestinians.

This moment, then, is a glimpse of the road not taken in US policy. Clinton's threats to the Palestinians turned out to be empty. The Palestinians not only refused to compromise, but launched a violent campaign against Israel a few months later. Following Clinton's original logic, the US should have rushed to demonstrate American support for Israel and impose a diplomatic cost for Palestinian behavior. Instead, the opposite happened – the US reverted back to evenhandedness, holding both sides responsible for ending the "cycle of violence."

Jerusalem, Israel
July 31, 2000

US President Bill Clinton's remarkable interview on Friday with Israel Television's Channel 1 has been greeted with anger by Palestinians and cynicism by many Israelis. The critics in both camps, and on both sides of the Israeli political spectrum, are bristling at what seems to be a transparent attempt to extract Prime Minister Ehud Barak from a political corner. As a political intervention, Clinton's move may back-fire. In terms of the peace process, however, being an "honest broker" should not exclude periodic departures from mechanical neutrality.

In his interview, Clinton began by revealing that he was planning a "comprehensive review to improve the US-Israel strategic relationship." With this, he signaled that the US effort to help "modernize the IDF" was officially being brought out of mothballs, having been set aside by the collapse of the Syrian talks and the flap over the just-cancelled Israeli radar sale to China.

Also on the security side, Clinton lauded Barak's withdrawal from Lebanon and pledged to help Israel with the security implications of that move, including helping the government of Lebanon take control over the area Israel evacuated.

The biggest bombshells, however, were Clinton's unsolicited comments on moving the US Embassy to Jerusalem and barely veiled threats regarding a Palestinian unilateral declaration of independence.

On Jerusalem, Clinton claimed that he has "always wanted to move our embassy to West Jerusalem," but had not done so because he did not want to undermine the US role as "honest broker." "But in light of what happened," Clinton explained, "I've taken [the embassy policy] under review." It is a shame that the timing of this announcement – just before a crucial week of Knesset votes for Barak – has led to its automatic discounting as a legitimate, as opposed to political, step in support of the peace process. The Palestinians have cried foul, claiming that Clinton's move reveals the US to be the "Zionist agent" they knew it was all along. Clinton's announcement, however, far from violating the US role as honest broker, should be regarded as the logical consequence of the lopsided behavior of the two sides at Camp David.

By all accounts, Barak surprised even the Palestinians by smashing Israeli taboos regarding Jerusalem at Camp David. It is not entirely clear what Barak agreed to, as opposed to 'agreeing to consider.' What is clear is that Israel was willing to negotiate in earnest over Jerusalem in an honest attempt to achieve a comprehensive peace.

Palestinian Authority Chairman Yasser Arafat, by contrast, was reportedly not willing to negotiate on the basis of numerous proposals made by the United States, leading both Israel and the US to conclude that agreement could not be reached.

The question now is what are the consequences of Arafat's decision not to stray substantially from the maximalist declarations he has been making for years, and continues to make following the summit. In such a case, an honest broker might conclude that the Palestinians were not serious about obtaining a peace agreement, so there is no reason for US policy to continue bending over backwards toward the Palestinians on Jerusalem.

The US, it should be remembered, has greatly weakened Israel's position in negotiations over Jerusalem by not recognizing Israel's presence in any part of the city. It was one thing, all these years, to assert that Israel must negotiate over the eastern part of the city, quite another to refuse to accept Israel's designation of her own capital. Even today, passports and birth certificates issued to American citizens in Jerusalem imply that the city is floating in thin air by listing the place of issue or birth as 'Jerusalem,' rather than 'Jerusalem, Israel.' Moving the US Embassy to Jerusalem now would not undo the damage done to Israel's negotiating position on a matter central to Israel's interest. It would, however, signal to the Palestinians that there is a price to be paid for a refusal to make serious compromises on extremist positions.

Similarly, Clinton's polite threat in case of a unilateral declaration of independence also squares well with the role of a broker trying to press both sides toward a comprehensive agreement. According to Clinton, not only would US assistance to the Palestinians be put at risk, but the "entire [US-Palestinian] relationship." At Camp David, the Palestinians put into question not only their willingness to compromise on Jerusalem and the "right of return," but whether they are really willing to agree to a complete end to the conflict. Clinton and Barak, reasonably or not, seem to be willing to give Arafat another chance. If that chance is not taken, however, moving the embassy should be the least of the consequences for rejecting peace.

◆   ◆   ◆

The September 2000 Millennium Summit at the United Nations was quite an event, and the hot diplomatic item was the Mideast peace deal that did not happen that summer at Camp David, but still seemed to have a prospect of coming together. Because of their respective roles at Camp David, Ehud Barak was the man of the hour, and Yasser Arafat was in the diplomatic doghouse – an unusual reversal of roles at the UN.

The irony is that Arafat only escaped his diplomatic isolation not by softening his Camp David positions but by launching the terror offensive that began a few weeks later, and continues nearly three years after that.

When this editorial was written, the deal seemed to be hung up on the future of the Temple Mount, the ancient platform built by Herod two thousand years ago of which the Western Wall, Judaism's holiest site is a part, and on which the al-Aksa mosque and the Dome of the Rock, both Muslim shrines, sit.

A Tale of Two Speeches
September 8, 2000

It is the year 2000 and 150 world leaders gather at the United Nations for the largest summit the planet has ever seen. The Middle East, as is its wont, monopolizes the limelight. The world looks on as the fate of a speck within a speck, the Temple Mount within the Old City of Jerusalem, hangs in the balance.

Some observers might wonder: What is it about this tiny place, no bigger than a few football fields, that there are proposals to parcel sovereignty over it in at least three ways – one arrangement for its outer wall, another for buildings sitting on it, and a third for the courtyard in between?

Such attempts to slice sovereignty into microscopic pieces cannot obscure the reality starkly revealed by the speeches of Prime Minister Ehud Barak and Palestinian Authority Chairman Yasser Arafat: Arafat speaks of sharing the city, but is unwilling to do just that; Barak speaks of keeping the city whole and yet is willing to explore ways for both parties to meet their needs.

With world leaders as his audience, Barak became the first Israeli leader to acknowledge Palestinian ties to Jerusalem. "We recognize that Jerusalem is also sacred to Moslems and Christians the world over, and cherished by our Palestinian neighbors," Barak declared. "A true peace will reflect all these bonds."

Arafat, in contrast, referred to Jerusalem as "the cradle of Christianity and the site of Prophet Mohammed's ascension to heaven," but pointedly omitted any Jewish connection to the city. Adding insult to injury, Arafat accused Israel of "attempts to Judaize Jerusalem."

Incredibly, Moslem clerics and Palestinian negotiators still question the Jewish connection to the Temple Mount, as if the 2,000-year-old structure was built to hold the Islamic shrines that appeared there almost seven centuries later. Denial, however, will not change the facts that Jerusalem was first made a capital by King David 3,000 years ago, and that his son, Solomon, built the First Temple there, on the hilltop where Jewish tradition holds that God stopped Abraham from sacrificing his son Isaac.

In a perhaps unparalleled commemoration of a particular historical event, every year Jews fast and sit in mourning on the floor of synagogues all over the world and, by candlelight, read the Book of Lamentations, an entire book of the Hebrew Bible describing the destruction of Jerusalem, centuries before Mohammad was born.

There is no comparison between the centrality of Jerusalem to Israel and the Jewish people, and the peripheral role the city played in Islamic history. Barak, however, was right to recognize that Palestinians have come to "cherish" Jerusalem, if only to highlight the Palestinian unwillingness to acknowledge any Jewish moral or historic claim to the city.

In his UN speech, Arafat claimed that, "We have agreed to share the city, in contrast to the attempts at monopolizing it." In doing so, he played upon the common impression that by arguing for splitting Jerusalem, the Palestinians are being reasonable, while Israel is selfishly claiming the entire city. In reality, it is Arafat who is unwilling to discuss anything short of full Palestinian sovereignty over what makes Jerusalem holy to Judaism and Islam: the Temple Mount.

Over the past 30 years Israel has bent over backwards to give the Islamic authorities (Wakf) control over the Temple Mount – to the point of allowing the Wakf to dig a huge hole in its surface with heavy machinery without any archaeological supervision and in blatant violation of Israel's Antiquities Preservation Law. Given Israel's longstanding willingness to delegate religious and civil authority over the Temple Mount, one might ask, why should ceding full sovereignty to the Palestinians be a show-stopper?

The reason is that, just as for 2,000 years of exile Jerusalem symbolized the Jewish yearning to return to Zion, Palestinian recognition of the Jewish connection to ancient Jerusalem would recognize the moral and historic right of Israel to exist in this land.

Accepting the Jewish connection to Jerusalem is tantamount to abandoning the Arab notion that the Jews are squatters on a land that is foreign to them, sort of Crusaders with computers who will go as quickly as they came.

Without recognizing Israel's ancient connection to Jerusalem, the Palestinians can cling to the notion that Israel exists only by might, not by right. It is no coincidence that the name 'Jerusalem' means 'City of Peace.' Arafat's willingness to make tough concessions in Jerusalem is the best measure of his willingness to enter into a real peace with Israel.

We can see the southernmost Jerusalem neighborhood of Gilo from the roof of our apartment. Jerusalem is a city of hills and valleys; Gilo is one hill away. At night, sometimes, we could hear the shooting between Israeli forces in Gilo and the Palestinians who were firing from Beit Jala, a neighborhood of Bethlehem just across a valley and within the range of simple machine gun. Our children would generally sleep through the noise, so we were spared having to explain to them what was going on so near to our home.

Beit Jala is the only neighborhood bordering Jerusalem that was in full Palestinian security control, what was called "Area A" under the Oslo Accords. The Palestinians chose to shoot from this area either because they knew Israel would not enter with its forces, or as a deliberate attempt to induce Israel to reenter Palestinian-controlled territory, which would provoke a crisis with the United States.

Blind Restraint
November 15, 2000

As four more Israelis were buried yesterday, including a 42-year-old mother of five who was gunned down gangland-style in a car near her home, it was painful to watch the helplessness of the government.

The choice between massive retaliation and total restraint is a false one; it is time for Israel to be less concerned about "burning bridges" and more concerned about forcing an end to the Palestinian attacks.

For over a month, Israelis have watched in dismay as the Lebanon that they thought they left behind has been neatly copied, only closer to home. Schoolchildren in Jerusalem's Gilo neighborhood study behind sandbags and concrete barriers, and their parents feel as if Jerusalem has become as exposed as Kiryat Shmona. More fundamentally, Israelis are being taught by their government to become used to a steady flow of casualties, and constantly reminded that there are "no military solutions" to such guerrilla warfare.

The Lebanon quagmire ended in a unilateral withdrawal and solemn assurances that any renewed attacks would be met with swift and massive retaliation against the nations responsible. The Palestinians, clearly, are attempting to produce a similar total Israeli withdrawal to the pre-1967 lines.

It does not help that Israelis see little comparison between the Lebanese and Palestinian situations. Israel had no claim or interest in remaining on Lebanese territory and no Israelis lived there. Israel's presence in Lebanon was purely military and tactical. The moment a better way could be found to protect the northern border, remaining there was more a sign of weakness and defeat than leaving.

Unfortunately, the precipitousness of Israel's flight from Lebanon, in the context of the utter collapse of our South Lebanese Army allies, made the withdrawal look nothing like a deliberate strategic choice. Now Israel is in the uncomfortable position of having to force the Palestinians to unlearn what for them was the graphic lesson of Lebanon: that Israel can be slowly bled into withdrawing from territory.

Israel's current policy of restraint tends to confirm the relevance of the Lebanese model in the Palestinian mind. To Palestinians and Israelis alike, the constant reminders by government ministers, generals, and pundits of the lack of a military solution bring back strong memories from Israel's Lebanon experience. In Lebanon, Israel's military options were limited by the nature of guerrilla warfare. In facing the Palestinians, in addition to the practical difficulties of dealing with hit-and-run attacks, there are the twin desires not to burn bridges with them while not succumbing to Yasser Arafat's attempt to broaden the conflict.

At the end of the day, according to the current mantra, both sides will return to the negotiating table. This may well be true, but it is not an argument for blind restraint. For Arafat, not only are the use of force and negotiations consistent, they are two sides of the same coin. Israel need not respond in kind, but neither can Israel act as if the need to defeat Arafat's attack is irrelevant to the negotiating process.

Arafat shows no concern that making Israel bleed will prevent a return to the negotiating table – on the contrary, he believes his

31

negotiating position will be strengthened. Israel should also not be concerned that vigorously defending itself will close the door to future negotiations.

Israel's moral and strategic desire to limit innocent Palestinian casualties is a valid, even necessary, reason for military restraint. But Israel has not yet taken numerous military and non-military steps that have little or no risk of producing such Palestinian casualties.

Israel is still transferring millions of shekels of tax remittances to the Palestinian Authority, still allowing cement to be delivered for construction in Gaza, and still facilitating much of the Palestinians' oil, electricity, and telecommunications infrastructure. Official Palestinian television and radio stations continue to incite further violence and Palestinian military training camps remain untouched.

Just as a situation as complicated as the current one has no simple military solution, it also has no solely diplomatic one. The current armed intifada must be made too costly for the Palestinians to continue by both military and diplomatic means. Excessive military restraint by Israel, coupled with President Bill Clinton's refusal to unequivocally fault the Palestinians for their attack, will allow the death toll to climb and further distance the prospects for peace.

2. Israel Alone

From the start of the war in Israel in late 2000 up to 9/11.

Rosh Hashana, the Jewish new year, is a two-day religious holiday. Religiously observant Israelis, who do not listen to the news over the holiday, emerged from this cocoon of time in synagogues and with their families to hear of the deadly rioting of both Israeli Arabs and the Palestinians in the territories.

For all the talk that violence would come, the actual descent into war after peace seemed to be within grasping distance was a severe shock. And it was not just any war, but one that swiftly moved from clashes with security forces to suicide bombings in Israeli buses, cafés, streets – almost anywhere people congregate. This is when it seemed that Oslo had died and our long September 11 began.

Arafat's Victims
October 2, 2000

The period of the Days of Awe, framed by Rosh Hashana and Yom Kippur, has been likened to a trial in which the Jewish people must defend itself before God, who is a merciful judge. The prayer book leaves little to the imagination, warning that in these very days God decides who will live and who will die, and spelling out the path of repentance that can, even at the eleventh hour, elicit a positive verdict.

The violent riots of the last few days clarify that the peace process has reached a similar stage in which the stakes are life or death, and not in a metaphorical sense. But while God works in mysterious ways, the reason for the deaths of the 29 Palestinians and two Israeli border policemen who lost their lives since Friday is painfully simple and clear: Palestinian Authority Chairman Yasser Arafat is once again attempting to negotiate with violence.

The supposed reason for the Palestinian riots – Likud leader Ariel Sharon's visit to the Temple Mount on Thursday – should be dismissed outright. First, it is inconceivable that the visit of anyone anywhere excuses deadly violence, unless one accepts the notion that the Palestinians are hopelessly violent people who cannot be held to normal standards of civilized behavior.

Second, the violence began with the bomb that killed an Israeli soldier in Netzarim the day before Sharon's visit. Third, and most significantly, violence of the scope recently seen – the worst rioting since 1996 – is effectively an act of will by the Palestinian leadership, for which Sharon's visit at most provided a convenient rallying cry.

Sharon's visit to the Temple Mount backfired, both because he is being widely blamed for provoking violence and because the hundreds of police needed to secure him illustrated the difficulty Israel has in exercising its sovereignty over the area. Even though most Israelis, including perhaps Prime Minister Ehud Barak, agree that the Temple Mount must remain under Israeli sovereignty, now many middle-of-the-road voters will have trouble believing that Sharon is capable of being a sincere participant in the peace process.

The United States, however, made a cardinal error by joining in the chorus of blaming Sharon. By saying, "Sharon's visit to the site caused these tensions," the State Department clearly implies that the violence was justified, no matter how strenuously it claims otherwise. Nothing could invite future violence more than any American understanding expressed for it, because a major goal of the violence is to elicit international sympathy for Palestinian demands.

Similarly, Israeli Arab MKs are making a mistake by openly expressing understanding for violent rioting by Palestinians and by Israeli Arabs. The Israeli Arab community cannot have it both ways: It cannot increasingly act with the Palestinian leadership against Israel and wage a successful battle for inclusion and respect within Israel.

The vast majority of Israeli Arabs, it is fair to estimate, want and deserve to improve their lot within Israel. By showing more interest in demonstrating solidarity with the Palestinian Authority, some Israeli Arab leaders are harming both their own constituents and the peace process. Few trends could be more poisonous to support for the peace process within Israel than the specter of Israeli Arabs becoming an arm of a future hostile Palestinian state.

Nor is this violence in the Palestinian interest, mainly because Palestinians are doing most of the dying. The gruesome televised pictures of the death of a 12-year-old Palestinian boy and wounding of his father who tried to save him indicate the depths to which the Palestinian use of violence for political gain will sink.

In any case, the ultimate responsibility for all the deaths among all sides lies with the party that has chosen to use violence as a negotiating tactic.

In fact, terming the violence a 'negotiating tactic' might dignify it too much. Many analysts believe that Egypt could not have made peace with Israel before claiming victory in the Yom Kippur War. Now Arafat is presumably torn between those who count the intifada of the 1980's as the Palestinian "War of Independence" and those who believe more blood must be let before accepting the peace agreement that is now more or less on the table. If so, the question becomes how many Palestinians and Israelis must die – not to change the terms of an agreement – but for Arafat to conclude that the time has come to make peace.

◆ ◆ ◆

The previous day Shoshanna Reis, 21, and Meir Bahrame, 35, were killed, and 60 wounded when a car bomb was detonated alongside a passing bus on Hadera's main street during rush hour. Two days before, a roadside bomb exploded at 7:30 in the morning alongside a bus carrying children to school from Kfar Darom, an Israeli settlement in the Gaza Strip. Miriam Amitai, 35, and Gavriel Biton, 34, were killed and 9 others, including 5 children, were injured – 5 of them seriously.

It is remarkable, looking back, that the Americans lecturing Israel about the "excessive use of force" passed largely without comment at the time. The reason was that the Israeli government, led by Ehud Barak, did not complain and indeed seemed to be in close coordination with the Clinton Administration. It is also striking how unsupportive the US could be toward Israel's need to fight terror, and what this says about attitudes toward terror before September 11, 2001.

The Cost of Evenhandedness
November 23, 2000

Last night's grisly bombing in Hadera demonstrates that Palestinian Authority Chairman Yasser Arafat's limitation on attacks from Palestinian areas, far from being a cease-fire, means that Israel itself is a free-fire zone. If US President Bill Clinton's pallid tolerance of Palestinian aggression continues, Israel will have no alternative but further military escalation.

On Monday morning, an Israeli school bus was bombed, killing two teachers and maiming at least three children for life. That day, Israel responded with missile strikes pinpointed on the headquarters and training bases of Fatah, the Tanzim, and Force 17, the forces that have led the armed attack. The State Department did not tarry in its response: Israel should "understand that the use of excessive force is not the right way to go." Though it was the strongest retaliation against the continuing wave of Palestinian terrorism until this writing, the response to the bombing of children clearly fell in the category of a dramatic signal rather than sustained warfare. No one believes that attacks against mostly empty buildings seriously raises the price of Palestinian aggression or will degrade their ability to carry out future attacks. Even the subsequent killing of a mid-level Fatah military leader cannot be considered more than minimal tit-for-tat retaliation, as opposed to an attempt at the decisive use of force.

Within Israel, the government's policy is rightly seen as one of maximum restraint, given the massive pressures to, as the slogan goes, "let the IDF win." Even the reporters at the US State Department were having some trouble understanding what spokesman Richard Boucher would consider a proper response, given his strong implication that Israel had acted excessively.

When asked how the US felt about the economic measures Israel has taken, Boucher replied, "We don't believe that squeezing the Palestinians economically is the right course of action." Nor is the US pincer action limited to the military and economic fronts.

When Foreign Minister Shlomo Ben-Ami had the temerity to suggest, in effect, that the international "fact-finding" mission be linked to a cease-fire on the ground, the US responded - no dice. "We understand Israel's concern that it will be difficult for the fact-finding committee to operate in a violent atmosphere," White House spokesman P.J. Crowley said. "At the same time we believe the fact-finding commission can play a role in assessing the reasons for the crisis."

The US position can be summarized thus: You, Israel, have no right to defend yourself either militarily, economically, or diplomatically. The best thing you can do, friend, is to sit quietly as your soldiers, citizens, and children are picked off and blown up, and wait for Yasser Arafat to return to the negotiating table.

It would be some, however minor, comfort if the US refusal to support even minimal and largely symbolic Israeli efforts at self-defense were a function of State Department evenhandedness run amuck, not the will of the president. Unfortunately, there is no basis for such a conclusion.

Clinton has become so involved in the Arab-Israeli struggle that he is informally referred to as the peace process' "desk officer." More fundamentally, it is Clinton himself who has been unwaveringly evenhanded since the Palestinian attack against Israel began.

On Sunday, when asked point-blank by CNN whether the burden for getting back to negotiations lay on one side or the other, Clinton offered, "I can't really say more than that it's a troubling, difficult, and painful situation, and we've got to find a way to end the violence. You don't have to end every single instance of it, but there has to be a dramatic reduction in the violence before the parties can talk again and make commitments again that could constitute a peace agreement."

The theme that both sides are equally responsible for "the cycle of violence" is repeated ad nauseum by Clinton and all senior administration officials, including Secretary of Defense William Cohen during his visit yesterday. The implications of the US refusal to call aggression and terrorism by their name is as simple as it is deadly: Israeli and Palestinian blood will continue to flow.

Before he became president, Bill Clinton told Jewish groups that his beloved pastor made him swear on his deathbed never to turn his back on the Jewish state. This story captures Clinton's image, both here and in the US, as the best friend Israel has ever had.

In the spirit of the Thanksgiving holiday Americans celebrate today, Israel must never take for granted that critical and unique bonds of support exist within the US. At times like this, however, Clinton's bear hug foreign policy costs lives. The assault on Israel will only end when the US supports Israel's right to minimal self-defense and imposes a steep diplomatic price on continued Palestinian aggression.

◆ ◆ ◆

Whenever Israel is being attacked or threatened, there are always two general directions for US policy: urging Israeli restraint or backing Israel's right to respond. At this time, the US took the former approach regarding Palestinian attacks and the latter with respect to threats from Syria. The former approach worked quickly to deter Syria; the latter has allowed the Palestinian offensive to continue for almost three years, resulting in the deaths of thousands of Israelis and Palestinians.

A Timely Warning
December 5, 2000

On Sunday, US Ambassador to Israel Martin Indyk warned that war could break out in the Middle East. The US has already taken some important steps to pressure Syria not to play with fire on the Lebanese border. But the US penchant for speaking like a disinterested analyst rather than an engaged leader signals impotence, when in reality there is much the US can do to prevent the conflict it fears.

Speaking to a Jewish audience in Baltimore, Indyk stated that "what has happened in the last nine weeks is that some in the Arab world are playing with the idea of resorting to the military option." He noted that the US is concerned about Saddam Hussein's threats against Israel. Indyk could have added to his list Iraq's increasing acceptance in the Arab world, the erosion of sanctions, the tightening relations between Syria and Iraq, the withdrawal of Egypt's ambassador to Israel, and the anti-Israel riots and protests in Jordan, Egypt, and Morocco.

It is important that the US has begun to acknowledge the marked and precipitous deterioration in the regional situation, and even more important that, in the case of one potential flashpoint, has begun to engage with some degree of seriousness. The US is signaling that it shares Israel's concerns regarding Syria's encouragement of attacks by Hizbullah across its northern border and recognizes that Israel will have to retaliate, even at the risk of war.

American ambassadors in Lebanon and Syria have told those governments that Israel will respond against the forces that support Hizbullah in Lebanon if they do not ensure that Hizbullah ceases its attacks. This includes Syrian military targets in Lebanon, and perhaps radar systems that support those forces from within Syria as well.

By warning Syria that Israel will have to act militarily, rather than warning Israel against taking such action, the US is placing the full responsibility for a possible Israeli-Syrian conflict on Syrian shoulders. This should have been the approach toward Yasser Arafat's orchestrated attack against Israel as well, which would have ended some time ago if the US had implicitly backed Israel's right of military response.

What is not clear is whether the relatively subtle US approach toward Syria will be sufficient to produce the desired result. Syrian President Bashar Assad may well look at the US reaction toward the Israeli-Palestinian conflict and conclude that, if a shooting war begins, the US will revert to evenhanded calls to end the "cycle of violence," rather than support Israel's right to self defense.

If the US wants to be sure that Assad is not confused by mixed signals, some further steps to prevent war are in order. First, the US should tell the Lebanese government that if it continues to allow Hizbullah free rein, the US will place Lebanon on its list of "terrorist-supporting countries."

Putting Lebanon on the US terrorist list would accomplish a number of purposes at once: It would accentuate Lebanese government responsibility for Hizbullah, punish Lebanon politically and economically for embracing Hizbullah, and signal to Syria that the slight US movement toward taking Syria off the terrorism list had reversed direction.

In his speech, Indyk accused Syria of giving a 'green light' to Hizbullah to attack Israel. Speaking frankly about Syria is important, but the US should go further. It should back Israel's formal complaint to the UN Security Council and push for UN action against Syria and Lebanon.

Syria should understand that not only will its support of aggression against Israel not be tolerated, but its days of military occupation of Lebanon are numbered. The greatest pressure the US can put on Syria is not by implying support for Israeli action, but by taking its own diplomatic action against Syria's illegal occupation of Lebanon.

If at one time Syria could claim that it was restoring order or somehow balancing Israel's presence in Lebanon, now its presence has no leg to stand on. The people of Lebanon might be excused for asking why the world can rise up against Israeli occupation, while their own suffering under the Syrian thumb is met with a resounding silence. Syria's occupation of Lebanon should become an international agenda item on its own merits, but Syria's support for aggression against Israel should add urgency to this effort.

◆ ◆ ◆

The plan discussed here for Jerusalem was part of the "Clinton Parameters" described by Clinton to the parties two days before, but this information was not yet public. By this time, the Jerusalem neighborhood of Gilo had been under fire for weeks from Beit Jala, a Palestinian-controlled area of Bethlehem.

It did not take a lot of imagination, in other words, to see how Jerusalem could be turned quickly into Belfast or Sarajevo if it were ever divided again. Yet since the Barak government was willing to accept such a division, it will be difficult for any subsequent government to argue otherwise.

Keep Jerusalem Whole
December 25, 2000

In the cabinet meeting yesterday, Prime Minister Ehud Barak reportedly denied that the United States has submitted a bridging proposal that has been widely reported in the press. What the US has put forward is 'just ideas,' says Barak. If so, it is not too late for Israel to reject these 'ideas' and limit the damage that has already been done.

According to the US proposal, which Jerusalem Mayor Ehud Olmert says is supported by, not forced upon, the Israeli negotiating team, all of the capital's Arab neighborhoods and most of the Old City would come under the full sovereignty of the future Palestinian state. The Jewish Quarter of the Old City, including the Western Wall, would remain Israeli, as would all the Jewish neighborhoods built since the 1967 Six Day War. The formula for the Temple Mount is still murky, but it seems Israel would retain some 'connection' to it rather than any formal sovereignty.

It is painful to even describe these possible concessions, let alone consider what life in Jerusalem would be like under such conditions. A sovereign country does not simply hand over half its capital, let alone half of the city that symbolizes its sovereign existence, unless it has been utterly defeated. This is precisely the most dangerous part of the proposal: the stench of defeat that surrounds it.

The unmistakable impression given by Israeli largesse under fire is that what took almost two decades for Hizbullah to accomplish in Lebanon took only two months of low-level warfare by the Palestinians. The 'Aksa intifada' has been fought by both sides with two legs hobbled and one hand tied behind the back; both sides know that the other has held back most of the force available at its disposal.

On the Palestinian side, this sense of power and 'restraint' is intoxicating, and will not end with a 'peace agreement' based upon extreme Israeli concessions reached at the point of maximum Israeli self-imposed weakness. Within days, weeks, months, or years, the Palestinians will succumb to the temptation to make life in Jerusalem unlivable. This temptation will be great, because it will be so easy – a potshot here and there, a few stones, perhaps a small bomb or two. It will not take much, because Israel will have no remedy for an agreement designed with only one scenario in mind – a perfect peace.

A Jerusalem that is both intricately divided and completely open might have worked if the two countries in question were the United States and Canada, or Sweden and Norway. Nor is the problem limited to the fact that we happen to live in the Middle East. The Palestinians, according to a recent Bir Zeit University poll, overwhelmingly (74 percent) believe that, even with east Jerusalem in their hands, Israel has no right to be in west Jerusalem. This same poll found that 91 percent of Palestinians believe there could be no peace unless Israel recognized the Palestinian 'right of return.' The point is that even in an agreement in which the Palestinians commit to the 'end of the conflict,' there will still be plenty of room for interpretation. If Israel does not accept the Palestinian interpretation, the conflict, judging by the experience of Oslo, will continue. Israel, therefore, cannot sign an agreement that leaves the Palestinian hand squeezing the jugular of Jerusalem itself.

It is tempting to regard the Jerusalem proposals as ratifying the status quo. After all, all Jewish neighborhoods remain Jewish and all Arab neighborhoods remain Arab. But the status quo is that Arab and Jews live peacefully, if separately, side by side, in the same city. That peace depends on Israeli control in and around Jerusalem. The effect of the proposals is to give the Palestinians the ability to rend the peaceful fabric of Jerusalem with barely a shrug or the lifting of a finger.

Those who think that Jerusalem is divided now because Israel made the mistake of not further developing and integrating the Arab areas of the city, and because most Jews never set foot in most Arab sections, perhaps do not remember what it was like to live in a truly divided city. If there was one pillar to the Israeli consensus regarding a future peace, it was the oath that Israel would never return to the walls and barbed wire of pre-1967 Jerusalem again.

If the contemplated agreement goes forward, Israelis may wake up one day and realize that the only thing worse than a city in conflict with a wall down the middle is a city in conflict without any dividing wall and no possibility of erecting one. Ehud Barak continues to swear that he will not concede any Israeli vital interest. If keeping Jerusalem whole is not a vital interest, what is?

In the waning days of the Clinton and Barak governments, and after the Palestinians' post-Camp David terror offensive had already begun, there was a frenzied rush to reach a final status agreement. At that time, it seemed that the talks would collapse despite Israeli concessions, but that there was some chance the Palestinians would take their state and run with it.

The strange thing was that Barak and his ministers were already trying to sell Israelis on the agreement they thought might come, not by extolling the virtues of peace, but by raising the specter of war if Israel did not sign. At that time, no one dreamed that within three years Saddam Hussein would be gone and American divisions would be sitting in Baghdad. Contrary to the Barak model, defeats for Arab radicalism bring peace closer, while Israeli concessions from a position of weakness tend to push peace further away.

Stop Threatening Us
December 28, 2000

Two types of offers cannot be refused: Those that are too good to turn down and those that are made, Mafia-style, with a gun to the head. Prime

Minister Ehud Barak is making both types of offers, the former to the Palestinians, the latter to his own people.

Barak has consistently pledged to leave "no stone unturned" in the search for peace, while at the same time refusing to compromise Israel's vital interests. By accepting a withdrawal almost to the 1967 lines, including dividing Jerusalem and abandoning the Jordan Valley, the pretense of safeguarding Israel's vital interests has been thrown to the winds.

Instead, what we see is a desperate effort to take the maximalist offer made at Camp David and sweeten it further, to the point that it becomes an offer the Palestinians cannot refuse.

Since the Palestinians may cling to the dream of flooding Israel with millions of descendants of refugees, and remain convinced that the Jewish people has no connection to the place Jews pray towards three times a day, they could still well refuse an offer Israel should never have allowed to be made. But if an agreement is reached, then Barak's other offer kicks in, the much more ominous offer to the Israeli public.

It is already clear that Barak's offer to his own people, despite many associated sweeteners, will not so much be a vision of peace as the specter of war. In an interview over the weekend, he vowed that he would not allow Israel to be "be dragged into rivers of blood and fire" as a continuation of the "blindness" of previous governments would have done. Yesterday, Foreign Minister Shlomo Ben-Ami was quoted as saying, "If we don't reach an agreement, there will be war here – it will be Kosovo, the UN will come, NATO will come, who won't? Either we reach an agreement or an arrangement will be forced on us."

Another cabinet minister, Binyamin Ben-Eliezer, came at this theme from another angle, claiming that postponing a final status deal would only result in a worse deal for Israel. Finally, Barak outdid himself and his lieutenants by making the Big Threat. At Sunday's cabinet meeting he warned the ministers that in five to 10 years Israel could be facing "an entirely new Middle East" featuring nuclear weapons, fundamentalist regimes and a surge in organized terrorism.

The first question raised by these threats is why we are hearing them from our own leaders, not only from Saddam Hussein or, perhaps, the French foreign minister. If an agreement were ratified in this context, the Arab world would learn that not only had a certain segment of Israel's leadership been forced into an agreement against their will, but the people of Israel had succumbed to potential threats, not from Arab leaders, but from their own.

Barak, of course, is not the first to wave the nuclear rationale for the peace process; it was considered a cornerstone of Yitzhak Rabin's thinking. Nor should the possibility of a series of peace agreements that solidifies Israel's position in the region be dismissed as a component of Israel's strategy toward growing non-conventional threats.

But it is one thing for Israel to make agreements, even painfully generous ones, from a position of strength, and quite another to admit to being forced into concessions that cross the reddest of red lines. The 'sky is falling' argument cuts both ways: A secure peace, yes; suing for peace, no.

The United States has for years pressed Israel to "take risks for peace," meaning give up physical components of security in exchange for more abstract, strategic ones. This only works, however, if the physical concessions truly improve Israel's strategic position. The litmus test of such an improvement is whether the Arab rejectionists see Israel's indestructibility increasing, or on the contrary, whether those bloody dreams dashed in 1967 and 1973 have been revived.

We cannot bank on the demise of the radical regimes in Iran and Iraq, but neither should we assume that such regimes are more permanent than the Soviet Union seemed a short time before it collapsed in a heap.

In any case, a peace agreement that does not project strength on Israel's part becomes more dangerous, not less, in the face of a growing non-conventional threat. Peace agreements will not prevent the world Barak describes from emerging, but a forced retreat to less defensible borders will make contending with such a world more difficult for Israel.

◆ ◆ ◆

The mood conveyed here explains why Ariel Sharon, who a year before would have been considered completely unelectable, beat Ehud Barak by a landslide in the subsequent elections. It was one thing for Barak to make extraordinary concessions at Camp David, even after his coalition no longer held a majority in the Knesset. It was another to continue to make concessions under fire, and ignore each rejection by the Palestinian side.

As a result, Israelis came to see Barak as more reckless and dangerous than Sharon, a politician who had developed a reputation for exactly these traits on the opposite side of the political spectrum. During the Netanyahu years, Sharon had been a gadfly to the right of Netanyahu's right-wing government. At the negotiations over the Hebron agreement (a subset of Oslo), Sharon refused to shake Yasser Arafat's hand.

Some two decades before, Sharon was banned from his post as defense minister in the government of Menachem Begin, after a commission of inquiry found that he should have prevented the massacre by Christian Phalangists in the Palestinian refugee camps called Sabra and Shatila in Lebanon. The defense ministry lawyer who defended Sharon before the commission told me that none of the military or intelligence experts who advised Sharon before he decided to send the Phalangists into these camps predicted that a massacre would take place, and that the main Israeli concern was that the Phalangists would be no match for PLO forces that controlled the camps.

Once Sharon was elected, he surprised practically everyone by moving sharply toward the center with statements such as "restraint is a component of power" and, most recently, that it is time to "divide the land of Israel" and "end the occupation."

Two Fallen Soldiers' Zionist Legacy
January 1, 2001

It is just as well that the advent of the new millennium was celebrated a year ago, rather than today, the day that sticklers for detail say it actually begins. The mood here is hardly celebratory, as it seems that this moment is at best a low point and at worst just the beginning of a difficult year ahead.

This is a moment in which Justice Minister Yossi Beilin, in yesterday's *Washington Post*, is proclaiming that dividing Jerusalem and relinquishing sovereignty over the Temple Mount is "the fulfillment of the Zionist dream: the establishment of a state in which Jews will be able to live, as a majority, a life of normality." It is a moment in which Foreign Minister Shlomo Ben-Ami told his confused ministry colleagues that we had reached "the end of territorial Zionism" – making one wonder if the next stop in the negotiations is to convert Israel into a Web site.

From these comments, and Prime Minister Ehud Barak's policy in general, we are to learn that the reason for the lack of peace is Israeli territorial acquisitiveness and that, if only we were to free ourselves of that which is most dear, then the conflict would be over.

45

The brutal irony of the Barak-Beilin-Ben-Ami approach is that, as the supposed price of peace becomes steeper, the likelihood of peace actually recedes. A central reason for this is what is considered by the United States and some Israelis to be an enlightened choice: Barak's decision to reverse his pledges not to reward violence or negotiate under fire.

Barak's denials notwithstanding, it is clear to all that Yasser Arafat has improved the deal offered him at Camp David by launching an armed attack against Israel. Rewarding the Palestinian attack, even if it has ended, all but ensures that the Palestinians will continue to use violence to assert their demands, including demands that they may have supposedly renounced. The government's decision to make further concessions as the attacks continue only reduces the prospects for peace.

Perhaps the worst part of negotiating under fire is the demoralizing effect it has on Israelis. As it happens, the moving stories of the soldier and border policeman just buried are bracing reminders of what our leaders may regard as a passe form of Zionism.

Capt. Gadi Marsha immigrated from Ethiopia as a child and rose to lead the trackers' unit of the Southern Command. He gained the admiration of the Beduin soldiers under his command, in addition to his skills as an officer, by fasting with them during the month of Ramadan.

Sgt.-Maj. Yonatan Vermullen grew up in Israel in a Christian family that came to support Israel during the 1973 war, and decided to move to Israel when his family returned to Holland. As a resident rather than a full citizen, he had to work hard to be accepted as a volunteer to the army, and once accepted volunteered for the dangerous work of a Border Police sapper.

It is probably safe to say that Marsha and Vermullen shared the Zionist visions of Beilin and Ben-Ami to the extent that they, too, wished that someday Israel would live in peace and security. Yet it is doubtful that a Zionism that does not project a basic level of confidence and self-respect will be capable of attracting and sustaining the sense of purpose exhibited by these young men.

Now that the Palestinians have thoughtfully rejected Barak's already too-generous acceptance of the Clinton plan, even the mistaken rationale for negotiating under fire no longer exists. Yesterday, the cabinet hinted at shifting gears toward a 'time out' and pursuing 'unilateral' options, but pretended that the Palestinians were considering the Clinton parameters.

Negotiating under fire was a mistake that is better corrected late than never. The Palestinian legislature and numerous Palestinian leaders have heaped abuse on the Clinton parameters. The government's seeming refusal to take no for an answer can only imply that Israel is willing to see the Clinton parameters move even further in the Palestinian direction. It will not be easy to unteach the lesson that violence pays, but the longer we wait, the harder the long road back will be.

◆ ◆ ◆

I wrote this, my first signed column, with great trepidation. Though I had written hundreds of unsigned editorials before this point, I had no idea if I could write a weekly column, with a distinctive voice that was different from the pronouncing-from-on-high tone that editorial writers are supposed to take. Anonymity can be a comfortable thing; I was not as eager to drop it as one might expect.

When this was written, about six months after the collapse of the Camp David summit between Bill Clinton, Ehud Barak, and Yasser Arafat, and less than four months after the ensuing wave of Palestinian terror began, no one imagined that it would last over two years.

The name of the column, "Interesting Times," seemed particularly apt since Israelis had plunged so quickly from the sense that peace was on the way to a new and vicious war. At the same time, the previously unelectable Ariel Sharon seemed poised to win the upcoming balloting, both Barak and Clinton were on their way out, and Israeli-Palestinian negotiations continued apace in the midst of an election campaign and terrorist attacks. The challenge I describe at the end, of articulating a "conceptzia" (world view) that neither negates the possibility of peace nor pursues it unrealistically, remains essentially unmet.

Interesting Times: Shlomo and the Conceptzia
January 19, 2001

I live in Jerusalem. Even during my normal distracted morning rush to drop off our daughter Noa at her kindergarten, I can't help but notice the dramatic mountain ridge on the horizon. That ridge is in Jordan, on the other side of the Dead Sea, and to see it I must look over the entire Palestinian state-in the-making.

47

The view of what will be not one, but two, foreign countries confronts me first thing in the morning. The land is beautiful, the view of sleepy villages pastoral, but the consciousness of remaining hostility is inescapable.

Now a sheet is being circulated in Noa's kindergarten asking parents whether to continue paying Shlomo, the guard hired recently to protect our children.

Three choices appear on the sheet: drop Shlomo now, keep him for another month, or sign him up for a full year.

Pressed for a strategic assessment before the morning mist burns off the Dead Sea, I sign under the most pessimistic, better-safe-than-sorry column.

The middle, one-month-only option is well ahead in the polling.

The majority's choice is a sign of confusion, hope, and stubbornness. On one level, the Israelis seem to have become used to the idea that settlers and Jerusalemites will be shot at and bombs will go off periodically in other parts of the country. On the other hand, the public's willingness to vote for Likud leader Ariel Sharon seems to reflect not just a desire to punish Prime Minister Ehud Barak, but a stubborn belief that something can be done to improve their security.

Deeper still, there may be a realization that we are not just approaching an election verdict, as momentous as that is, but are on the verge of the second great sea change in Israeli history.

Almost 28 years ago, the Yom Kippur war became a watershed event for Israel and Egypt.

For Egypt that war, despite the victory myth subsequently built around it, was a stunning defeat that convinced Egyptian president Anwar Sadat that there was no alternative to making peace with Israel. For Israel, that war led to an even more pervasive rethinking that has culminated in Barak's mad dash to ink an Israeli-Palestinian pact.

Pre-1973 Israel was symbolized by Golda Meir, the last of an unbroken dynasty of Labor party leaders who had ruled the country since its founding.

Until then, Israel was a largely bolshevized society, in both positive and negative senses: it was mobilized behind the notion that it had no alternative but to stand strong against the threat from its Arab neighbors, and it brooked no quarrel with the pervasive party-state-economy-society apparatus that had built the nation.

When Egypt and Syria succeeded in surprising Israel that October, it was not just a particular intelligence appraisal that collapsed – conceptzia as it became known in Hebrew – but the way Israelis saw themselves and their world.

Menachem Begin's election victory in 1977 not only swept out a particular Labor government, but ended forever the presumption of one-party rule.

At the same time, the election of a government of the Right helped precipitate a 'peace movement' that had been quietly brewing since the 1967 war.

I place 'peace movement' in quotes not to disparage it, but because the distinction between that movement and its opponents has never been about the desirability of peace, but over whether peace is possible. The name of Peace Now, the flagship organization founded in 1978, says it all: peace is not something that depends on our enemies changing their spots, but is within our grasp.

The idea that peace is like a brass ring just beyond our reach has reached its crescendo at this moment. Barak has boldly tested the proposition that peace can be obtained by essentially fulfilling every Palestinian demand but one, the one that novelist Amos Oz said recently 'would mean eradicating Israel.'

The pre-1973 conceptzia was that peace was not attainable, so Israel had no alternative but to be indestructible. The post-1973 conceptzia, as embodied by the Oslo accords, was that peace could be obtained by satisfying Palestinian grievances.

The day after the elections, regardless of who wins, the challenge will be to build a new, more mature conceptzia that combines elements of the pre-1973 fortress Israel with the peace-or-bust Israel that has emerged since.

It might be farfetched to read all this into a sign-up sheet at a kindergarten, but the fact that such issues arise in mundane places is a sign that, more than usual, we live in the 'interesting times' of that famous Chinese curse.

I look forward to attempting to decipher these times with you, with the conviction that they ultimately hold even more promise than they do peril.

◆ ◆ ◆

For the first nineteen years of Israel's existence, until 1967, Jerusalem was a city divided by barbed wire and high concrete walls. The Clinton parameters, issued in the last days of his administration after the Camp David summit had failed and the current Palestinian offensive had already begun, envisioned dividing Jerusalem again along the lines of the intricate existing patchwork of Jewish and Arab neighborhoods.

Stand Firmer for Jerusalem
January 19, 2001

Since there likely will be no final status deal before Israel's election, last week's massive rally in Jerusalem, for Jerusalem, might seem as overtaken by events. Unfortunately, nothing could be further from the truth. Indeed, the rally marked the beginning of the long road back from the legacy of Bill Clinton and Ehud Barak.

The Oslo Accords established Palestinian statehood as a given in the quest for peace; the struggle now will be over whether Camp David II and its aftermath will be allowed to create a similar presumption regarding the division of Jerusalem.

The outlines of the post-election, post-Oslo-era debate can already be seen. True believers in the path taken by Ehud Barak will say that regardless of what happens between now and a future peace deal, the eventual deal will be along the lines of the Clinton parameters. The other camp, which now includes a solid majority of Israelis, believes a deal based upon the division of Jerusalem is currently, perhaps indefinitely, unworkable, unacceptable, or both.

Some recent snap polls seemed to indicate that there was a majority for dividing Jerusalem by asking questions like, "Do you favor giving up Arab neighborhoods in Jerusalem?" The results of such polls are misleading because they do not distinguish between people who would be willing to redraw Jerusalem's borders to exclude some outlying Arab neighborhoods and the much more radical approach proposed by Bill Clinton.

A more accurate picture is revealed by a recent poll by the Tami Steinmetz Center for Peace Research, which asked more specifically about Clinton's proposal: Turning over every Arab neighborhood to full Palestinian sovereignty, including most of the Old City, creating a patchwork of Jewish and Arab sovereignty. Phrased this way, two of every three Israelis polled answered negatively.

And so, last week's was more than an ordinary opposition rally.

For one thing, a clear majority of Israelis side with its cause. Secondly, the organizers went through pains to depoliticize what had become a very political issue at the most political of times – just before the election.

The driving force behind the rally was former minister of interior Natan Sharansky, who is no stranger to such mass rallies. Over a decade ago, Sharansky defied the doubts of the American Jewish community and brought 250,000 people to Washington to rally for Soviet Jewry during a visit by Mikhail Gorbachev to the US capital. At that time, the emigration of 50,000 Soviet Jews a year was considered an outrageous pipe dream; a decade later about one million had won their freedom.

Today turning back the wheel of the peace process – without giving up the cause of peace – may seem to be an equally impossible task. What Barak and Clinton have inadvertently revealed, however, is that each turn of the wheel in the current direction leads further from peace, and that the hope for peace lies in the other direction.

A realization is dawning that even "the most far-reaching offer Israel can make," as Amos Oz wrote last week in the *New York Times*, is not enough for the Palestinians. The next realization should be that the attempt to make ever more far-reaching offers was fatally flawed, because the Palestinians just moved farther away from us.

Oz insists that the place for Israel to stand firm is against the Palestinian 'right of return,' which would mean simply "eradicating Israel." But for the Palestinians the 'right of return' is no more or less of a red line than an Israeli retreat to the 1967 lines, including exclusive Palestinian sovereignty on the Temple Mount. Even if the Palestinians were to sign an agreement that left pockets of post-1967 territory in Jerusalem and elsewhere in Israel's hands, there is little reason to believe that they would resist the temptation to make life in those pockets untenable.

The hope for peace lies in Israel unifying behind its own definition of vital interests, and convincing the Palestinians that Israel will stand on its own right to live in this land no less than they will. One of those vital interests is a unified Jerusalem. The rally, therefore, was not just about keeping Jerusalem whole, but about creating a new paradigm for the peace process: instead of reaching farther, standing firmer.

◆ ◆ ◆

The irony of Sharon's tenure as prime minister is that he seems not to have had the ambitions that I suggested for him here, and yet may be headed toward accomplishing more than the more ambitious prime ministers who preceded him. Sharon's real ambition, it seems, is a stable form of cold war with the Arab world, rather than the more formal and comprehensive peace that his predecessors sought (see "Sharon's Not So Secret Plan," pages 192-195).

I still wish he were more ambitious regarding the economy, rather than placing all his bets on improving the security situation.

Interesting Times: Destiny
March 23, 2001

Caught a segment of "Jay-walking" the other night in which comedian Jay Leno gets a laugh at the expense of young people who lack what we like to call common knowledge. This time Jay showed some college-age kids a classic picture of Franklin Delano Roosevelt. The picture continued to draw a total blank, even after Jay threw in the hints 'FDR' and 'president.'

I would like to think that kids here would know that David Ben-Gurion was our first prime minister, not a guy named after the airport. Though Ben-Gurion and FDR were almost contemporaries, the icon from Sde Boker seems less relegated to ancient history, if only because two of his disciples now run the country. If Ariel Sharon and Shimon Peres have something in common, it is that both considered Ben-Gurion a mentor.

Following his victory lap in the United States, Sharon will need to take a page from Ben-Gurion's book and perhaps even from that of a more recent US leader, Ronald Reagan.

Like Reagan, Sharon is an older, avuncular leader inheriting a country in what Jimmy Carter famously called "malaise" (see also 'stagflation,' 'Iranian hostage crisis,' and 'Soviet invasion of Afghanistan'). Twenty years later, Reagan is to be credited with launching a wave of American prosperity and global ascendancy.

Israel's problem, though seeming to be one of security, is closer to America's problem in the 1970s than meets the eye. The challenge posed by the Camp David intifada (let's call it that, because the Palestinians now admit its purpose was to bury the deal proposed there) is only indirectly military in nature. The more direct battle is over whether Israel has the right to defend itself. Fundamentally, it is a battle over whose victory is inevitable: Israel's struggle to live in peace as a Jewish state or the Palestinian attempt to replace it with a state of their own.

Like Seventies Americans, contemporary Israelis are loath to admit that they are in the ideological equivalent of a showdown at the OK Corral. 'Detente' was the watchword then, and now we, too, have been captured by the idea that peace can be finessed by bridging what amounts to a case of bad blood.

The heart of the Reagan turnaround was a rejection of the inevitability of American mediocrity and decline. Though dubbed the 'Great Communicator,' Reagan was not a particularly eloquent man. Two much-maligned words – "evil empire" – were enough to send an entire edifice of moral equivalence into a tailspin.

Reagan revolutionized America by being optimistic, standing on principle, and thinking big. Three acts from his first two years in office defined his presidency: enacting tax cuts, firing striking air traffic controllers, and pitching missile defenses.

Sharon should start his Reaganite revolution by banishing defeatist notions that have become commonplace. Even Defense Minister Binyamin Ben-Eliezer reacted to the latest atrocities by urging the public not to expect "magic solutions" – translation: get used to violence, because we can't stop it.

It is OK to demand patience, but Sharon's message should be that PA Chairman Yasser Arafat's attack against Israel will be defeated for everyone's sake, including the Palestinians. Sharon's first task is to restore the sense that Israel can shape its own destiny. Sharon should understand, as Reagan did, that the first step out of a national rut is making people believe not only that you can, but that you must and will change what had seemed inevitable.

Ben-Gurion understood this well. In 1944 he wrote, "Resisting fate is not enough. We must master our fate; we must take our destiny into our own hands! This is the doctrine of the Jewish revolution – not non-surrender to the Galut but ending it."

The Palestinians, to their credit, seem to possess this spirit. I would wish them well if the objective of their revolution was limited to creating their own state. But so long as the Palestinian leadership insists on displacing our destiny with their own, we need Ben-Gurion's history-shaping spirit as much as ever.

Like Reagan regarding the Soviet Union, Sharon must calmly speak the truth, not only about the Palestinian leadership, but the radical dictatorships that seek to terrorize the entire region. Like both Reagan and Ben-Gurion, he must aim beyond survival and security and seek prosperity and growth – both economic and demographic.

There is nothing inevitable about our security situation, economy, or political system. Sharon's landslide election and warm welcome by the US cap his startling rehabilitation as a political figure. To paraphrase Ben- Gurion, however, rehabilitation is not enough. Like Reagan, Sharon must prove that the oldest leaders can sometimes be the most revolutionary.

◆ ◆ ◆

Shalhevet Pass, a 10-month-old baby, was shot in the head in her stroller by a Palestinian sniper perched on a hilltop in Hebron. This piece, like others written shortly after the current war began, tries to grasp a hatred that could include the deliberate targeting of young children.

Interesting Times: Haunting Hatred
March 30, 2001

Normally my well-honed emotional defenses screen out such morbid thoughts, but this week I could not help being haunted by the assassination of baby Shalhevet. As I looked at the cherubic face of our own 10-month old daughter, Shalhevet's wide eyes and round face flashed through my mind.

I also found myself thinking about the last seconds of Naftali Lanzkron (13) and Eliran Rosenberg (15) who were speaking face-to-face, in Hebrew, with a Palestinian when he blew himself up.

What is striking about these crimes is not just their monstrosity, but the dehumanizing hatred that it took to carry them out. There was no level of abstraction here – no faceless anonymity between the murderer and his victim. Whether from afar through a telescopic site, or from up close, the killers looked at the faces of the children whose lives they were about to snuff out.

This hatred is particularly unfathomable because it is so unrequited. Sure there are Israelis who hate the Arabs back with similar intensity, but at the level of societies there is no comparison.

In 1984, my brother Alex, may his memory be a blessing, traveled to Jordan just before moving to Israel and being drafted into the IDF. After visiting Mount Nebo, the spot where Moses stood tantalizingly close to the promised land, Alex looked for a place to put his sleeping bag. He headed for a nearby spring, where a man named Muhammad guarded a broken pumping station. They sat for hours, communicating by means of Alex's broken Arabic.

As Muhammad lamented the sadness of war, since Jesus, Moses and Muhammad were all brothers, Alex thought to himself, "Great, here is a simple devout Moslem whose Islam makes wars seem wrong." This idyll was quickly shattered when Muhammad elaborated that the Jews were 'Satan' and that Israel was a foreign implant that would disappear without American backing.

In a letter home, Alex reported, "The whole conversation was rather unreal, moving from the abstract of total brotherhood among men, to total hatred of a manipulating people who were in fact the devil. All from a very generous, hardworking man, who didn't even have the grudge of the Palestinians against Israel, as he was Jordanian. His hatred came from his Islam and his understanding of the world, which in turn came from Arabic radio."

The intensity of Arab hatred for Israel is damning, since many assume that hatred generally runs from the victim to the victimizer. But if hatred were produced mainly by what people did to each other, then Israeli hatred of Arabs would be as intense as theirs is of us. If Israel is hated for perching on a tiny fraction of what the Arabs consider their exclusive domain, then Israel might be expected to hate even more those who seek to destroy the only Jewish state.

As a society, however, we not only cannot bring ourselves to hate them, we have trouble believing that they hate us. Not just since the Rabin-Arafat handshake in 1993, but since 1967, the peace process paradigm has been that the Arab world is no longer bent on Israel's destruction, but just wants to negotiate the 'secure and recognized' borders envisioned by UN Security Council Resolution 242.

By signing peace treaties with Egypt and Jordan, Israel seemed to be steadily implementing its dream of secure boundaries and closing the book on the 1967 war. But Arab hatred reminds us that as far as the Palestinians, the rejectionist Arab states, and both the intelligentsia and the masses in Egypt and Jordan are concerned, the conflict is still stuck in 1948.

In Cairo, an anonymous wedding singer sold a million and a half copies over three weeks of a song with the catchy title, 'I Hate the Israelis, I Love Amr Moussa.' In Jordan, Israeli journalists attempting to cover the recent Arab summit were expelled because their security could not be guaranteed.

The English poet Lord Byron once said, "hatred is by far the longest pleasure; men love in haste, but they detest at leisure." We can take solace in the fact that many of the old hatreds within Europe are gone, though wars in the Balkans show that they too can be rekindled. Nations are not doomed to live or act according to their hatreds.

Admitting Arab hatred does not imply that we must reciprocate, or give up the possibility of peace and security. Arab hatred cannot be surmounted, however, by pretending that, deep down, our desire for peace is shared by the other side. Peace should not wait until Arab hatred has dissipated, but it cannot be built as if hatred did not exist.

◆ ◆ ◆

Another example of the "power of context" I refer to below is the critical relationship between the regional climate and the prospects for Arab-Israeli peacemaking. This is why America's war to dismantle the terror network is the most important component of the peace process, while the diplomacy that is usually given the credit is mainly reaping the harvest of confronting Arab radicalism.

Interesting Times: The Tipping Point
April 20, 2001

Look at the world around you. It may seem like an immovable, implacable place. It is not. With the slightest push – in the just the right place – it can be tipped.

So ends a remarkable book that, as one reviewer put it, "changes the way you think about, well, everything." In *The Tipping Point, New Yorker* writer Malcolm Gladwell pulls together everything from the crime rate in New York, the sudden hipness of Hush Puppies shoes, the revolution-ary impact of Paul Revere's midnight ride, and a rash of teen suicides in Micronesia, to demonstrate that social phenomena often propagate much like epidemics. The implications of this are far-reaching because, as Gladwell convincingly argues, both medical and social epidemics are not inevitable forces of nature, but are exquisitely sensitive to being "tipped" by seemingly trivial environmental factors.

The notion that ideas spread like viruses is not a new one, and Gladwell's "tipping point" is similar to the concept borrowed from nuclear reactions called "critical mass." What makes the book so inter-esting, though, are the disparate real-world examples Gladwell dissects along the way, and his discoveries of what made particular phenomena "tip."

The murder rate in New York City, for example, did not drop gradually, it plummeted like a stone – over five years in the mid-1990s, it dropped by 64 percent. Epidemics are not linear things, they explode rapidly and collapse just as rapidly when the tipping point is reached.

What makes things tip is not always obvious. When citizens were being gunned down at an alarming rate, for example, most people might have excused the New York police for not paying too much attention to nuisance crimes such as subway graffiti and fare-beating, or those annoying people who would wash windshields at stoplights and demand payment.

Yet the murder rate in New York did collapse just after authorities scrubbed the graffiti off the subways and cracked down on other sorts of seemingly trivial breaches of public order. It seems absurd that something as simple as clean subway cars can influence whether more New Yorkers decide to commit murder, but evidently it did.

The explanation is what Gladwell calls the "Power of Context" – New York's would-be criminals were influenced by an atmosphere of anarchy and decay that had developed in the public sphere. Restore the trappings of order and, presto!, actual order returns.

Parochial being that I am, I immediately combed my mind for local examples of tipping points. Maybe the epidemic of violence in our schools could be tamed by working on lesser symptoms of anarchy, such as broken windows and tardiness? Going more macro, wouldn't it be nice if the Arab-Israeli conflict, for example, could be tipped like a pinprick deflating a balloon?

The original intifada started one fine day in late 1987, following a road accident involving Arabs and Israelis. Some have argued that a terrorist attack by a glider-borne Palestinian a few days before was taken as a sign that Israel had let its guard down. The glider attack may have been the tipping point for the intifada.

On the positive side, Egyptian president Anwar Sadat's visit to Jerusalem might be considered an act that revolutionized both Israeli and Arab attitudes toward the possibility of peace. Sadat's visit shows that once there is a sincere desire for peace, it is possible for a leader to cut through many layers of enmity with bold but simple actions. The coldness of the Egyptian-Israeli peace does not contradict this point, because the peace itself has proved quite durable despite remaining Egyptian hostility toward Israel.

In more current terms, what the 'Power of Context' suggests is that Oslo and Wye agreement provisions on ending Palestinian incitement should not be treated as optional items that are okay to let slide, while the real meat is security cooperation. Incitement could be to peace what graffiti was to New York crime – only more so, since incitement is designed to promote violence, while crime is an unintentional by-product of graffiti.

Palestinian and Israeli negotiators seem to agree that Arafat was not ready for the compromises expected of him at Camp David. The lesson for the next run at peacemaking should be to front-load the requirement to end incitement before attempting another final status negotiation. If this sounds farfetched, it's not – it's pure Oslo. Incitement was to end before final status talks began. After all, how can Arafat ever be ready for peace before he stops preparing for war?

◆　◆　◆

By this time, Israel had been under terrorist attack for half a year, but there was still much disbelief that the dreams built up during the Oslo era could have been turned to a nightmare so quickly. This was the first Independence Day Israel celebrated while under attack. The challenges of continuing with daily life described here are reminiscent of the first days after the September 11 attacks that came a few months later, when Americans were groping with how to live normal lives after having endured such a massive and unexpected terror attack.

58

We developed our own rituals for living under terrorism in Jerusalem. Since our three daughters were all very small at this time (they were born in 1996, 1998, and 2000) we did not have to worry about them wandering around on their own. We stopped taking buses, going to the center of town, avoided shopping malls and restaurants that had no security guard.

In an article in Redbook *("What it's like to live with danger," January 2002), my wife Wendy Singer wrote of our lives, "I can't say that I walk around feeling uptight all the time, but when I'm in a public space I am intensely aware of every passerby. Suicide bombers often disguise themselves as Orthodox Jews or Israeli soldiers. ... When I leave a public space, something in my body relaxes. Only then do I realize how tense I have been, how wary of being in a crowd."*

Wendy did find a project that let us feel that terror was not confining us to our homes. The city of Jerusalem, at this time, sported about eighty artistically painted concrete lions all over town, similar to the cows that were placed around Chicago and New York. She decided that she would photograph our children with each of the lions. Now we have a photo album with all these pictures, none of which suggest that they were taken in defiance of the threats around us.

Interesting Times: Grilling Rituals
April 27, 2001

In a normal year, the power of rituals is less obvious. In a normal year, the patriotic rollercoaster running through Remembrance Day and Independence Day is more of a non sequitur to daily life in modern Israel. This year, it is these twinned days that are what the doctor ordered, while daily life seems slightly out of place.

Rituals are clumsy things. They come along at prescribed times and demand that you be happy or sad, or think about things beyond yourself, like God and country. Rituals depend on the law of averages; if enough people do the same thing often enough, eventually it will affect some of them.

The most powerful ritual I have come across is the *shiva*, the seven-day period of mourning under Jewish law. It is a circumstance perfect for ritual, because when someone very close to you dies, choice – the opposite of ritual – is not what you want. The laws of *shiva* are brilliant because they force you to concentrate on mourning for seven days, allowing you to resist the modern inclination to move on too quickly. During the *shiva*, you do not have to try to recover, your job is not to recover.

Unlike other rituals, *shiva* has no timing problem, because it is linked directly to the circumstances that demand it. Calendar-linked rituals have the odds stacked against them. It is not so natural, on fine spring days, to remember the Holocaust, or the fallen in Israel's wars.

This Remembrance Day, the sense of the need to sacrifice and the lack of peace was not as anachronistic as it might have seemed a year ago. But if Remembrance Day gained power from its connectedness to the moment, Independence Day gained from its disconnectedness, from its power to help Israelis to defy the moment, head for the outdoors, and barbecue the day away just like every other year.

Contrary to popular opinion, the widespread impulse to grill meat is not the main thing that sets our Independence Day apart from national days elsewhere. What is distinct about our day was highlighted by, of all people, Ukrainian President Leonid Kuchma, in a recent interview by the *Jerusalem Post*. Not thinking he was saying anything unusual, I am sure, Kuchma ended his interview by congratulating Israel on its 53rd anniversary, "a truly extraordinary accomplishment."

Kuchma was not congratulating Israel for what it had accomplished; for Kuchma, Israel's reaching the ripe old age of 53 was itself "truly extraordinary."

Until about six months ago, Israelis were under the impression that national existence was an accomplishment, but not an ongoing one. The question of existence was behind us, and all that was left was wrapping up the details, like permanent borders.

Now it seems that the people we thought we were making peace with are not interested in dividing up the Land of Israel, but in fighting us for it. On Monday, after Arafat had condemned the suicide bombing in Kfar Saba and claimed he would work against mortar attacks, the official Palestinian newspaper *Al-Ayyam* featured a chilling picture: two small children, one a baby sucking on a pacifier, wearing large headbands with Arabic inscriptions. The older child's headband read, "Palestine from the [Mediterranean] Sea to the [Jordan] River" (translation by Palestinian Media Watch).

The Palestinian decision to reject compromise does not mean that Israel is any more threatened than it was six months ago. Like Saddam

Hussein choosing to invade Kuwait before his nuclear bomb was ready, Yasser Arafat has done us a favor by revealing his intentions before fully consolidating a Palestinian state.

What the current Palestinian offensive does mean is that Israel will have to work harder and wait longer than anticipated before the Palestinians come to terms with Israel's permanent presence in the region. We wanted peace in a hurry (as in 'Peace Now'), but we will have to settle for going back to being patient and invincible.

All of this tends to bring back to Independence Day its pre-peace process quality of defiance and, as Kuchma suggested, notching another year under our belt. For Israel, the Palestinian success in turning the clock backwards is disturbing, but something we can live with. For Palestinians, it locks in a much grimmer present, and postpones the long climb up from tyranny and poverty.

◆ ◆ ◆

Palestinian and Israeli nationalism have more in common than meets the eye. The Palestinians have been copying our path toward statehood, including the parts that Israel should wean itself away from.

Interesting Times: What Next?
May 18, 2001

Kids have minds like steel traps. They will spot inconsistencies in your behavior in a flash, and they remember what you say better than you do, whether or not they choose to listen. They may be little, but they are learning machines, snapping up vocabulary and drawing lessons about the world effortlessly and at a furious pace.

Compared to Israel and the Jewish people, the Palestinians are in their political infancy – indeed their state is yet to be officially born. At this time of conflict between us, neither side would admit it, but there is much of a parent-child relationship between Israel and the Palestinians. This relationship is most evident when the Palestinians copy us, as in this week's marking of what they call 'al-Nakba' – the Catastrophe.

On May 15th, the 53rd anniversary of Israel's founding, Palestinians mimicked Israel's Remembrance Day by standing in silence while sirens blared. To differentiate themselves, perhaps, Palestinians held up a 'V' symbol with their hands, rather than the contemplative, head down pose struck by many Israelis.

The Palestinians ape Israel, not just with physical acts of commemoration, but with the place of memory in the national myth. The 'Nakba' is the Palestinian answer to the Holocaust – the suffering that is integral to the nation's birth and legitimacy. Nations that are born through an act of will, such as Israel, the United States, and the still nascent Palestine, need some crucible to mobilize and bind them together.

Every foreign leader is brought to lay a wreath at Yad Vashem, reinforcing Israel's self-image as a nation built upon the ashes of the Holocaust. Israeli school children are brought to Poland on a 'March of the Living' to affirm the triumph over Nazism that Israel represents.

The notion of Israel as an antidote to Auschwitz is true and right, and Israel must never forget its role as the living depository of the memory of the six million who perished. Yet even in Israel's case, it is fair to ask whether an appeal to suffering is a sufficient source of sustenance for national rebirth.

Jerusalem philosopher David Hartman makes a compelling argument that "it is politically and morally dangerous for our nation to perceive itself essentially as the suffering remnant of the Holocaust... Stories of persecution will not inspire our grandchildren to be Jews. We have to offer them a dream, a vision that is morally and spiritually compelling." According to Hartman, "It was not Hitler who brought us back to Zion, but rather belief in the eternal validity of the Sinai covenant."

Even after half a century, we have not learned how to remember without letting memory and survival themselves become our overwhelming purpose. Yet Israel can approach this task with an enormous advantage: a clearly defined sense of peoplehood bound together by a shared language, religion and history.

The Palestinians, by contrast, have a much more acute problem: their peoplehood is almost completely a derivative of their struggle against Israel.

Without Israel, ironically, there would be no Palestinian people, except perhaps in the sense that 'Californian' is distinct from 'American.' If the Jews had not returned to Palestine, this land would have been a minor backwater within the sea of the Arab world, perhaps a province in southern Syria.

One might think that the Palestinians would be interested in cutting the umbilical cord that attaches their identity to Israel. Our overreliance on victimhood pales beside the Palestinian inability to move beyond being victims of Israel.

Though it is obviously not pleasant to see Palestinians protesting Israel's founding as a 'catastrophe,' adding layers to the mythology of Palestinian victimhood is more of a problem for them than for us. Building nationalism on victimhood hurts Palestinians in two fundamental ways: it blocks Palestinian statehood by dissuading Israelis of the possibility of a 'two state solution,' and it defines Palestinians as more of an 'anti-people' than a people.

Imitation may be the sincerest form of flattery, but it is flattery Israel can sometimes do without. We want our kids to copy the best parts of us, but for some reason it does not always work out that way. With kids, the only way to deal with unwanted imitation is to stop doing the behavior yourself. We cannot and should not stop remembering our own suffering, but we can do a better job of developing the more constructive and inspiring side of our national purpose. 'Never again' is not enough; we must also ask: 'what next?'

◆ ◆ ◆

We tend to forget that one of the most odious UN conferences ever convened ended just a day before 9/11. Some people may believe that those attacks came out of the blue. But the warning signs were there, and not just in the previous terrorist attacks.

The original conference statement painted Israel as a racist state and legitimized the use of violence against it. Only after the American delegation walked out in protest was the statement substantially improved. As indicated here, however, the pre-9/11 Bush Administration did not act unequivocally toward Israel's right to defend itself against terror attacks.

Build on the Durban Victory
September 10, 2001

Despite a last minute turnabout at the edge of the abyss, the Durban conference on racism should go down in infamy in the annals of international relations. Thanks to the US walkout, the adopted declaration reads like the Israeli national anthem in comparison with the original text pushed by the Arab states. Durban should be seen as an American victory over diplomatic terrorism, with real lessons for the fight against the actual terrorist offensive facing Israel.

Let there be no mistake, without the US and Israeli walkouts from the UN conference, the remaining nations would not have been "shamed... out of acting like complete doormats for bigotry," as *New York Times* columnist William Safire put it. South Africa succeeded in pushing through a text whose only mention of the word 'Israel' is to recognize our right to security. But this success came only after the pre-walkout failure of Norway to gain agreement on a very similar text.

The South African text contains almost nothing of the vicious anti-Israel diatribe in the original draft but bears some scars from the rejected draft. The attempts to minimize the Holocaust or charge Israel with genocide are gone, for example, but why does a statement that the Holocaust "must never be forgotten" belong in the Middle East section of the declaration? The Holocaust is not just a parochial matter of concern to Jews and Israel, but the ultimate 'crime against humanity.' And what is a recognition of "the inalienable [Palestinian] right to self-determination" doing in a declaration on racism?

These, however, are quibbles in the face of the transformation of the Durban declaration from blatantly denying Israel's right to exist to a call for an 'end of violence' and for the rights of both Israelis and Palestinians to live in peace and security. What was a cry for jihad has become a call for peace.

Now that American leadership has delivered such a stunning victory in Durban, it would be a shame if the lessons from that victory were not applied to the situation in the Middle East. First, it should be acknowledged, the two challenges are not just related, they are the same challenge.

The same exact countries and leaders that were behind the near-fiasco in Durban are now reportedly saying, in the words of Saudi Ambassador to the US Prince Bandar, that "America's standing in the Arab world is at its lowest in 30 years." At Durban, the US could have attempted some blighted compromise out of concern for its 'standing in the Arab world.' To its enduring credit, it showed it is not concerned about kowtowing to sowers of hatred, but about remaining true to its own values and interests.

For the US to be victorious against the real wave of terrorism directed at Israel, it must act in the same way it did at Durban – unabashedly stand with Israel. Despite the bitter protests against US policy in the Arab world, the US is not currently shoulder to shoulder with Israel on terrorism the way it was against the hate-language of Durban.

The US has condemned Palestinian terrorism without equivocation and has blocked all Palestinian attempts to benefit from terrorism in the UN Security Council. As importantly, President George W. Bush has revoked Yasser Arafat's frequent guest pass to the White House and has clearly placed responsibility for ending terrorism on his shoulders.

At the same time, however, the US has criticized every measure Israel has taken to defend itself against Palestinian terrorism: withholding taxes, closures, pinpoint killings of terrorists, and brief incursions into Area A.

Bush has never called what Israel is doing legitimate self-defense, and the US has shown extreme reluctance to even indirectly endorse Israeli actions.

The Arms Export Control Act states that US weaponry can only be used for purposes of 'legitimate self-defense.' Sensing a contradiction, journalists have for months been asking why, if the US is opposed to targeting terrorists, the administration has not called Israel on a violation of US law.

The simple answer to these questions would have been that Israel is acting in self-defense and therefore entirely within US law. But the State Department continued to evade the issue, saying no determination had been made. On August 17, Secretary of State Colin Powell finally sent a letter to Congress that seemed to settle the issue, but also served to highlight American ambivalence. The letter did not say that Israel is using American weaponry for self-defense, only that "we believe a report is not required." The letter added ominously that the US "has been monitoring Israeli actions carefully and will continue to do so."

In this context, yesterday's statement by Secretary of Defense Donald Rumsfeld, who expressed complete understanding for Israeli actions, could mark a critical watershed in US policy. On Fox News Sunday, after five Israelis were killed in three terrorist incidents, Rumsfeld said, "I think that any time people are doing suicide bombings and blowing up your people at bus stops and in restaurants, you certainly cannot sit there and tolerate that. You have an obligation to your people to take action to try to reduce that level of violence or to eliminate it if humanly possible."

Rumsfeld's unabashed support for Israel's right to self-defense takes a page from the American victory in Durban and applies it to the fight against terrorism. If his remarks are echoed by the president and the secretary of state, the pressure on Arafat to end his offensive will increase significantly. Ironically, the more the US supports Israel, the more the arrows of moderate Arab states will be directed at Arafat rather than the US. Standing for principle is a winning policy, and everyone ultimately wants to be with the winner.

3. America Attacked

From 9/11 to the Iraq war.

On September 11 , it was difficult to absorb what had just happened. I remember hearing that an airplane had crashed into the World Trade Center and thinking it must have been a terrible fluke. Then hearing that a second plane had crashed into the second tower, and knowing it must have been terrorism. Finally, watching in horror as the towers collapsed, another plane plowed into the Pentagon, and a fourth crashed in Pennsylvania after the passengers struggled with their hijackers.

Given the failure to enlist the UN Security Council in the effort to oust Iraq's Saddam Hussein over a year later, the call here to employ the UN seems misplaced. I still wonder what would have happened if the US had moved more quickly at the UN in those first days.

In any case, our fundamental realization in these first few hours stands the test of time: that this was a global war against evil, and that the first task was to revive such moribund moral categories.

The New Evil Empire
September 12, 2001

Yesterday, December 7, 1941 – a date which will live in infamy – the United States of America was suddenly and deliberately attacked... No matter how long it may take us to overcome this premeditated invasion, the American people in their righteous might will win through to absolute victory... I ask that the Congress declare that since the unprovoked and dastardly attack by Japan on Sunday, December 7, a state of war has existed between the United States and the Japanese empire.

– US President Franklin D. Roosevelt, after the attack on Pearl Harbor

We live today in a different world. As German Chancellor Gerhard Schroeder has stated, someone has declared war on the United States. The war against terrorism, however, is a world war as surely as the war that was fought half a century ago.

As we look with horror at the devastating attacks on the United States, the hearts of all Israelis are with the American people. Even we Israelis, who have been battling a wave of terrorism for almost a year, have trouble fathoming what has befallen tens of thousands of innocent people in America.

We are sickened, once again, by scenes of Palestinians dancing in the streets, this time celebrating the deaths of Americans. We have trouble fathoming the hatred directed at us, so we can only imagine the bafflement and pain of Americans attempting to contemplate the baseless hatred directed at them.

Some Americans, like some Israelis, may be tempted to think about what they have done wrong, what they might have done to cause people to take so many lives along with their own. The answer is that America has been attacked not for what it has done wrong, but for what it has done right, and for being the hope of the entire world.

Concepts such as good and evil have long gone out of fashion, but we must relearn how to think in these terms. We have become used to rounding the corners off everything, so that what used to be a chasm between good and evil has been whittled down to a matter of opinion. But the fact that there are people in this world who would crash an airplane full of innocent people into a building full of innocent people should revive the concept of evil.

There is a new 'evil empire' – the empire of terror.

When confronting evil, the appropriate emotions are anger and determination, not understanding and moderation. The terrorists were evidently thinking as big as they could; the American response should be no less ambitious.

The United States will obviously seek out the organizations that have declared war on it and the states that give them moral and material support. But the world is not a court of law and the United States cannot limit itself to acting based on a level of proof that may never be found.

Rather, the United States should state, as Roosevelt did in 1941, that as of yesterday's attacks a state of war 'has existed' between the United States and the 'evil empire' of state-sponsored terrorism.

In this war, the diplomatic front is at least as crucial as the military one. The United States, as strange as it may sound, should take this opportunity to restore the United Nations to its original purpose.

The highest purpose of the United Nations Charter was to band the nations of the world together against international aggression. While that purpose was long ago distorted beyond recognition, it is time to finally breathe life into it.

The United States should demand that the Security Council use the strongest measures in its arsenal – mandatory 'Chapter 7' sanctions – against any nation that supports international terrorism. Making sure that such sanctions are imposed on known terrorist states may be a long battle, but fighting this battle will put these nations on the defensive and provide the appropriate background for military actions the United States will have to take. Any nation that opposes the American effort should be told that its relations with the United States will be affected accordingly.

Terrorism is a global scourge that must be fought globally. Until now, the democracies have fiddled with and indulged the states where terrorism has been cultivated and grown. America's goal should be, one way or another, to defeat or remove the regimes that have declared war against her. If the democracies do not unite to defend themselves, our world will become as tragically unrecognizable as the New York skyline.

◆ ◆ ◆

Reading this now, it is hard to believe that the world's newspaper of record, which is also the newspaper of the city that had just been so devastatingly attacked, could editorialize as it did at that time. Fortunately, most Americans shared their president's view that they were in a war that must be won, not psychologized.

Michael Kelly, whom I quote below, later died while covering the war with US forces in Iraq. His rapier pen is sorely missed.

69

Defining the Enemy
September 13, 2001

As Americans try to recover from and comprehend the most devastating terrorist attack ever, it is not surprising that US leaders are groping for a new language and way of thinking to confront the new reality.

There is general agreement that America is and must be 'at war.' But the pledge of President George W. Bush and many others to "find those responsible and bring them to justice" sounds not like war, but a police action against criminals.

The distinction between fighting a war and bringing criminals to justice is not a merely semantic one. It is a distinction over the nature of the enemy.

America's first task is defining the enemy. In this war, the enemy's attempt to distort and obscure its identity is its primary line of defense.

The enemy is not merely Osama bin Laden or whatever terrorist organization carried out the monstrous attack. The enemy is the states that sponsor terrorists and the ideology that animates them.

Imagine for a moment that bin Laden is proven to be the immediate culprit and the US were to successfully bomb him and his organization out of existence. Would terrorism have been defeated? No – such a success would be the equivalent of destroying a kamikaze or Nazi unit while leaving the wartime governments of Japan or Germany in place.

If the bin Ladens of the world are defined as the enemy, terrorism has won; if the governments that sponsor terrorism are the enemy, then terrorism can be defeated. As Israel learned in Lebanon, it was impossible to defeat Hizbullah while that organization's Syrian, Iranian, and Lebanese sponsors were effectively held immune from attack.

The idea that regimes, not just organizations, must be held responsible may seem obvious. Indeed, Bush has stated that the US will "make no distinction between the terrorists who committed these acts and those who harbor them." But even before the rubble has ceased to smolder doubts are being expressed.

In its editorial on the attack, the *New York Times* mused that "this is an age when even revenge is complicated, when it is hard to match the desire for retribution with the need for certainty." What retribution? What need for certainty? To talk about retribution and certainty is to act as if the task after Pearl Harbor was to prove which unit had attacked

America and to punish that unit – rather than to defeat and replace the governments of Japan, Germany, and Italy.

In a second editorial, the *Times* argued that "part of the challenge for the United States is to recognize that the roots of terrorism lie in economic and political problems in large parts of the world." This is errant nonsense.

As Michael Kelly points out in the *Washington Post*, "The whole world was stolen from somebody, most of it repeatedly; there are claims and counterclaims and counter- counterclaims for every inch of the planet that is desirable and for much that is not." If poverty, corruption, tyranny, suffering, ethnic conflict, and territorial disputes were the sources of terrorism, sub-Saharan Africa would be the terror center of the world.

To 'recognize the roots' of terrorism is to harbor the notion that terrorism can be justified. Worse, it directly fulfills the goal of terrorism, which is to blackmail the world into addressing 'grievances.' The obstacles to addressing real suffering are the regimes that are behind terrorism, which not coincidentally oppress and impoverish their own people.

For the free world, the war against terrorism cannot be limited to punishment, retribution, or sending signals. Those who sent the terrorists to attack America would be only too pleased to absorb a less than tit-for-tat cruise missile attack in response.

The free world must recognize that it is in a war of self-defense whose goal is victory. The concept of a war against terrorism is meaningless without the goal of removing terrorist regimes. The exact combination of diplomatic, economic, and military tools to be deployed toward this goal is a legitimate matter of debate. But a war against terrorism that avoids the issue of regime change in countries such as Iraq, Iran, and Afghanistan cannot be won, because it has not even really been joined.

◆ ◆ ◆

This, my first column after September 11, is a reminder of those first few days in which the shock of the attack was still raw, and no one really knew how the US would respond. My criticism here of Bush's initial bunker-hopping in the first few hours generated a fair number of angry e-mails, most of them assuming I was a left-wing opponent of the president.

As it happened, Bush has more than amply corrected for his somewhat skittish behavior that day. I was surprised that no one else seemed to question that Bush headed for a nuke-proof bunker in Nebraska rather than the White House on the day itself. I still wonder whether there was a single general or White House advisor who was worried about sending the wrong signal – both to the terror network and Americans – by acting as if even the White House was not secure enough for the President.

Interesting Times: Design to Win
September 14, 2001

The day after, I had the same traumatic, disoriented feeling I had after my brother fell in battle and after Yitzhak Rabin's assassination. How could the sun still be shining? How can daily life just continue, as if nothing happened? The sickening scenes of the collapsing twin towers and the gaping hole left in their place did not just terrorize America, but us, sitting here in Jerusalem. It was a successful attack on the entire world.

Terror must be understood as the most potent form of psychological warfare.

Terrorism is a way of bypassing the armies that countries build to defend themselves and directly attacking the morale of the enemy. Terrorists know that the ability to fight is irrelevant if the will to fight has been defeated.

If we think of the fight against terrorism only in military terms, we have fallen into their trap. Israelis show instinctive understanding of this when they fight back by continuing with their normal lives. Workers labored around the clock to reopen Jerusalem's Sbarro pizzeria as quickly as possible, devastated by a suicide bombing a month ago. The reopening this week was an occasion of pride and defiance, attended by President Moshe Katsav and United States Ambassador Daniel Kurtzer.

Most Americans, like Israelis, will have the instinct to deny terrorism the victory of affecting their way of life, but this instinct must be cultivated and reinforced. President George W. Bush, unfortunately, displayed a blindness to this psychological aspect of the fight against terrorism when he let his security people keep him away from the White House.

The president, as the explanation goes, was shuttled from one place to another, including a nuclear missile base in Nebraska, because of unnamed threats against the White House and Air Force One. This is not convincing.

72

There is no doubt that Air Force One could have been more than adequately defended from a civilian airliner by a fighter jet escort; the same is the case for the White House itself.

Grounding every American civilian airliner, closing the borders, sending the president into bunkers, all these are victories for the terrorists. The actions taken on the civilian side were perhaps necessary precautions, but the president should not have been swayed from his path by a single inch.

The generals were thinking about how to maximize the security of the president, but by ignoring the psychological aspect, they unnecessarily weakened America's national security.

The choice of where to fly Air Force One was just the first of many that will demand understanding of the psychology of terror. It is not too late for Bush to learn from his mistake. Indeed, he must, because the president bears great responsibility for setting America's mood, and by extension, the mood of the world.

It is not enough to say, over and over again, that America's spirit will not be broken; what matters is acting that way. The twin towers were not just a financial center. They were, as George Will writes, "like Manhattan itself, architectural expressions of the vigor of American civilization." President Bush should announce a national competition to design a new World Trade Center, with the stipulation that the new center capture the soaring spirit of the towers that were destroyed, and of America's belief in itself and the new age.

There will be those who advocate a squat, secure, structure that can withstand the impact of numerous hijacked planes. The winning design should be exactly the opposite: a complex designed for a world that has defeated terrorism, not one that has been cowed by it.

There are 189 members of the United Nations. Roughly five of them use terrorism as an instrument of national policy. America's goal should be to reduce the number of governments that support terrorism to zero by the time the new soaring, wispy, inspiring World Trade Center is rebuilt. This goal may sound utopian, but it is both realistic and necessary.

If we accept the inevitability of terrorist states, we are dooming ourselves to a futile attempt at turning our cities into bunkers. This time the weapon was hijacked airplanes, a weapon so low-tech that it could have been used in the 1940s. We know that the technology is already available to make September 11 look like child's play.

The United States alone, the 184 non-terrorist states together, or some combination in between, have the might to make it impossible for a handful of tin-pot dictatorships to sow terror and remain in power. The first step is for America to show that it is not only saying it is unbowed, but has set a deadline for and is betting on its own victory.

◆ ◆ ◆

After 9/11, soon after the initial shock and anger had a moment to lessen, the media began to ask the question "why do they hate us?" It is impossible to ask this question without more than a tinge of self-doubt, as if America were at fault for being attacked. The tendency of democracies to self-blame and doubt when confronted by dictators who know no such compunctions is nothing new, and connects the American and Israeli experiences in confronting terrorism.

Rosh Hashana 5762
September 17, 2001

Starting tonight, the Jewish people begin the Days of Awe – the 10 days beginning with Rosh Hashana and ending on Yom Kippur. It is a time of closure and of new beginnings, a time of solemn judgment, mixed with the confidence that God is a merciful judge who gives us the benefit of the doubt.

The year we are finishing is one of the worst in memory. Last Rosh Hashana was when the violent Palestinian violence began, and the failure of the Camp David summit was sealed in blood. And now this bloody year has been capped by the unimaginable attacks on the United States.

It is a difficult time to develop a spirit of renewal or to engage in personal spiritual cleansing. What form of self-inspection is appropriate when our country and our Western society are under attack?

What is not appropriate is the kind of self-incrimination that terrorism is meant to generate – self-doubt and questioning whether there is something we did to deserve being attacked. Our attackers have no right to murder us. The idea that terrorism is generated by grievances that are either justified or fulfillable is a poisonous myth.

If anything, the evidence indicates that the opposite is the case. At Camp David and in the negotiations that followed, Israel made it clearer than ever before that it was not only ready, but determined to address Palestinian grievances to the maximum extent possible, short of committing suicide. And it was this offer that was met by a wave of Palestinian terrorism, this time courtesy of the proto-state that Israel agreed to establish as a down payment toward peace.

The Palestinian resort to terror at precisely the moment when Oslo's 'two-state solution' was about to be concluded, coupled with the redoubling of Palestinian demands for a 'right of return,' indicates that the real 'grievance' remains not the 'occupation,' but Israel's existence.

Similarly, regarding the wider attack on Western civilization, as represented by the economic and military centers of American power, it is clear that is what is objectionable about the West is not this or that policy, but its very existence. The 'grievance' of the bin Ladens of the world is that the US stands in the way of their dreams of a radical Islamic empire that is not 'subservient' to Western notions of freedom, human rights, and democracy.

So what kind of self-examination, as individuals or as a society, is called for in a situation like this? Perhaps our sin is not that we have neglected the grievances of others, but we have not given enough weight to our own? Have we been naive about the threats to our countries and to everything we believe is right?

After all, if we truly believe in democracy, human rights, and eliminating poverty, why have we been so passive when it comes to advancing our values?

Why do we not seem to attach any value to our own grievances against those who not only deprive their own peoples of freedom, but attack us for having the temerity to call them on it?

Hillel's famous dictum, "If I am only for myself, then what am I?" is one of the most powerful expressions of the ethos of Western civilization. But his dictum also asks, "If I am not for myself, then who will be for me?" Hillel clearly understood that the first imperative is to be good, but to be good, one also has to survive.

As we think about the coming year, perhaps we should consider that we too have grievances and that these grievances are actually more legitimate than the ones our enemies try to throw at us. Further, that by not giving sufficient weight to our own grievances, we are not only endangering ourselves, but are depriving many more less fortunate people of the hope that Western power and values represent.

May this year be a year that we reexamine ourselves and not only fix our faults, but recognize and fight for our virtues. Shana Tova.

◆ ◆ ◆

President George W. Bush has not only set goals for the war as we advocated here, but has since taken a significant step toward fulfilling them by ousting Saddam. Yet the war against the terror masters has not received the cooperation we had hoped for, nor has it been directed as widely and simultaneously as it might have been. The next challenge is to remove the regime that started it all and remains the largest state-sponsor of terrorism, the mullahcracy in Iran.

Drain the Ponds of Terror
September 25, 2001

President George W. Bush gave the best speech he has ever given, has about the highest approval rating in American polling history, and has the American people squarely behind him in an all-out war against terrorism. Looking from afar, we marvel at the unity and determination of the American people, and salute them with all our hearts.

Yet the very awesomeness of American power, when brought together for a single aim, raises the stakes enormously. Behind American unity lies a raging debate: How widely should the net be spread? Who are America's real targets? How will victory be defined?

The president, to his enduring credit, prepared the American people for a comprehensive war against terrorism, not just against the one man whose face is on the cover of almost every news magazine in America: Osama bin Laden. There is no doubt that this man must be eliminated. It is clear, however, that the elimination of one terrorist, or one terrorist's network, does not a war on terrorism make.

Bush clearly understands this. Speaking to a small group of US senators in a way that says even more than his fine speech to Congress, Bush said: "When I take action, I'm not gonna fire a $2 million missile at a $10 empty tent and hit a camel in the butt. It's going to be decisive." Decisive is the right word. But what does it mean to be decisive in the war against terror?

Decisive means eradicating state-sponsorship of terror. And eradication means rejecting the notion that the US and its allies must choose which terrorist states to go after, rather than change the rules for all of them at once. The Bush administration is wisely giving even the guiltiest regimes, such as Iran, a chance to change their ways. The rules were different before September 11. But now new rules have to be written, and they have to be enforced not just by the US but by Europe – at a minimum – as well.

The rules should be that any country that hosts or supports terrorist groups (including religious organizations that advocate terrorism), whose passports or diplomatic pouches are used by terrorists, or that does not cooperate in hunting down or handing over terrorists, will be treated as a terrorist state.

All terrorist states should be subject to complete ostracism by Western nations: no diplomatic relations, no trade, no banking transactions, and no air travel.

If the US declares it will be working with its close allies to define what it means to be a terrorist state and the draconian sanctions that will be taken against such states, there will be a scramble by countries to comply with the new rules even before they are enforced. America's NATO allies will not stand in the way on this if the US is determined.

The demonstrated determination of the West to use all its economic and diplomatic clout against all terrorist states will produce a number of 'converts' and isolate the toughest nuts to crack. We already know one leader that will be in the holdout category: Iraq's Saddam Hussein.

It is impossible to decisively beat terrorism without removing the Mother of All Terrorist Regimes. Serious students of the issue, such as former CIA director R. James Woolsey, are convinced that Saddam was behind the September 11 monstrosity. OC Intelligence Maj.-Gen. Amos Malka may be have been too hasty in exonerating Iraq in this case. There is certainly a convincing case that Saddam was behind the first attempt to topple the World Trade Center in 1993.

But in the unlikely event that Saddam had no role in this latest attack, he is certainly no less worthy of removal than he was before September 11. Saddam had to go even before this, because he is openly defying the UN Security Council's efforts to disarm him of weapons of mass destruction and therefore poses a terrorist threat much greater than Osama bin Laden. Saddam is busy building a nuclear, biological, and chemical umbrella for terrorism. Most importantly, Saddam is much weaker than he is made out to be. He already does not control the 'no-fly' zones maintained by the US and Britain. With considerably less force than was employed during the Gulf War, the US could help the Iraqi National Congress take over most of Iraq and recognize it as the legitimate provisional government.

Within a short time, most of Iraq's military would defect to the opposition, and Saddam would effectively be transformed into the mayor of Baghdad. Most of his much vaunted missile sites would be out of his control, and he would be too busy fighting for his life to continue his race to rearm. The US and the Iraqi opposition would both commit to keeping Iraq whole and to holding free elections to determine Iraq's new government.

The combination of setting and enforcing new rules for terrorist states and toppling Saddam should be at the core of America's plan to eradicate state-supported terrorism. Hunting for bin Laden is necessary, but it is like angling for a particularly big fish, when what is needed is to drain the pond. The pond can be drained, using only a fraction of the economic and military power available to the West. Doing so now will be immeasurably cheaper, in blood and treasure, than the alternatives, and will change the world we live in radically for the better.

◆ ◆ ◆

The story of the peace process has been of the Palestinians trying to get what they want, a state, without giving Israel what it wants, peace. Avoiding such an unfair and unworkable deal might seem to be straightforward, but it has not been. Often, Israel's own willingness to overlook Palestinian violation of agreements has been a great part of the problem. Following the June 2003 Aqaba summit, the test of the "road map" will be the same as it was for Oslo: will the Palestinians get away with not fulfilling their part of the bargain?

Learn from Oslo's Mistakes
September 28, 2001

On Wednesday morning, Foreign Minister Shimon Peres paved Yasser Arafat's way into the post-September 11 'good guys' club by meeting the Palestinian leader in Gaza. The cheering Palestinian crowds and Arafat's embrace of terror had put him on the wrong side of the post-September 11 divide - just as his backing of Saddam Hussein had done during the Gulf War. Israel, of all countries, threw Arafat the rope he needed, in exchange for another promise to stop terrorism.

We have been through this before, not just because Arafat has promised a cease-fire six times in the last year, but because Israel did the same thing in 1993. At that time, Arafat was broke and isolated following his backing of Saddam, and Israel essentially promised him a state in exchange for a permanent cease-fire.

Now the wizards of Oslo admit that they made a small mistake: not holding Arafat to his key commitments, such as ending incitement and confiscating illegal weapons. The post-Oslo mantra is that the agreement fell apart because both sides were undermining the territory-for-peace bargain. Instead of educating for peace, the Palestinians educated for war, while Israel – according to conventional wisdom – was trying to keep territory by building settlements, rather than moving toward dismantling them.

The facile equation between incitement and settlements is invalid on both legal and practical grounds. Legally, the Palestinians' incitement was expressly prohibited, while Oslo did not restrict the growth of either Palestinian or Israeli communities in the territories that were under dispute. Practically, when push came to shove at the Camp David and Taba talks, Israel was willing to withdraw from over 95 percent of the territory, while the Palestinians were completely unprepared to give up on the 'right of return' or compromise in any meaningful way.

Most dramatically, months of vicious anti-Israel incitement in the Arafat-controlled Palestinian media laid the groundwork for the Palestinian reembrace of violence and terrorism one year ago.

What relevance does all this history have to the current moment? Plenty.

The agreement just reached between Peres and Arafat has not been released, but one has to wonder whether ending incitement is a serious part of it.

On September 11, as it happens, the Arafat-controlled newspaper Al-Hayat al Jadida published these thoughts: "The suicide bombers of today are the noble successors of the Lebanese suicide bombers, who taught the US Marines a tough lesson. These suicide bombers are the salt of the earth, the engines of history. They are the most honorable people among us." This week, the police recommended indicting the Palestinian-appointed mufti of Jerusalem, Sheikh Ikrama Sabri, for calling for the destruction of Israel, the US, and the UK in a sermon in al-Aksa Mosque on the Temple Mount.

What will happen if the cease-fire holds, but the glorification of suicide bombers as the "salt of the earth" continues? Will Israel and the United States jointly say to Arafat, 'Sorry, talking now while preparing to shoot later won't wash?'

The circumstances of the Peres-Arafat meeting do not bode well for the prospect of holding Arafat to a higher standard. Just a short time ago, Prime Minister Ariel Sharon had an embarrassing photo-op with US President George W. Bush at the White House, where it seemed that Bush wanted to see the Mitchell plan move forward even though Palestinian attacks had not been brought down to zero. Now Peres was not willing to hold Arafat even to Bush's low standard before meeting him.

The collapse of Oslo and the events of September 11 demand that Israel and the United States not make the same mistakes again. Just as the US is changing the rules regarding terrorism globally, Israel and the US must change the rules regarding what is tolerated locally, on the Israeli-Palestinian front. The litmus test for whether the rules have really changed should not only be zero terrorism and incitement, but attention to an element that Oslo brazenly ignored: the need to 'educate for peace.'

There is little point to returning to the negotiating table if the Palestinians are not willing to do what Israeli society has been doing for years: preparing the public for making compromises in order to achieve peace. Incitement is the opposite of 'educating for peace.' We've seen what happens with the former; now, if we have the chance, let's insist on the latter.

◆ ◆ ◆

This piece was triggered by the flak Italian Prime Minister Silvio Berlusconi received for daring to speak of the "superiority" of Western civilization. I also took the opportunity to introduce one of my favorite Jewish thinkers, Eliezer Berkovits. If you think that religion should be more about making a better world and better people, and less about ritual, theology, and good intentions, Berkovits is an inspiring guide. The essay I mention below by David Hazony in the Summer 2001 issue of Azure *is the best summary of his thinking that I have seen (www.shalem.org.il/azure/11-hazony.htm).*

Interesting Times: The West is Best
October 5, 2001

After September 11, Hollywood rushed to electronically 'white out' the Twin Towers from upcoming films, presumably so as not to bring up unpleasant memories for the viewer. Watching Steven Spielberg's movie *AI* in Israel this week, our feelings were not so spared.

The movie takes place far in the future, when robots have become so like humans that they actually become the most sympathetic characters in the story. Manhattan, inexplicably, has already been engulfed by the ocean, but the Twin Towers are still standing there in celluloid.

It is painful to think that the towers that in Hollywood's mind would survive thousands of years, through floods and ice ages, did not make it even until the release of the movie. Despite the popularity of disaster films of all kinds, based on fires, meteorites, earthquakes, or the general breakdown of society, even Hollywood did not anticipate the reality of September 11.

The star of *AI* (short for 'Artificial Intelligence') is a robot boy, masterfully played by Haley Joel Osment, who competes for the love of his human 'mother.' In the end, the borders between human and robot are blurred, as mechanical creations become capable of the whole range of human emotions. The robots, if anything, emerge as a sort of idealized form of humanity – wanting to please, immortal, and free of human venality.

What is thought-provoking about *AI* is that it flips the usual Hollywood take on technology on its head. Rather than the machines-run-amuck vision of films such as *2001* and *Westworld*, Spielberg seems to be using machines as a contrast that finds people to be morally wanting.

Though movies have no shortage of evil human characters, Hollywood tends to portray humanity as a whole – when in conflict with technology, nature, or other worlds – as basically good. Spielberg's presentation of humanity is more of a mixed bag, which is actually in keeping with a Jewish view of human nature that is especially relevant to our new-old post-September 11 world.

In an essay on philosopher Eliezer Berkovits's contribution to Jewish thought in the current issue of *Azure*, David Hazony writes that "the mistaken belief that man can be made good solely through preparation of the mind is, in Berkovits's view, the salient tragedy of Western civilization." Berkovits claimed that the great moral failure of the West was to confuse intellectual enlightenment with moral advancement.

"There seems to be little [moral] difference between ages of greater and lesser enlightenment," Berkovits argued, "except that as knowledge increases, man grows in power proportionately and becomes proportionately more dangerous."

A case can be made that political and economic progress is correlated with moral progress, in that human rights have flourished mainly in developed countries. But Berkovits rightly questions the Western view that morality is a natural byproduct of what we call 'progress.'

In contrast to Immanuel Kant and even to Jewish philosophers such as Martin Buber and Abraham Joshua Heschel, Berkovits measured morality by good results, not by good intentions. And according to such a results-oriented standard, the West must be judged not just by the positive results it produces at home, but by its willingness to defend and promote morally superior values.

It is often pointed out that the tolerance and openness of democratic societies is both their strength and their weakness. The West certainly must not give up what has made it great, but it would not be a bad time to question whether, as a teenager might put it, it is possible to become so open-minded that your brains fall out.

Italian leader Silvio Berlusconi took a lot of flak for asserting that the West was 'superior' to Islam. He may have been a bit crass, but he may also have been on the right track.

What Berlusconi actually said was that, in a war against terrorists spouting a particular breed of Islam, 'we should be confident of the superiority of our civilization.' The West produced Hitler and Stalin, and Islamic civilization has at times been more tolerant of minorities, including Jews, than the Christian world. But Berlusconi is right that to win this war the West must first believe in itself.

When confronting evil, old-fashioned righteous indignation, rather than tolerance, is the order of the day. A meaningful notion of progress should include what is often thoughtlessly dismissed as 'cultural imperialism.' The issue is not whether countries have a right to reject McDonalds or Disneyland, but whether the West should more actively offer hope for the freedoms it enjoys to the billions of people who do not.

◆ ◆ ◆

When a Russian aircraft carrying many Israelis crashed shortly after 9/11, the immediate fear was that another major terror attack had occurred. Ukraine's defense minister later admitted that his forces had mistakenly downed the plane during a military exercise.

Another measure of this skittish time was Ariel Sharon's "Czechoslovakia" speech, accusing George W. Bush of appeasing the Arab world at Israel's expense. This is an important episode to keep in mind, because it shows that the moral clarity Bush employed in subsequent months was not as much in evidence in these initial stages of the war.

From a tactical point of view, Sharon's speech was unnecessarily confrontational and, to some extent, unfair. Sharon could have sent a warning signal with greater subtlety and effectiveness.

Sharon's Warning Shot
October 5, 2001

Whatever caused the crash of Sibir Airlines Flight 1812 from Tel Aviv to Novosibirsk, the tragic results are, unfortunately, certain. Seventy-eight passengers and crew are dead, among them over 50 Israelis. That most of these Israelis came to live here only recently only compounds the tragedy, and heightens Israel's responsibility to determine what happened.

Given the attacks of September 11, and that witnesses from a nearby Armenian aircraft reported seeing an explosion from the Russian plane, the prospect the plane was downed by a terrorist attack initially seemed to be a real one. But American satellite surveillance reportedly proves that it was an errant Ukrainian missile that downed the plane.

Ukrainian Prime Minister Victor Yushchenko should be given some credit for pledging a quick and thorough investigation into the tragedy, given that his defense minister had categorically denied the possibility that a missile from a Ukrainian military exercise could have brought down the plane. It is also encouraging that, according to Prime Minister Ariel Sharon, Russian President Vladimir Putin has pledged to include Israel fully in the investigation that has already begun.

It is imperative that there be complete cooperation among Ukraine, Russia, and Israel, and any foreign intelligence agencies that can shed light on what happened. The sooner the cause of the crash can be positively determined, the better it will be for relations between the nations involved, and at least the added burden of uncertainty will be lifted.

Forced to confront tragedy upon tragedy, Sharon also addressed yesterday's terror attack in Afula, in which three Israelis were murdered and seven wounded, just a day after two Israelis were murdered in another terror attack in Elei Sinai.

Sharon's statement that the cabinet had authorized "all necessary measures" in response seemed to be an explicit warning that Israel's policy of restraint has reached its limits.

Most striking, however, was Sharon's direct accusation against the United States: "Do not repeat the dreadful mistake of 1938, when enlightened European democracies decided to sacrifice Czechoslovakia for a 'convenient temporary solution.' Do not try to appease the Arabs at our expense. Israel will not be Czechoslovakia. Israel will fight terrorism."

The Bush administration will no doubt be surprised by Sharon's hurling what is the most painful arrow one ally can aim at another, the charge of Munich-style abandonment. Aside from the element of surprise, however, the Bush team is hardly in a position to argue that Sharon's charge is unjustified.

Sharon is absolutely right that it is morally and strategically bankrupt for the US to act as if its alliance with Israel is a liability in the war against terror, while praising Arab regimes that have been fanning the jihad against America for years. The excuse that stiff-arming Israel is needed to build a coalition does not wash – where is it written that the US needs the permission of Arab states to act in its own self-defense? If anything, lessening the bonds between the US and Israel at this moment stinks of weakness, when what is needed is reassertion of America's commitment to defend its interests across the board, including Israel's security.

President Bush's speech at the State Department yesterday was encouraging in that he reiterated that America would not only 'have no compassion for terrorists,' but would have 'no compassion for any state that sponsors [terrorism].' But when it comes to the terror Israel is confronting, Bush went mushy, saying only 'that in order for there to be peace, we must reduce the level of violence.'

Israel's problem is not some amorphous 'level of violence' but a terrorist offensive as unacceptable as that facing the US.

The fact that Sharon had to accuse the US of appeasement at this time should be a serious warning signal for US policy. If any two countries should be tightly coordinated in the war against terror – against both nations – they are the US and Israel. If the Bush administration does not want to be surprised by such accusations in the future, it should stand shoulder-to-shoulder with Israel, not push it into a corner.

◆　◆　◆

I wrote this to help Americans, shocked to find themselves in the circle of terror, retain a sense of perspective. Along the way, I surprised myself by managing to express why I moved to Israel almost seven years before. My point was that September 11 might create in America something akin to what attracted me about Israel.

Interesting Times: The Advantages of Adversity
October 12, 2001

To most Americans, September 11 came out of the blue, literally and figuratively. They, and we, never had a chance to say goodbye to the era that was, the decade between the Cold War and the War on Terror that in retrospect will seem like a happy, innocent time, like the 1920s and the 1950s.

In Israel, we didn't have such a carefree decade – it was more like a few months. Remember when it seemed that Ehud Barak could do no wrong, peace seemed to be on the way, there was almost no terrorism, and the Israeli economy was riding the Nasdaq boom? But even when times were harder here than they were in America, what was good for America was good for us, and even the sight of success was encouraging.

Now America has become Israel. Americans whose only contact with the world of terror was the metal detector at the airport, now are learning to think and talk like Israelis, for whom living with and fighting terror is a part of the national consciousness.

Like Pearl Harbor, September 11 brought America into an ongoing war.

Now, as then, it is obvious in retrospect that even if America did not join the war, the war would still come to America. Now, as then, America has been attacked not for what it does, but for what it is and stands for.

For Americans, a staggering 78 percent of whom reportedly have never set foot outside of their country, the abrupt transition from peace to war must be as difficult as it is incomprehensible. But distraught Americans should comfort themselves that even this situation that no one would wish for could change America for the better.

I was born in and grew up in the US, except for four early teenage years when I lived in Israel with my family. When we returned to the US in 1977, I distinctly remember the contrast between the Israeli peers I left behind, and the American high school kids I joined. At 16, my Israeli peers were just two years away from a three-year stint in the army. For my American friends, what passed for a maturing introduction to the real world was four years in college, though higher education was more akin to an extension of adolescence.

My Israeli friends were kids at heart, hardly dour, and not obviously burdened by their futures. But their imminent participation in the real world task of defending their country made Israeli kids more interested in engaging life than in creating artificial risks with drugs or alcohol.

Though I had been a foreigner in Israel, I felt somewhat out of place when I returned to America, and eventually, like all my brothers, moved back to Israel. What ultimately brought me back to Israel was a sense of purpose that felt lacking in America, partly because of the lack of adversity.

Israelis and Americans alike, of course, often do not understand why anyone would leave the promised land of ease and plenty for the Promised and of strife and small expensive apartments. Indeed, such a move does not make sense if one's goal is to make life easier.

I haven't been back to the States since September 11, but I imagine that even today, I would enjoy the ease of a world in which people are polite on the phone, the customer is always right, and everything works as smoothly as humanly possible. I'm certainly not against Israel having all these things.

For Israelis, 'America' is an adjective synonymous with paradise. We aspire to be like America, and in many ways, we should. It is insane that we have a government that comprises half of our economy, and even worse that no one cares. Don't get me started.

But now Americans may develop something that still attracts me about Israelis – a richness and appreciation for life born of having more at stake. Trading 'reality television' for reality has advantages, even if reality is less pleasant.

It is perhaps no coincidence that Israelis could be the most well-traveled people in the world and Americans among the least. On the Israeli side, this is mainly a function of living in a country about the size of a Texas ranch, and breaking loose following the need to grow up quickly in the army. But Israelis also travel more because they are, by necessity, already more a part of the wider world. An America forced to be more outward-looking will be good for Americans and even better for the world.

◆　◆　◆

The refusal to see Israel's struggle as a component of the wider war against militant Islam continues to be a fundamental Western weakness in that war. The Arab-Israeli conflict has been the place where the use of terrorism has been, if not accepted, essentially tolerated and amply rewarded. It is questionable whether the attempt now (June 2003) to push forward a diplomatic "road map" without fully removing Yasser Arafat from power will work, because it depends on transforming a regime that, even more than the Taliban, has supported terrorism.

Arafat is our Taliban
October 16, 2001

Prime Minister Ariel Sharon has famously labeled Palestinian Authority Chairman Yasser Arafat as "our bin Laden." Actually, this is an exaggeration. Arafat is our Taliban. Though Arafat and the Taliban are obviously not cut from the same Muslim fundamentalist cloth, their relationship to terrorism is similar. The United States and Britain decided to start bombing the Taliban regime, because it was difficult for them to tell who controlled whom: bin Laden or the Taliban.

The Taliban-run Afghanistan is now, with good reason, the prime global example of a state that harbors terrorists. But the Taliban itself is not generally accused of engaging in terrorist acts (unlike cases of Syrian, Iraqi, and Libyan intelligence agents who have been directly involved with terrorism). Like the Iranian and Syrian governments, which actively backed terrorist groups as an arm of their foreign policies, the Taliban and bin Laden seem to have a symbiotic relationship, with each using the other for its own complementary purposes.

Arafat's relationship with Hamas and Islamic Jihad may be more complicated, but in the end no less intimate than that between the Taliban and bin Laden. Over the past year, Arafat and his supposed radical opponents engaged a tandem strategy of terror. Arafat's forces, such as Fatah-Tanzim and Force 17, would gun down Israelis on the roads in Judea, Samaria, and the Gaza Strip, and controlled the manufacture and distribution of mortars that were fired on Israeli communities. Arafat's 'opposition' would focus on suicide bombing in Israel proper. When Arafat decided it was in his interest to call a cease-fire, he would convince his 'opposition' that suicide attacks were not in the Palestinian interest.

Whatever power struggle there may be between Arafat and Islamist Palestinian forces, when it comes to terrorism there is a division of labor between them. In this respect, Arafat is worse than the Taliban: he does not just harbor and cooperate with terrorists – the organizations he leads engage in terrorism themselves.

In a 'cease-fire,' ironically, Arafat's connection to terrorism could actually become more obvious, since Arafat's idea of a 'cease-fire' has been, at best, stopping suicide bombings within Israel. Arafat has never said that he would stop terrorist attacks against Israelis living in the disputed territories. It is this form of terrorism, which has mainly been carried out by Arafat's own forces, that the Organization of Islamic States just proclaimed is not terrorism, but "resisting occupation."

It is in this context that British Prime Minister Tony Blair's meeting with Arafat yesterday was particularly disturbing. Blair, in the great tradition of his country, has been America's staunchest ally and among the most eloquent in explaining the need to defeat terrorism. As Blair said, "What happened in America was an attack not just upon the United States, but upon the civilized world."

But Blair should know better that the war against terrorism can be fought by continuing to allow the terrorist to play divide and conquer. Both Britain and the United States have been drifting toward a distinction between two types of terror: 'global' terror directed at the West in general and 'local' terror geared toward achieving more limited local aims. A take-no-prisoners war is being fought against the former, but the world's most prominent symbol of the latter – Yasser Arafat – is welcomed into 10 Downing Street.

September 11 should have destroyed the supposed dichotomy between local and global terror. Before September 11, one might have argued, however cynically, that 'local' terror would never spread, and would stay 'local' if the West did not oppose it too vigorously. Now it should be clear that if 'local' terror is a successful and quasi-legitimate way to address local grievances, there is nothing stopping the use of terror in the war for the ultimate grievance, that of Islamists against the West.

In this respect, Sharon's retracted Czechoslovakia analogy was right on target. Appeasement is the attempt to address 'little' grievances in the hope that the big grievance will go away. Appeasement has a bad name not just because it is wrong, but because it is not prudent – it does not work.

An international effort to compel the Palestinians to accept statehood and peace with Israel based on authentic compromise – which the Palestinians refused to do at Camp David – could enhance Israel's security and contribute to the war on terrorism. But any attempt to ingratiate the Arab world at the expense of Israel's security will reward terrorism on a global scale, leading to more terrorism against Israel, Arab regimes, and the United States. The war on terrorism will not withstand the bombing of one Taliban and the coddling of another.

❖ ❖ ❖

Rehavam Ze'evi was the Minister of Tourism and the head of Moledet party, a small extreme right-wing party that had just resigned from the unity government led by Ariel Sharon and Shimon Peres. He was gunned down in the hallway of the Hyatt hotel, where he stayed when in Jerusalem. His assassination seemed like a watershed event at the time, but Israel ended up taking dramatic action against terrorism only in April the following year, after the massacre at a Passover seder in Netanya's Park Hotel.

After the Assassination
October 18, 2001

Six years ago there were four Israeli leaders whose lives of service spanned the history of the state. Now Rehavam Ze'evi, like his colleague from the Palmah, Yitzhak Rabin, has been assassinated. The other two veteran leaders, Ariel Sharon and Shimon Peres, now face what is perhaps the most fateful hour of their careers.

Ze'evi's extreme brand of politics masked an unusual array of qualities. Shimon Peres described him as having the "soul of an author, an historian." He had an encyclopedic knowledge of the land and its history, and had edited 65 books published by the Defense Ministry and the Eretz Yisrael Museum in Tel Aviv. Avraham Burg hailed his skills and dedication as a parliamentarian.

Other politicians cited his honesty, loyalty, and trustworthiness in an arena not known for such traits.

Ze'evi was a soldier in the literal and best senses of the word. After rising through the ranks to become a major-general and OC Central Command, he carried into the political world the same dedication to defending his country. He will be missed not only by his allies, but by his political foes.

Today thousands will pay their last respects as Ze'evi lies in state at the Knesset, in which he served since 1988. At his grave at the Mount Herzl Military Cemetery, Israel's leaders will eulogize him, and find it difficult to separate the life of this leader from the challenge left by his assassination.

Just two days ago, Ze'evi's resignation caused the government's foundations to quiver. By leaving, Ze'evi had set in motion a process that would force the government to change tactics in the military-diplomatic fight against Palestinian terror, or fall. Ze'evi's assassination has both unified the government and presented the same choice in much starker relief.

Now Israel has no choice but to destroy the PFLP, the Palestinian terrorists who claimed responsibility for his assassination. Just as the

Taliban was given an ultimatum to cough up Osama bin Laden or be destroyed, Yasser Arafat's regime must crush the terrorism in its midst or be destroyed as well.

Israel has no choice, because the assassination of an Israeli minister, if followed by the flurry of threats and limited measures that came after previous atrocities, will signal that Israel has lost the will to defend itself.

Until now, Israel has acted as if it must choose between defending itself and its relations with the United States. America's war on terrorism should have eliminated this choice, since the US should understand that Israel's self-defense is an integral component of this war. Instead, the opposite has happened: Israel has come under even greater pressure to cease "provocative" acts.

Both wings within the government have acted as if choosing between self-defense and American support is a given, with Israel's decision being between two dangerous evils – tolerating terror or international isolation.

The task of the government, following this horrific assassination, is not to make this choice, but to confront the choice itself. The United States should be told that if the West does not force Arafat to end terrorism completely – both his own and his opponents' – than Israel will have to do the job itself.

In essence, Israel will be demanding that the United States confront the Arab world's attempt to legitimize terror against Israel under the rubric of "resisting occupation." National Security Adviser Condoleeza Rice made a start when she stated that "Syria cannot be against al-Qaida, but in favor of other terrorist groups" and when she rejected attempts to "draw distinctions between types of terrorism." But the real test is whether the US stops treating Israel's self-defense as part of the larger war on terror, rather than as a troublesome "cycle of violence."

Israel's job now is to convince the United States that it will act without US support, but that it would be much better for the US, Israel, and the war on terrorism if our two nations acted in tandem.

Reacting to the assassination yesterday, former foreign minister Shlomo Ben-Ami said that Arafat had received "too cheap an entrance ticket" to the good-guy side of the post-September 11 global divide. Israel should tell the US that there are only two choices: setting Arafat's ticket price at ending terror, or Israel stopping terrorism for him.

The United States must understand that Israel supports the war on terrorism completely, but cannot accept terrorism against Israel being exempted from this war.

Arafat, like the Taliban, must choose between supporting terror and between being branded a terrorism-supporting regime by the United States. If the US does insist on such a choice, then Arafat will essentially be hiding behind the skirts of the United States. This would be a betrayal of America's commitment to Israel's security and of America's own war on terrorism. The test of whether this is a war on terrorism, or just one terrorist organization, is now.

◆ ◆ ◆

In the first weeks after 9/11, the strong sense in Israel was that America's war against terrorism had gotten off on the wrong foot. The Bush Administration was busy forming a coalition to depose the Taliban regime in Afghanistan, which was good, but it was making friendly noises toward other terror-supporting regimes, such as Iran, Syria, and the Palestinian Authority.

It is instructive to note how far US policy has evolved in the right direction since this low point. The US of late supports Israel's right to self-defense, recognizes that Yasser Arafat is not reformable, and places much more of the onus for peace on the Palestinians and the Arab states. But the process of transforming the US approach to the Arab-Israeli conflict to bring it into sync with the wider war against the terror network is still not complete.

Interesting Times: Dear George
October 26, 2001

In his *New York Times* column (October 23), Tom Friedman wrote a mock letter from President George W. Bush to Prime Minister Ariel Sharon and Palestinian Authority Chairman Yasser Arafat that seemed to capture administration thinking. "We're fighting for our self-defense," Friedman/Bush wrote, "when your friend America is at war for its survival, there is only one question Israel should ask: How can we help?... We know bin Laden didn't attack us to liberate Palestine... [but we need you to] get off our radar screen! Our resolve is being tested by our enemies, we don't need it tested by our friends." Here's how Sharon should respond...

Dear George,

I appreciate your frank letter, believe me, I know how you feel. I know that you have dedicated your presidency to crushing the bastards who attacked America, and to ridding the world of the scourge of state-sponsored terrorism. There is no country in the world that is cheering you on more, from the bottom of our hearts.

I know how you feel because my whole life has been dedicated to the same fight, and I was elected to win this fight for the people of Israel. I do regret publicly blowing a gasket with that Czechoslovakia speech, but it was out of frustration that we have not been working hand in glove in the same battle.

My frustration came from the same 'they don't get it' feeling that you have about us. You think I 'don't get it' because I'm not willing to make things easier for you. That's neither true nor fair. We have and are willing to make great sacrifices in the war on terror, and we regard your war as our war too. What we are not willing to do is sacrifice Israeli lives for the mistaken belief that compromising our security will help you fight terrorism.

I realize that you know full well that neither bin Laden nor your Arab coalition partners really care about the Palestinian cause. The fight that you have taken on is much bigger than that – it's about whether bin Laden can whip up the entire Arab world into battling you, their 'Great Satan.'

You know that what the Arab leaders are worried about is their skins, not what is going on here. I could be hugging Arafat tomorrow and it wouldn't move the Arab world one more inch into your corner.

That said, I know that you want quiet. So do I, to put it mildly. But there are only two ways for us to 'get off the radar screen:' for Israel to tolerate terrorism or for Arafat to stop it. Friends don't ask friends to tolerate terrorism. More importantly from your perspective, no leader could accept such a request, and implying that I should makes matters worse.

If you don't believe me, don't take my word for it, ask Arafat's confidant, Abu Ala. He said point blank that the Palestinians wouldn't "provide the Israelis with the ladder to climb down from its high position, as American pressure will in any case make Israel withdraw." Arafat figures, why should he crack down on terror if you are willing to protect him from us no matter what?

Don't you get it? Restraining us does not put pressure on both sides - it cancels out the pressure you are trying to put on Arafat. The pressure on us is superfluous in any case, because we are not trying to destroy the Palestinian Authority.

All we were trying to do – in addition to killing and capturing a lot of terrorists – was to expand the deals we cut in Beit Jala and Hebron across the board. As you know, we said we'd leave those places if the Palestinians stopped shooting from those areas, and if they didn't we'd come back permanently. I stuck with those deals, even though it lopped off the right wing of my government. But we can only cut a wider deal like that with the Palestinians if they know we can come back at will and won't have you all over our backs.

Your spokesman said that the situation here is different from Afghanistan, because in our case both parties have signed agreements. But this difference only holds when both sides are committed to negotiations, not when one side has blown up the negotiating table and resorted to terrorism.

I know that even we aren't acting as if Arafat is our bin Laden, because you don't talk about negotiating with bin Ladens, you just kill them. We're not even treating Arafat as our Taliban, because you've decided to get rid of the Taliban and we're still trying to reform Arafat. But the only chance we have of reforming Arafat is if you don't take away our stick. Throwing us to the wolves won't keep the coalition together; but stopping us from ensuring quiet will certainly help break it apart.

Sincerely,
Ariel

◆ ◆ ◆

British Prime Minister Tony Blair is now identified with his staunch support for the US-led campaign to oust Saddam Hussein. But as seen here, it should be remembered that Britain was initially among the countries urging the US not to target Saddam. Also, the moral clarity shown by Blair toward the war in Iraq has not fully extended to his approach toward Damascus or towards Israel's efforts to defend itself.

No Damascus Conversion
November 1, 2001

British Prime Minister Tony Blair has been one of the most forceful and eloquent spokesmen of the West since September 11. Blair has done his nation proud by embodying the NATO declaration that an attack on one is an attack on all.

Britain is supporting America not just in words, but in deeds, and doing so despite a large Muslim population and close historic ties with the Arab world.

The solidity of Blair's support, despite being ideologically closer to the previous American government than to the Bush administration, should hardly be taken for granted given the European antipathy toward America that was rising before September 11. In June, Anne Applebaum wrote in the *Spectator* of a "pan-European wave of hatred for the American president and his foreign policy." A just-released Hudson Institute paper by Irwin Stelzer notes that, "From Bianca Jagger to Jacques Chirac, Europe's elites are making it clear that America, under whose umbrella they need no longer cower lest the Russian bear turn nasty, is their international enemy No. 1."

September 11 transformed this 'wave of hatred' into a wave of sympathy – who would have imagined a French president in New York pledging his solidarity with America in English? But Blair is still in a league of his own in terms of supporting the US. In a speech geared to bolster support for the war effort in Britain, Blair told the Welsh Parliament this week that, "It is important that we never forget how we felt watching the planes fly into the twin towers. Never forget how we felt imagining how mothers told children they were about to die." He warned that "the terrorists will kill again unless they are stopped." Finally, Blair declared that the terrorists "have one hope – that we are somehow decadent, that we lack the moral fiber or will or courage to take them on; that we might begin, but we won't finish; that we will start, then falter; that when the first setbacks occur, that we will lose our nerve. And they are wrong."

These are stirring words, words to remember and live by. For all this, Britain in general and Blair in particular deserve tremendous credit. But Britain's leadership role as America's closest ally in Europe also magnifies the significance of any difference in strategy between the two countries.

In the struggle to define the aims and tactics of the war on terrorism, Britain is clearly pulling in a particular direction.

Even in his original speech to Parliament just three days after September 11, Blair hinted that the war on terror must be limited to those linked to that specific attack: "[We] will want to identify, with care, those responsible. This is a judgment that must and will be based on hard evidence." Speaking on ABC's *This Week* program last Sunday, British Foreign Secretary Jack Straw was much more specific: "Iraq has not been targeted. You only take military action where there is the clearest possible evidence of culpability... I have seen no evidence which links the Iraqi regime to... what happened on September 11." As absurd as it may seem, America's staunchest ally seems to be setting up a firewall protecting Saddam Hussein from the war on terrorism. One can only hope that this is a temporary stance, given that a war on terrorism that neatly cordons off Saddam is like spackling over leaks in a dam while ignoring a huge crack down the middle.

The other sign of a difference in approach between the US and Britain was the almost immediate visit by Straw to Iran, and now Blair's visit to Damascus. It is incongruous, to say the least, that the first visit of a British prime minister to Syria in at least 30 years should be now, just a few weeks after the worst terror attack in history. Even if Syria was not directly involved in September 11, beating a path to Damascus now is like calling on a major mafia boss while launching a war against organized crime.

Even a mafia boss, however, might have the sense or decency not to defend his criminal activities in front of a visiting leader. Syrian President Bashar Assad displayed no such sense, and instead delivered a stinging rebuke to Blair's call for an "an end to terrorism in all its forms." After his talks with Blair, Assad declared that, "Resistance to liberate land is a right that no one can deny... We cannot separate the terrorism that we see every day that Israel practices against the Palestinians." Given that Syria is a leading proponent of the Orwellian notion that blowing up discos and pizza parlors is not terrorism, but killing those who do is, the result of Blair's visit should have been predictable. The only real justification of such a visit would have been to present Syria with a clear ultimatum: Stop supporting terrorism or become a target in the war against terrorism. Perhaps the US and Britain are making a 'good cop, bad cop' division of labor in this war, but that only works if even the good cop does not forget that he is a cop.

◆ ◆ ◆

Over a year after Bush's key speech at the United Nations rejecting the notion of "good terrorism," the Arab world still has not moved decisively against either the rhetorical or financial support for terrorism from their countries. At the Sharm summit of June 2003, Bush did not extract from the Arab leaders, as Charles Krauthammer put it, "a single concrete action, not even a gesture, toward Israel." He also acquiesced to a Saudi veto of Sharon's presence at the summit. The gap between rhetoric and results is still a large one, so far.

Let's Roll
November 12, 2001

US President George W. Bush's address to the United Nations on Saturday was to the world what his September 20 address to Congress was to the United States: a clarion call to vanquish the scourge of state-supported terrorism. With his speech to Congress, Bush became America's leader in a new way. With his UN speech, he became the leader of the forces of good in the world.

As in many other speeches by him and other leaders, Bush railed against the evil of terrorism. What was different about this speech, however, was an end to the polite tolerance for those who support and justify terrorism. As Bush simply said, "A murderer is not a martyr, he is just a murderer." At first, the United States acted as if it could 'agree to disagree' about what terrorism is. When the Organization of Islamic Countries condemned terrorism without criticizing US actions in Afghanistan, Bush hailed their statement, even though it blatantly justified terrorism against Israel as "resisting occupation." Now Bush seems to have realized that Arab/Islamic attempt to justify terrorism cannot be swept under the carpet.

"We must unite in opposing all terrorists, not just some of them," Bush told the assembled leaders. "There is no such thing as a good terrorist. No national aspiration, no remembered wrong can ever justify the deliberate murder of the innocent. Any government that rejects this principle, trying to pick and choose its terrorist friends, will know the consequences."

97

Across from the UN headquarters in New York, the words of Isaiah's vision of peace – of swords being beaten into plowshares – are chiseled in stone. If there ever were words that deserved to be chiseled alongside that prophetic vision at this moment, they are Bush's words abolishing the notion of good terrorism. The war on terrorism may have physically begun in Afghanistan, but the ideological gauntlet was thrown down only now at the UN.

Without mentioning the Arab world by name, Bush called them at their game. Alluding to the incredible attempts to blame Israel or the CIA for the September 11 attacks, Bush said, "We must speak the truth about terror. Let us never tolerate... malicious lies that attempt to shift the blame from the terrorists themselves... To inflame ethnic hatred is to advance the cause of terror."

Those who had been concerned that Bush would make the mistake of rewarding Yasser Arafat with a meeting before Arafat had cracked down on terror need not have worried. As National Security Adviser Condoleeza Rice explained, "There are responsibilities that come with being the representative of the Palestinian people... You cannot help us with al-Qaida and hug Hizbullah – that's not acceptable – or Hamas." Nor is the US buying the idea that terrorism can be fought with another Middle East peace plan. "There's no doubt in my mind," Bush said with visiting British Prime Minister Tony Blair November 8, "We'll bring al-Qaida to justice, peace or no peace in the Middle East."

At the UN Bush called for two states, Israel and Palestine, living peacefully together. But he made clear that "peace will only come when all have sworn off forever incitement, violence, and terror." Bush has it exactly right: making peace depends on fighting terror, not the other way round. The reason is that anti-Israeli terrorism is just an extension of the rejection of Israel's right to exist, just like anti-American terrorism is an attempt to destroy everything that America stands for. The utter rejections of Israel and America are forms of meta-terrorism – they aim not just to kill civilians, but to wipe out societies and civilizations.

Bush seems to understand this. In an address to the nation on November 8, he stated, "Our nation faces a threat to our freedoms, and the stakes could not be higher. We are the target of enemies who boast they want to kill – kill all Americans, kill all Jews, and kill all Christians. We've seen that type of hate before – and the only possible response is to confront it and to defeat it."

Bush concluded with an appeal for the sense of "courage and optimism" exemplified by Todd Beamer, one of the passengers on United Airlines Flight 93 who lost their lives thwarting the hijackers from turning a fourth aircraft into a guided missile. Beamer's last words heard over an open phone line were a prayer and the exhortation, "Let's roll." Bush's call to Americans should resonate no less in hearts around the world: "We will always remember the words of that brave man, expressing the spirit of a great country... We cannot know every turn this battle will take... But we have our marching orders: My fellow Americans, let's roll."

◆ ◆ ◆

The liberation of Afghanistan was a clear precedent for the liberation of Iraq, as we argue here. We did not anticipate, however, that the campaign in Iraq would come about only 17 months later – a longer gap than expected – and that the US would not ally itself with local opposition forces, the way it did in Afghanistan. As it turned out, internal Administration disputes prevented the US from supporting the Iraqi opposition before the war, and ensuring that there was a government in waiting for the day after Saddam. This is making the transition to a new government in Iraq more difficult, but no less worthwhile.

Next Stop, Baghdad
November 15, 2001

Every time despots fall, we in the West are amazed that our own propaganda was right. During the Cold War, many people who cared about freedom and human rights could not bring themselves to believe that life was really so oppressive on the other side of the Iron Curtain. Then came the emotional fall of the Berlin Wall and the explosion of freedom throughout Central Europe.

The stories about life under Taliban rule were even harder to believe, almost a caricature of oppression. Prison for trimming a beard? Music outlawed? Women locked up in their homes? Now, before the dust has settled from the Taliban fleeing Kabul, we see a frenzy of Afghans cutting off their beards, blasting music, and women emerging from perpetual house arrest.

The recurring theme of the liberated residents of Kabul is rebirth. A shopkeeper, who had been thrown in jail for a week just for trimming his beard, said, "I feel like I've just been born – it's my second life!" A teacher, who secretly went house-to-house teaching her girl students, hoped to return to her classroom.

Many liberated Afghans remain wary of the Northern Alliance, whose rule was marked by corruption and infighting. Many had initially welcomed the Taliban, hoping they would bring security and order. Rooting the Taliban out of southern Afghanistan may not proceed as swiftly. And it is far from clear that whatever new government emerges will bring the peace and development that the Afghan people so sorely need.

Some will dismiss the liberation of Afghanistan as being tainted by ulterior motives. But there is no reason to pretend that America helped the Afghans eject the Taliban mainly out of concern for their freedom, rather than as a way station in the war against terrorism. What we should learn, though, is that freedom is no less sweet when achieved as a byproduct of other objectives.

We should also keep in mind that the scenes of a tremendous weight being lifted off Kabul will only be replayed with grander exuberance on the day that Baghdad or Teheran is liberated.

The Taliban may make Iran's mullahcracy look moderate, but that regime also rules with an iron fist. And the stories we hear from survivors of Saddam Hussein's sadistic brutality are just the tip of the iceberg of what will emerge when he falls.

Human rights alone, except in the case of South Africa under apartheid and right-wing dictatorships in Nicaragua, Iran, and the Philippines, has not been thought of as sufficient cause for the international community to demand a change of regime. It so happens that the regimes in Iran and Iraq are as, if not more, brutal than any of the regimes that were considered kosher for toppling. And there are plenty of other brutal regimes that draw little international attention of any kind.

The world is hardly consistent when it comes to doing something about freedom and human rights. But the fact that freedom seems to come into the spotlight only when other objectives are in play does not negate its relevance as a justification for international action.

The regimes in Teheran and Baghdad represent the combination of oppression and aggression that should make them prime candidates for overthrow, like the Taliban in Afghanistan. Of the two, Saddam Hussein is both the most brutal to his own people and dangerous to the world.

Accordingly, the US should not be shy about saying that, after Kabul, the next place to bring the jubilation of freedom should be either Teheran or Baghdad. It is hard to say which will come first, because like in Afghanistan, the US will play a supporting role to local liberation movements. The fall of the Taliban represents a particular combination of American force in support of a local uprising. In other places, the combination will be different, but the same principle can work.

What should be recognized, as Michael Ledeen argued in OpinionJournal.com yesterday, the war on terrorism is actually a revolutionary war of the sort that the US is uniquely equipped to fight. "While we will have to act quickly and urgently against secret terrorist organizations and suicidal fighters," Ledeen wrote, "our ultimate targets are tyrannical governments, and our most devastating weapons are the peoples they oppress."

The recent phenomenon of soccer games – the only opportunity for Iranians to congregate in large numbers – turning into anti-government rallies is a sign that Iran is ripe for the kind of bottom-up revolution that swept Central Europe. In Iraq, if the US decides to wholeheartedly back the opposition as it did the Northern Alliance, most of Saddam's army will defect and he will quickly lose control of most of the country. Once Saddam has been transformed into the mayor of Baghdad, it is only a matter of time before his regime will fall. The pursuit of freedom, it turns out, is not just an adjunct to the war on terrorism, but at its very heart.

◆ ◆ ◆

Bernard Lewis is a rarity. His place at the pinnacle of his profession, the study of the world of Islam, is undeniable. Yet he is among a small minority in his field that understood and did not downplay radical Islam, and therefore one of the few scholars worth listening to about the post-9/11 world.

Interesting Times: The Unbelieving West
November 30, 2001

Since September 11, Westerners have been scrambling to learn about Islam, in order to understand what we are up against. Unlike the crop of instant experts, Princeton's Bernard Lewis does not need to play catch-up. Lewis is widely recognized as the West's preeminent scholar of Middle Eastern studies. His most recent analysis in the *New Yorker* ("The Revolt of Islam," November 19), is therefore worth studying like a Talmudic text, a few lines at a time.

Lewis begins with a historian's somewhat wistful description of the West's tone-deafness to history, as compared to the Arab penchant for historical allusions. For most Americans, the Vietnam War is history, World War II is ancient history, and everything before that is prehistory. But, Lewis writes, when Osama bin Laden, in his October 7 videotape, spoke of the humiliation Islam has suffered for "more than 80 years," he could be fairly sure that Muslim listeners would "pick up the allusion immediately and appreciate its significance."

Lewis explains that bin Laden was referring to the 1918 defeat of the last great Muslim empire, the Ottoman sultanate – including the occupation of Constantinople, the capture of its sovereign, and the partitioning of most of its territory between the British and French empires. Lewis notes that the leader of the Ottoman empire was "not only a sultan, the ruler of a specific state; he was also widely recognized as the caliph, the head of all Sunni Islam, and the last in a line of such rulers dating back to the Prophet Muhammad in 632 CE." The Turkish abolition of the caliphate in 1924, after 13 centuries, "under the double assault of foreign imperialists and domestic [Turkish] modernists," was felt throughout the Muslim world.

So why attack New York and Washington and not London and Paris? Because that's thinking like a Westerner, not a Muslim. Muslims "tend to see not a nation subdivided into religious groups, but a religion subdivided into nations." The comment of a young Afghan refugee emerging from a Saudi-funded Islamic seminary in Pakistan is instructive: "We are happy that many kaffirs [infidels] were killed in the World Trade Center. We targeted them because they were kaffirs, unbelievers."

In a twist of fate that Israelis should readily understand, at the end of the long list of Islamist "grievances" against the West, there is one mega-grievance: the existence of the West. If Israel disappeared, the US withdrew all its troops from the region, and all Arab regimes were replaced by Taliban clones, the conflict with the West would not end – it would just be getting rolling. The "kaffirs" would be ripe for the plucking.

Muslims remember that over the centuries in which Europe was described as "medieval," Islamic civilization was the most advanced in the world. And throughout this period Islam divided the world into two parts, the House of Islam (where Islamic law prevailed) and the House of War (the rest of the world). "Between the two," explains Lewis, "there was to be a perpetual state of war until the entire world either embraced Islam or submitted to the rule of the Muslim state." What guidance can Lewis' historical review give us toward managing Islam's endemic aggressiveness?

One lesson is that the obligatory Islamic state of war ("jihad") can be interrupted by "truces" that were essentially the same as the peace treaties European powers made between themselves. Even the famed 12th-century Muslim conqueror Saladin struck a deal with the Crusader king of Jerusalem. Put simply, defeat is a powerful cure for jihad.

But Lewis's other suggestion is that the West pay attention to the Middle Easterners who "increasingly complain that the US judges them by different and lower standards than it does Europeans and Americans, both in what is expected of them and in what they may expect... in terms of political freedom." Lewis notes that Israel was blamed for the massacre of hundreds of Palestinians by Lebanese militiamen at Sabra and Shatilla "as if those who carried out the deed were animals, not accountable to the same human standards as Israelis;" the US preference for "a more amenable tyrant" in Iraq rather than backing a popular revolt; and the Western courting of Syria's late president Hafez Assad despite his slaughter of 20,000 Syrians at Hama in 1982.

In Iraq and Iran "there are democratic oppositions capable of taking over and forming governments," notes Lewis. "We could do much to help them, and have done little." It is not too late to make amends.

◆ ◆ ◆

At this writing (June 2003), Sharon's cabinet has recently approved the US-backed "road map" through his cabinet and even told a meeting of his Likud faction that it is time to "end the occupation" and "divide the land." All this is being responded to as if it is the first time Sharon is speaking seriously about a Palestinian state.

As can be understood from this editorial, those surprised by Sharon's seriousness may not have focused on or believed what he has been saying for some time. Here, we advocate that Sharon expand his message to include support for democratization on the Palestinian side.

Sharon's New Tone
November 30, 2001

Seemingly oblivious to the bitter criticism from his own party on his stance, Prime Minister Ariel Sharon reiterated his support yesterday for a Palestinian state. Indeed, on the eve of his planned US visit, Sharon sounded particularly conciliatory. The Palestinians should take this side of Sharon seriously, even if some Israelis do not.

Sharon is sometimes accused of looking over his right shoulder, toward the ideological spot he occupied when Prime Minister Binyamin Netanyahu was in office. Now these two leaders have switched places, and it is Netanyahu who has attacked Sharon's support for a Palestinian state, calling it 'a prize for terrorism.' Sharon, however, has not flinched, and continues to argue what historically has been a Labor Party position: that a demilitarized Palestinian state is not an oxymoron, but a real and even desirable possibility.

Sharon named three conditions for Israel's recognition of Palestine: that it be demilitarized, established by agreement with Israel, and have borders consistent with Israel's security. The poll published today by the *Jerusalem Post* indicates that whether the Israeli public supports such a concept is tightly linked to whether the Palestinians can be trusted to uphold their agreements.

The poll, conducted by the Smith Institute this week, found that 47 percent oppose the formation of a Palestinian state regardless of whether the Palestinians could be expected to honor a peace agreement. An additional 34 percent of respondents support a Palestinian state only on condition the Palestinians fulfill a peace agreement. Since the poll also found that 65 percent of Israelis believe that a Palestinian state of any kind would be a threat to Israel, most Israelis seem not to trust the Palestinians to uphold agreements, and therefore would oppose a Palestinian state.

All of this tends to support Sharon's case that he is the Palestinian's best hope for a 'Nixon going to China' scenario: the seeming paradox that right-wingers end up making peace agreements while left-wingers find themselves going to war. Sharon explicitly encouraged this thinking yesterday, saying, "I believe the Palestinians are missing out on an exceptional opportunity." Sharon claimed that he is "one of the few who could broker a deal." Finally, he argued that he understands that "peace hurts almost as much as war. And it won't be easy to stand before the public [to defend an agreement], but I believe I can do this."

The skeptics cannot argue that Sharon has no evidence to back up his claim. It was Sharon, after all, who played exactly this role in defending Menachem Begin's agreement with Egypt, including the dismantling of Yamit. And it was Sharon who defied all expectations as prime minister by announcing a unilateral cease-fire, supporting the Mitchell plan, and making the case that "restraint is power." Like Netanyahu, Sharon has managed to raise the suspicions of both the Left and the Right, with each side choosing to believe its own nightmare scenario. The Left argues that all of Sharon's talk of agreements is a massive bluff, and that he will use the inability of the Palestinians to produce even a week of quiet to postpone negotiations indefinitely. The Right is concerned that Sharon is now looking for his place in history, and ironically presents the greatest danger to the settlement enterprise that he championed for so long.

Unlike Netanyahu, however, Sharon has managed to maintain in both sides of the Israeli spectrum a glimmer of hope and not just suspicion. Maybe this is a matter of a different political style or a function of the unity government. Perhaps, however, Sharon is benefiting from a deeper change in Israeli society, in which each side of the traditional divide has begun to doubt its own infallibility and see some merit on the other side.

On the Left, the failure of Camp David and the return of Palestinian terror has led many to discover about the Palestinians what Winston Churchill said about the Soviet Union: "I do not believe they desire war. What they desire are the fruits of war." On the Right, many have come around to the idea that Israel must separate from the Palestinians, and the only realistic way to do this is by creating a Palestinian state. A majority of Israelis seems to see the combination of Ariel Sharon and Shimon Peres as the best hope for creating a synthesis from the shards of both collapsed paradigms.

In this context, it is unfortunate that Peres feels the need to imply that his partner is oblivious to the "psychological" side of the conflict. Though it may seem mundane, no Israeli prime minister, including Peres himself, has ever said what Sharon said yesterday: "It is hard to be a Palestinian." Sharon should go even further, and express support for Palestinian dreams – not just for independence – but for freedom, democracy, human rights, and the rule of law.

In his speech opening his first Knesset session as prime minister, Sharon closed by quoting Abraham Lincoln's second inaugural address, 'With malice toward none, with charity for all, for firmness in the right as God gives to us to see the right, let us strive to finish the work we are in, to bind up the nation's wounds, to do all which we may achieve and cherish a just and a lasting peace among ourselves and with all the nations.' The left-wing may not believe it and the right-wing may think it naive, but Lincoln's spirit of firmness in war and generosity in peace is very Israeli, and clearly resonates with Ariel Sharon.

◆ ◆ ◆

The subsequent failure of the United Nations to back America's decision to enforce UN resolutions in Iraq is another example of how far that organization has fallen. In effect, it has become a protector of dictatorship and aggression more than a source of hope for the spread of freedom and prosperity.

Unworthy of the Peace Prize
December 11, 2001

Yesterday, the Nobel Committee awarded its prestigious Peace Prize to UN Secretary-General Kofi Annan and to the United Nations itself. According to Alfred Nobel's will, written in 1895, the peace prize in his name should go to the person who "shall have done the most or the best work for fraternity between nations, for the abolition or reduction of standing armies, and for the holding of peace congresses." It is difficult to see how this year's prize meets any of Nobel's three conditions.

It should not take a great feat of memory to recall that, just days before September 11, a day that shall be marked for its barbarity, the United Nations closed one of the most hate-filled international conferences in history. The Durban Conference Against Racism and Intolerance, though ostensibly a 'peace conference' of the sort that Nobel hoped to encourage, had been transformed into a hate fest against Israel and the Jewish people. 'Protesters' contributed to the ambience of the conference with signs saying 'Kill the Jews,' 'Hitler should have finished the job,' 'Zionism is racism,' and 'End Israeli apartheid.' At the last minute, and only after a walkout by the United States and Israel, vicious condemnations of Israel and attempts to belittle the Holocaust were removed from the resolutions. An endorsement of the Palestinian 'right of return' – a barely disguised recipe for Israel's destruction – remained in the final document.

In defense of its decision, the Nobel Committee might argue first that the UN's leaders should not be blamed for the terrible acts of some of its member nations, and in any case we were all less sensitive about these things before September 11. But UN officials, including Annan himself, could not bring themselves to unequivocally reject the Arab states' hijacking of a conference against racism and their transforming it into a weapon against their region's only democracy, Israel. By the time UN Human Rights Commissioner Mary Robinson held up an anti-Semitic book being distributed at Durban and proclaimed that she was 'a Jew,' it was too little, too late.

Nor does the idea that the UN has changed since September 11 hold water. On December 5, for only the second time in 50 years, the signatories of the Fourth Geneva Convention were gathered for one purpose: to condemn Israel.

Though the conference was held under Swiss, rather than UN auspices, the same Durban dynamic was at work there, and United Nations officials could not be found uttering a word of protest against this flagrant politicization of international humanitarian law. Again, the United States, Israel, and to their credit, Australia, felt compelled to boycott the meeting, which accused Israel of 'occupying' a land that is the subject of negotiations and which Israel offered to withdraw from in exchange for peace. The Palestinian use of terrorism against Israel was, of course, completely ignored.

Though Annan is personally no worse and perhaps, by some measures, better than many of his predecessors, it is hard to see why a peace prize should be given to officials who so regularly tolerate gross hypocrisy and double standards. Perhaps it is impossible to expect of a bureaucracy that represents every almost every nation in the world – democracy and dictatorship alike – to reflect something higher than those nations' lowest common denominator. In this respect, Annan's Nobel acceptance speech was at once encouraging and disappointing, in that it accentuated what the UN does not say or stand for when it counts.

Annan concluded his speech not just with platitudes about peace, but with a relatively ringing call for the real source of peace – democracy. "When states undermine the rule of law and violate the rights of their individual citizens," Annan declared, "they become a menace not only to their own people, but also to their neighbors, and indeed the world. What we need today is better governance – legitimate, democratic governance that allows each individual to flourish, and each state to thrive."

Annan unabashedly recognized that democracy has earned its place among universally desirable values, such as promoting human rights and ending poverty. Yet he and the UN have not taken the next step: speaking out against bands of dictatorships when they abuse their power in international bodies and make a mockery of international law. The UN should not be receiving a prize for peace, but should be shamed for straying so far from its ideals and its true potential.

◆ ◆ ◆

Israel's interception of the smuggling ship "Karine-A" was reportedly a key factor in President Bush's decision to call for a new Palestinian leadership about six months later.

On May 20, 2003, Israeli forces captured the "Abu Hasen," a ship bound for Gaza from Lebanon containing sophisticated explosives, missiles, and CDs explaining how to assemble "next generation" bomb belts, all courtesy of the Iranian and Syrian-backed group, Hizbullah. The 36 CDs captured included instructions regarding where a suicide bomber should stand in a bus in order to maximize casualties.

This latest ship was captured after the appointment of Mahmoud Abbas (Abu Mazen) as prime minister, and after the Palestinians had supposedly accepted the road map, committing them to end terrorism. Israeli officials said that Arafat is the only one who could have financed such an operation, and named Palestinian officials who specialize in smuggling and are linked to Hizbullah.

Arafat's Ship of Death
January 7, 2002

If ever there was a photo-opportunity demonstrating what is behind the hand that Yasser Arafat sometimes stretches out in peace, the tarmac full of captured weaponry displayed last night was it. The captured ship, the *Karine-A*, was reportedly purchased in October 2000 – just months after the end of the Camp David summit and at the same time Arafat was pledging his first cease-fire to Ehud Barak, Bill Clinton, Hosni Mubarak, and Kofi Annan at the Sharm e-Sheikh summit. Every time one thinks that Arafat's duplicity cannot be more apparent, he manages to reach new heights.

Arafat, as a diplomat might delicately point out, has a credibility problem.

His fingerprints are all over the ship, in the form of its Palestinian Authority ownership, the high-ranking PA commander who was the ship's captain, the large cost which could not be hidden, and the involvement of Arafat's right-hand man for smuggling operations. The idea suggested by an unnamed US official – that the ship was smuggling weapons to Hizbullah in Lebanon – is bizarre and shows how deeply denial can run.

The most obvious significance of this enormous weapons cache is that Arafat's real intention is not only to escalate terrorist attacks (over two tons of explosives were found on the ship) but to move beyond terrorism. As military leaders and analysts have pointed out, the only purpose of the relatively long range weaponry captured is to threaten Israeli population centers. Throughout the Oslo period until today, Arafat has been building a sizable army, in complete disregard for the personnel and weaponry limits imposed by the Oslo agreement.

The idea Arafat might be building his illegal army for defensive purposes does not wash. Arafat's simplest defense is not to attack Israel in the first place, in which case none of the closures and incursions into PA-controlled territory would be necessary. A much more plausible explanation – which Israel has no choice but to assume – is that he is bucking for a pivotal role in a general Arab war for Israel's destruction.

Even dovish proponents of a Palestinian state agree it must be demilitarized and may not form alliances with Israel's enemies, such as Iran and Iraq. Now we see that Arafat is not bothering to wait until he has a state to violate both conditions.

There are a number of strategic lessons Israel and the international community should draw from the hand Arafat has revealed.

The first is it is irresponsible to rely on any commitments Arafat might make that a Palestinian state would be demilitarized, even commitments made in the context of a future peace agreement. It is naive to believe any future agreement will constrain Arafat's determination to arm himself to the teeth any more than Oslo did.

In this arena, the experience with Saddam Hussein is instructive. For years, the international community operated under the assumption draconian international sanctions and inspections could keep Saddam from rearming. In the end Saddam – despite having much less international sympathy than Arafat – managed to free himself of most of his international shackles. The US and many other countries have accordingly come to the conclusion the only way to prevent Saddam from becoming a further menace to his neighbors is his removal from office.

In the Palestinian case as well, Arafat has proven legal and diplomatic constraints are impotent in the face of a regime determined to militarize as much as possible. The *Santorini* and the *Karine-A* were intercepted, but Arafat has been smuggling arms through underground tunnels, in his own helicopter, and by any other means possible. Given the experience with Arafat, it is not surprising the possibility of a Palestinian state that does not threaten Israel is being called into question. Yet even if one does not go so far as to reject the idea of a Palestinian state in principle, it should be clear agreements alone are not sufficient to guarantee its demilitarization.

As with Iraq, the only guarantee of real peace is not agreements but the nature of the regime that signs them. Saying Arafat is irrelevant may be a somewhat useful description of how he should be treated, but it is not really true. Arafat has demonstrated he will never lead a state at peace with Israel. For anyone who supports the idea of a Palestinian state, whether it is led by Arafat or another dictator like him should not only be relevant, but critical. The primary message of Arafat's ship of death is it is not possible to trust any agreement with the Palestinian people so long as it is led by the current regime.

◆ ◆ ◆

Bush's "axis of evil" speech, his first State of the Union address after September 11, was a foundation stone of the new post-Cold War architecture he was creating (see "Unlikely Compatriots," pages 146-148). The power of that one word, "evil," is striking. Its power comes from its contrast to the moral relativism that has become a pillar of modernity.

Oddly enough, one of militant Islam's main critiques of modernity is exactly its moral relativism. The paradox is that we need to cultivate a degree of intolerance in order to defeat the ultimate intolerance of our enemies.

Interesting Times: The Virtues of Intolerance
February 15, 2002

Europeans always thought of George Bush as a Texas yokel, and now they have their proof: his "axis of evil" speech to the US Congress. "Absolutist," harrumphed European Commissioner Chris Patten. "Simplistic," shot back French Foreign Minister Hubert Vedrine. Any rube knows that North Korea, Iran, Iraq are neither "evil" nor linked in an "axis," say European sophisticates, appalled that they must share the same planet with riff-raff who claim otherwise.

The Europeans, of course, know full well that the regimes fingered by Bush are about as evil as they come.

But even in America, words like evil are not normally used in polite company, let alone in public discourse. Modern people don't talk like that. Just a short time ago, the Clinton State Department decided to stop referring to the same states as "rogue regimes," preferring instead the less judgmental label: "countries of concern." Good people are tolerant, we Westerners like to believe. The march of progress is marked by an ability to understand the Other, and a commitment to cure humanity of the vicious hatreds that poisoned the last century. To the extent there are people who haven't gotten the message, say good Westerners, we certainly do not want to become like them.

If there is anything that is simplistic, however, it is acting as if tolerance is an absolute good. Of course tolerance is a necessary antidote to racism and all sorts of irrational phobias toward people and cultures whose only sin is to be different. But a form of tolerance that pretends there is no such thing as evil is itself wrong.

At some level, this is understood. Who today would argue with Edmund Burke's adage from over a century ago: "The only thing necessary for the triumph of evil is for good men to do nothing." Yet there is little doubt the West has preferred to err on the side of tolerance.

What George Bush has done, and Ronald Reagan before him with his "evil empire" slam at the Soviet Union, is similar to a child crying out that the emperor has no clothes. We can treat tyrants and terrorists as if they are acceptable members of the community of nations, but that does not change who they are. And it is impossible to begin to fight back without saying the truth: they are evil.

In a wonderful essay in the *Wall Street Journal* last week, Michael Novak recalled just how powerful that single judgmental word can be. "You know what caused the downfall of the Soviet Union?" reports Novak on a conversation with an ex-Soviet general, "That damn speech about the evil empire! That's what did it!" To the questioning eyes of one American, the general added: "It was an evil empire. It was."

As odd as it is to say it, intolerance, far from being an anathema to progress, is essential to it. Progress depends on intolerance for the status quo. In the ancient world (and in some cultures today) there was no notion there could be a better future – there was only Fate. The Western idea of progress began with two Jewish concepts: that time had a moral direction, and that one people could judge another.

The Bible said history is linear: Time began with creation, and its destination was a messianic era in which there would be peace on earth. The idea that history was going somewhere and that people could do something about it was new. Though taken for granted in the West, there is nothing inevitable about this notion, and it is not shared by all cultures.

An even more fundamental concept is that God's realm extends beyond a single people. All politics is local, we say, but in ancient times, so were all gods. The Bible vividly rejected such boundaries with stories such as that of Jonah, in which God could not be escaped by setting sail on a ship.

Without monotheism and its offspring – universal morality – the bedrock Western notion of universal human rights makes no sense. The idea of human rights is judgmental par excellence.

Bush seems to realize that without speaking of evil, it is impossible to make fundamental distinctions, such as between regimes that must be toppled before they obtain nuclear weapons, and countries in whose hands the same weapons can help produce peace. The significance of Bush's speech is not just in the regimes he singled out, but his frontal challenge to the idea that silence in the face of evil is sophisticated and willful blindness is moral.

The question of whether Israel must fight terrorism differently than the US because Palestinian terrorism is somehow different from that of al-Qaida is a critical one. President Bush has argued strongly against the idea of "good" terrorism, but as seen below, he has also slipped into implying that some terrorists might have more immunity than others.

Interesting Times: Is Anybody Listening?
March 15, 2002

Yasser Arafat's health may not be what it once was, but the world seems convinced that he is hard of hearing. 'YOU CAN HAVE A STATE,' said first Israel, then the US, and now a unanimous UN Security Council. 'You can stop fighting now,' the world keeps trying to tell Arafat, as if he is an unruly child, having trouble focusing.

The message to Arafat of this week's historic UN Security Council resolution was simple: stop terror and a state is yours. Israel, for its part, is completely on board – not a peep of protest from Jerusalem. So why is it not time to put away the guns and take out the confetti? Why does everyone assume the resolution will make no difference?

Part of the reason is that the Palestinians may be the first nation in history to be offered a state on a negotiating platter and yet insist on launching a war of independence anyway. At Camp David, Ehud Barak and Bill Clinton practically begged Arafat to take the state he said he wanted, with half of Jerusalem as his capital. Arafat was offered the 'Saudi plan' (withdrawal to the pre-1967 lines with minor adjustments) and turned it down – before the bullets started flying.

Some of Oslo's architects argue that Israel's offer was not good enough, but this is not serious. You cannot claim at the same time that the Palestinians are pragmatists who are ready to make a deal that Israel can live with, and yet they decided to launch a war rather than negotiate.

The more logical explanation is that Arafat does not accept the bargain on the table: a state for peace. If he wants a state at all, he wants a state without any agreement with Israel, or with an agreement that leaves the conflict open – that is, a state without peace. Neither of these choices should be granted any legitimacy, because they amount to not giving up on the dream of destroying Israel. Yet even the US has trouble admitting that Arafat's goals are illegitimate.

In an especially revealing exchange on Wednesday, President George W. Bush was asked if he thinks Prime Minister Ariel Sharon "shares your concern for those not involved in terror." Bush responded, "I do. But, unlike our war against al-Qaida, there is a series of agreements in place [between the Israelis and Palestinians] that will lead to peace. I certainly hope that Prime Minister Sharon is concerned about the loss of innocent life." In other words, Israel is not simply fighting terrorists who must be destroyed, but a once and future partner in peace agreements. And in this context, there is a question over whether Israel is fighting too dirty.

In reality, there is no reason to apply a different moral standard when fighting terrorism under different political circumstances – in all cases civilian casualties should be minimized and understood to be morally on the shoulders of the terrorists themselves, not those exercising their right to self-defense.

In the US, this understanding went so far as to deny even an interest in civilian casualties. Based on press reports, one American professor calculated that at least 3,800 Afghan civilians died in two months of the US fight against terrorism there. Yet at the time, *Fox News'* Brit Hume wondered: "Civilian casualties are historically, by definition, a part of war, really. Should they be as big news as they've been?" Another well-known journalist, *National Public Radio's* Mara Liasson answered: "No. Look, war is about killing people. Civilian casualties are unavoidable." Liasson suggested that the US should simply make clear that "we are trying to minimize them, but the Taliban isn't, and is putting their tanks in mosques, and themselves among women and children."

Arafat's dogged refusal to accept a state suggests that his goal is not a legitimate one. But even if it were, the moral calculus is the same in Israel's fight as in America's. The same journalists who thought it was obvious that the Taliban should be blamed for hiding among civilians should ask why Palestinian terrorists hide in crowded refugee camps.

There is a moral chasm between Israel and the Palestinians: Israel has been trying to minimize civilian casualties, the Palestinians have been trying to maximize them. Rather than "hope" that Sharon shares his sensitivity toward civilian lives, Bush should praise Israel for taking operational risks that the US would not have dreamed of taking in Afghanistan, and paying the price for it in the lives of its own civilians and soldiers.

This next editorial is a sober snapshot of the peak of terrorism in March 2002. It was published five days before the worst massacre of this period, at the Passover seder in Netanya's Park Hotel, which killed 29 people. In the month of March of alone, 125 Israelis lost their lives in terror attacks.

Rather than oust Arafat completely as this editorial advocates, Israel ended up launching Operation Defensive Shield throughout the Palestinian areas, and confining Arafat to his compound in Ramallah. Over a year later, and after the fall of Saddam Hussein, the push to remove Arafat has again been defused by the appointment of Mahmoud Abbas (Abu Mazen) as prime minister and the release of the US-backed "road map."

Israel's Moment of Truth
March 22, 2002

We are living through a case of human experimentation gone awry, as if this time the results will be different. In a span of 24 hours, 10 Israeli citizens have been murdered in suicide-massacres on a bus and a central Jerusalem street. Israel will not give in to this barbarism, but it will not end unless it is confronted rather than appeased.

In the six months since September 11, we have gone through a complete cycle that started with appeasement, switched to confrontation, and then back to appeasement. The cycle began with the sense that, at the moment the United States was gearing up to crush al-Qaida and depose the Taliban, Israel was told to restrain itself in order not to inflame the "cycle of violence."

The height of this first attempt to appease Palestinian Authority Chairman Yasser Arafat was US Secretary of State Colin Powell's November speech placing the state of Palestine at the center of America's vision for the Middle East. Then came envoy Anthony Zinni's previous mission, which was greeted by suicide-massacres in Jerusalem and Haifa on December 1 and 2.

At this point, while Prime Minister Ariel Sharon happened to be in Washington, US President George W. Bush switched tacks. Bush dropped the evenhandedness that he had inherited from the previous US administration and began to unequivocally back Israel's right to self-defense. The effect of Bush's switch was immediate and powerful. On

December 16, Arafat gave his first public call for an end to terrorism against Israel.

Arafat's speech was not followed up by any serious actions against terrorist organizations, but a period of relative quiet followed. But even though the number of terror attacks went down, and Israel cut back its military operations substantially, there was not a single terror-free day, let alone the week that Israel was demanding before entering into negotiations.

While it is commonly argued that Israel triggered the escalation that followed by killing Fatah-Tanzim leader Raed Karni, this claim does not stand up to examination. The underlying explanation is not any particular incident, but the continuation of a pattern that has existed for some time: Arafat turns down the flames under pressure, then turns them back up when the pressure subsides.

The reason for this is simple. Regardless of all the commitments he has made – from Oslo to Sharm, Mitchell, Tenet, and Zinni – Arafat has decided that the terrorism will continue until Israel withdraws under fire. With each cycle of terrorism leading to pressure, a 'cease-fire,' then more terrorism, Arafat hears more voices of desperation, more calls to internationalize the conflict, negotiate under fire, or withdraw unilaterally. Each time Arafat comes closer to 'proving' that pressure and force do not work, and Israel's only choice is to give in.

Now it is Israel's turn for a moment of truth. The government must face the fact that Arafat will not implement the Tenet or any other cease-fire plan as a result of inducements, such as relief from Israeli military pressure or a meeting with Vice President Richard Cheney.

Sharon must decide that he is willing to oust Arafat from power. This decision must be taken despite the risk to his two most critical relationships: with Foreign Minister Shimon Peres and George Bush. Sharon must tell Peres that he would very much prefer moving ahead together, but is determined to do so with or without him. Sharon must tell Bush that he has given restraint and diplomacy every chance to work, but that Israel cannot afford any more failed experiments, each of which costs dozens of Israeli lives and leads to further escalation.

Of the two, Bush will be more easily persuaded. The current American slide into enticing Arafat was not born of any belief that it would work, but out of a realization that Israel was acting tough enough to complicate American diplomacy, but not tough enough to win. If Sharon and Peres were together to tell Bush that Israel is ready to free the

Palestinians from Arafat's coalition of terror, the United States would back Israel. Even without Peres's support, the clear US interest would be the success of Israel's campaign.

It would obviously be preferable for Israel and the United States if this moment of truth could be postponed until after the US had ousted Saddam Hussein from power. But Arafat and Saddam know this as well, and they are unsurprisingly unwilling to cooperate with such a timetable. They know that it is impossible for the United States to project an image of invincibility while turning a blind eye to the pummeling of its ally, Israel. Arafat will keep escalating as long as the prospective campaign against Saddam gives him immunity from the US and Israel. As much as Israel wants to clear the way for Saddam's ouster, allowing her citizens to be slaughtered with impunity will not help.

◆ ◆ ◆

Given that 15 of the 19 terrorists who carried out the attacks of September 11 were Saudi citizens, the US approach toward Saudi funding of the clerical network that preaches hatred of America is surprisingly low-key. Perhaps there is more Saudi-US cooperation against terrorism than meets the eye, but the impression that the Saudis are not doing enough and will have to be confronted remains strong.

Terror's Other Infrastructure
April 4, 2002

US Secretary of Defense Donald Rumsfeld does not like to mince words, and he made himself clear – despite his own pledge not to add to the Bush administration voices speaking on Middle East policy. First, Rumsfeld took the opportunity to directly link the targets of America's war on terrorism with the Palestinian suicide-offensive against Israel.

Iraq, Rumsfeld noted, is "running around encouraging people to be suicide bombers and offering – I think I saw something like $10,000 per family. I would suggest that that is very actively trying to kill innocent men, women, and children. There's no question but that the Iranians were deeply involved in the *Karine A* – the ship that was captured by the Israelis that had tons of equipment for the purpose of conducting terrorist attacks. There's no question but that the Iranians work with the Syrians and send folks into Damascus and down the Damascus-Beirut Road and then into south Lebanon so that they can conduct terrorist attacks."

To Rumsfeld, matters are clear: Iraq, Iran, and Syria are "repressing their own people and denying them their rights and simultaneously going outside their country and attempting to finance and encourage and arm and equip people to go kill people in neighboring countries. "Showing his capacity for understatement, Rumsfeld added, "Now that is uncivilized behavior."

These statements, from President George W. Bush's enforcer in the war on terrorism, are the critical link between that war and Israel's struggle. At a time when it is fair to question whether Palestinian Authority Chairman Yasser Arafat has become an exception to the Bush Doctrine, Rumsfeld's remarks are a reminder that the surrounding states that back terror are only adding reasons for the US to target them. The nations Rumsfeld mentioned are certainly the worst actors, and the Hizbullah attack in the North yesterday reemphasizes the need to warn Syria in particular that it is not immune from its actions.

Then, too, Rumsfeld could not be more refreshing in implying that Israel is only following America's example: "When the United States is hit by terrorist attacks, you have a choice; you can say, 'Gee, that's too bad,' or you can go try to find the terrorists and do something about it." Would that our Foreign Minister Shimon Peres could say something like this, rather than sounding as if the ongoing IDF roundup of dozens of wanted terrorists is an exercise in futility. Speaking of the teenage girl who detonated herself in a Jerusalem supermarket recently, Peres wondered what 'infrastructure' she needed besides a poisoned mind.

But if Peres and the chorus continually claiming the futility of military measures is misguided, so is the idea that the ideological side of the terrorist infrastructure can be ignored. In his press conference, Rumsfeld was asked what should be done about other countries that are sources of funding for terrorists, such as Saudi Arabia.

Rumsfeld agreed that "any minor segment of that religion where it is taught that it is a good thing to strap weapons and bombs and plastic [explosives] around your body and go into shopping malls and restaurants and synagogues and kill people, that people who fund that are in fact contributing to the problem of terrorism... It's important for every country in the world, and people in the world who don't think that's a good idea, to stand up and say so."

But Rumsfeld also gave Saudi Arabia and Egypt a broad pass by arguing, "It isn't countries that do this... it's an individual mullah, and it's an individual financier who decides they want to send their money and help out those folks." This, unfortunately, lacks Rumsfeldian fervor and does not nearly do justice to the scope and significance of the problem. As the dean of Middle East experts, Bernard Lewis, recently told this newspaper, the Wahabi branch of Islam that bred Osama bin Laden and most of the suicide bombers attacking Israel is not a 'minor segment,' precisely because of the massive funding it has received, much of it from the Saudi royal family.

"Imagine that the Ku Klux Klan or the Aryan Nation were suddenly to come into possession of unlimited wealth and used it to establish a network of schools and colleges all over Christendom peddling their brand of Christianity, then you will have some idea of what's happened. Wahabism would have been a lunatic fringe in a marginal country. Because of oil it's become a world force."

None of this could have happened without the consent of the Saudi government; it cannot be reversed without holding that government fully responsible. The cleric who gives his blessing for mass murder is central to the infrastructure of terrorism. The war on terrorism cannot be complete until the regimes that tolerate the funding of such clerics are threatened by the same punishment as those who harbor the terrorists themselves.

◆ ◆ ◆

It is painful to me when I hear Israeli politicians claiming that our soldiers have died for nothing. I know how this feels for the families of the soldiers, because mine is one such family. I wrote this piece more for these bereaved families than for anyone else. The day this column appeared there was a suicide bombing in Mahane Yehuda, Jerusalem's main open-air vegetable market, that killed six and wounded 104 Israelis.

Interesting Times: Terrorism Can be Beaten
April 12, 2002

This week, the families of 13 soldiers from the battle of Jenin joined what is known in Israel as the 'family of the bereaved.' Also this week, opposition leader Yossi Sarid told the Knesset, and by extension the soldiers fighting and dying in the field, that the current war is useless, futile, and unnecessary.

I don't care much about Sarid, but I do care about the parents who are being told their children have died in vain.

At some level, I am consoled by the knowledge that the family of each fallen soldier knows full well that their son died in the most noble of causes: to save the life of others. These families can dismiss all the rest as politics, not something that diminishes the heroism of those who sacrifice their lives in the line of duty.

Still, these families are being buffeted by claims that serve to diminish the meaning of their sacrifice. The first claim is that their sons died in a Sisyphean struggle against terrorism than can never be won.

One answer to this debilitating thought is that Sisyphus never managed to push his stone to the top of the mountain, but he did keep that stone from rolling down and crushing the people below. Even if terrorism could not be beaten, it does not follow that it should not be fought. There is no doubt that by killing and capturing hundreds of terrorists, our soldiers saved civilian lives in a more direct manner than most soldiers in most wars.

But the war against terrorism is not Sisyphean: it can be won and the more it is fought the closer that victory draws. Those who claim there is no military solution to terror tend to err doubly: they discount the military contribution to diplomacy and the diplomacy they seek is misguided. In truth, terrorism can be ended by a variety of military and diplomatic means whose common attribute is denying the terrorists what they want. Anything that contributes to proving the futility of terrorism is an important part of achieving victory, certainly including the crushing of the nests where terror spawns.

The more difficult claim that these families must struggle with comes from a completely different angle: that their sons died on the altar of PR. As Lior Shavit told this newspaper at the funeral of Sgt.-Maj. (res) Menashe Hava on Wednesday, "I've buried four friends in the past few months, this has got to stop. We are losing so many soldiers because we are fighting house to house, instead of using fighter jets to destroy any section from which there is shooting."

This is more difficult to contend with because it is true. The soldiers who died in Jenin would likely be alive today if Israel had corralled the terrorists into the smallest possible area and then destroyed that whole area from the air. (Most armies would not have even bothered with the first step, and gone straight to bombing.) One could say that Israel did not do this only because it would look bad, and therefore these soldiers gave their lives for Israel's image. But this neglects the deeper significance of protecting civilian lives. The heroism of the battle of Jenin had three parts: killing terrorists, defending Israeli civilians, and minimizing Palestinian civilian casualties.

The Palestinians, at this moment, are attempting to make two contradictory claims: that in Jenin they fought like in Stalingrad and were massacred like in Sabra and Shatila. Neither is true. The Palestinians did fight, but not like an army that protects civilians - they fought from behind civilians who they deliberately endangered. Not only was there no massacre, but Israeli soldiers effectively showed more concern for Palestinian civilian lives than the terrorists did themselves.

Menashe Hava and his comrades did not die for Israel's image but to ensure that Israel continues to be a place worth fighting for. The weaknesses of democracies are also their strength. Even if the world will not give Israel a smidgen of credit for it, Israel must continue to be true to itself. In a world in which no one will believe in us, it is all the more important for us to be able to believe in ourselves.

◆　◆　◆

Israel should have pushed strongly for abolishing UNRWA, the UN agency that perpetuates the "refugee" status of millions of Palestinians, when the Palestinian Authority was created. It is mind-boggling that the Palestinians have gotten away with such cynical use of the suffering of their own people for so many years.

Abolish UNRWA
April 15, 2002

As pictures of the destruction in Palestinian areas beam out across the world, it is not surprising that US Secretary of State Colin Powell would see fit to meet with relief agencies and pledge US assistance to help relieve the Palestinians' plight. What is less understandable is America's choosing the United Nations Relief and Works Agency (UNRWA) as the conduit for $30 million in additional aid.

UNRWA was founded 52 years ago as a temporary agency to help the Palestinian refugees from the first Arab war to destroy Israel, in 1948. In a report he submitted in November 1951, UNRWA director John Blandford Jr. stated he expected the Arab governments to assume responsibility for relief operation by July 1952. The international community assumed the refugees should be resettled as soon as possible because, as Blandford put it, "Sustained relief operations inevitably contain the germ of human deterioration."

While Blandford's innocence is somewhat touching, he should have suspected foul play from the moment of UNRWA's creation. The UN, after all, already had an agency dedicated to helping refugees – the venerable UN High Commission on Refugees. On its own Web site, UNRWA explains why all the world's refugees have one agency and the Palestinians have another: "UNRWA is mandated to provide the Palestine refugees with humanitarian assistance, whereas UNHCR has the mandate... to seek permanent solutions for the problem of refugees by assisting governments."

With this, UNRWA admits its sister agency is in the business of solving refugee problems, while its job is to perpetuate one. As Ralph Garroway, a former UNRWA director, explained in August 1958: "The Arab states do not want to solve the refugee problem. They want to keep it as an open sore, as an affront to the United Nations and as a weapon against Israel. Arab leaders don't give a damn whether the refugees live or die."

Follow the money and it tells the same story. In its first 20 years, the US provided more than two-thirds of UNRWA's budget, while the contribution of the Arab states was minuscule. As recently as 1994, Israel gave more to UNRWA than all Arab countries except Saudi Arabia, Kuwait, and Morocco.

As if this weren't bad enough, UNRWA has now become a de facto accomplice in terrorism. Food storage areas have been allowed to become munitions depots and weapons factories, as the incursion last month into the Balata refugee camp showed. And UN administrators have ceded effective control of the camps to Palestinian gunmen – a fact not lost on the IDF as it attempts to destroy the terrorist infrastructure in Operation Defensive Shield.

It needn't be this way. If there is one thing that Israelis, Americans, Palestinians, and Europeans can ostensibly agree on, it is that the suffering of refugees should be alleviated both for humanitarian reasons and in the interest of peace and stability. Accordingly, on his last visit to Washington, Prime Minister Ariel Sharon pledged his support for a 'Marshall Plan' for the Palestinian areas. And Israeli governments of all stripes have been the driving force behind proposals to build proper housing for those stuck in refugee camps and joint industrial parks to provide Palestinians with jobs.

Yet the Palestinian embrace of the sword has put these efforts in jeopardy. Nothing could illustrate this nexus more starkly than Friday's terror attack at the Erez crossing. The Palestinian terrorist started firing indiscriminately at Israelis and Palestinians, killing border policeman Sgt. David Smirnov and a Palestinian worker. The Palestinian worker who was murdered was one of about 3,000 who work in the industrial area, one of the few examples of Palestinian-Israeli cooperation that has survived from Oslo's heyday.

In 1947, eight million Hindus fled Pakistan and six million Muslims fled India upon the creation of those two countries. The following year about 600,000 Arabs fled Israel and an equal number of Jews fled the Arab countries to Israel. The Hindu, Muslim, and Jewish refugees were all resettled by the war-torn countries they fled to, despite the poverty of those countries and the fact that no refugee agency was created to help them. Far from providing 'relief,' UNRWA's mission has added to the burden of Palestinians and Israelis alike. Rather than pledging more money to UNRWA, Powell should have yanked the US contribution and found a way to spend it on solving, rather than perpetuating, the Palestinian refugee problem.

◆ ◆ ◆

That democracies tend to avoid defending themselves is hardly new. Alexis de Toqueville recognized it over a century ago. This editorial, written for Israel's 54th Independence Day, argues that it is important to remember not only the weaknesses of democracies but perhaps the greater weaknesses of dictatorships.

How Dictatorships Perish
April 16, 2002

The annual intermingling of Remembrance Day and Independence Day is always poignant, but this year both days have added immediacy.

123

These days, it seems, almost every day is both Remembrance Day and Independence Day. As in the early days of the state and in 1967 and 1973, it is clear that Israel is fighting a war for its existence. We had hoped to be beyond this by now, but at least we know what we have to do.

Though Israelis are still split on important aspects of the conflict, polls indicate that 75 percent support Operation Defensive Shield. Despite all the noise made by the fewer than 300 men who refuse to serve, not only have Israelis responded to the recent reserve call-up in over-whelming numbers – at much higher rates than for routine call-ups in calmer times – but more than 4,500 have volunteered to serve. Israelis are also responding somewhat like Americans did after September 11 – by buying twice as many Israeli flags than for a normal Independence Day.

Israelis tinge their patriotism, however, with something that would be unthinkable for Americans: a doubt over the ultimate viability of their country over the long term. A poll taken this month among Israeli high school students found that 78 percent of the Jewish students plan to serve in the IDF, and of those, 55 percent want to serve in combat units.

Impressive. But the same poll found that only a slim majority of Jewish students (54 percent) were confident that Israel "definitely will" exist in 50 years, while 32 percent "thought it will," and a further 8 percent thought or were sure that Israel will not survive that long. Among Israeli-Arab high school students the results were even more striking: 54 percent either thought or were sure that Israel would *not* exist in half a century.

What can and should be said to the many students who doubt Israel's future?

It would be condescending to dismiss their fears which, after all, are hardly irrational, particularly at a time when the world seems to be showing so little understanding for Israel's predicament. It is not neces-sary, however, to resort to blind confidence to be optimistic about Israel's long-term future. To understand why, it is helpful to recall how recently even America questioned its future and how dramatically its fortunes turned around.

Though written by a French intellectual, Jean-Francois Revel's 1984 book, *How Democracies Perish*, struck a deep chord in America. "Democ-racy may," Revel wrote, "turn out to have been an historic accident, a brief parenthesis that is closing before our very eyes." Democracy was in danger because it was "the first [civilization] in history to blame itself, because another power was seeking to destroy it." Revel also marveled at the fact that democracy was "not only deeply convinced of the rightness of its own defeat, but that it should regale its friends and foes with reasons why defending itself would be immoral and, in any event, superfluous, even dangerous."

Israel is badly infected with exactly the sentiments that Revel feared would doom the West in its struggle with communism. Yet what is striking about Revel's warnings less than two decades on is how widely he missed the mark. It was not the whimpering West that imploded, but confident communism which collapsed.

The lesson for us is not that it is wise for a substantial part of our intelligentsia to blame Israel for Arab aggression and to incessantly question the efficacy of self-defense. Revel was right that the democracies risked defeat when they began to doubt the justice of their own cause. Where Revel erred was in his obliviousness to the inherent weaknesses of communism, which finally revealed themselves in a spectacular fashion just six years after his book appeared.

To Israel, the Arab world has for decades looked much like the Soviet bloc did in 1984: powerful, determined, immutable, unified, and patient. And Israel's minuscule size gives the Arab world an advantage that the Soviet Union never had – the ability to contemplate Israel's utter destruction, even at the cost of absorbing a retaliatory strike. Unlike the United States, Israel cannot afford to lose a single war.

Since our last Independence Day, however, this assumption of Arab invincibility must be questioned in ways that most Israelis have yet to appreciate. Despite the current US regression into evenhandedness between Israel and the Palestinians, America's war on terrorism promises to radically change the strategic landscape in Israel's favor. A year from now, it is a fair bet that Saddam Hussein will have been replaced by a pro-Western government in Iraq, and the monolith of Arab radicalism will have been shattered. More than ever, and whether the US admits it or not, Israeli and American interests have become inextricably intertwined. Yasser Arafat has presented George W. Bush with a simple choice: to decisively confront his leadership or to accept his toppling of the Bush doctrine. Bush cannot afford to make the wrong choice – not for Israel's sake, but for America's own.

◆　◆　◆

This piece was written during a brief period that marked one of President Bush's worst stumbles in the war against militant Islam. The period is bracketed by two Bush speeches. The first was on April 4, 2002, calling on Israel to end the military campaign that had begun one week before, after the Passover Massacre in Netanya. In this speech, Bush said he would send Powell to the region to jumpstart diplomacy.

In the second speech, on June 24, 2002, Bush switched tacks completely, calling for a new Palestinian leadership and making Palestinian statehood contingent on democratization. This was a sea change, because it marked the first major US break with decades of failed diplomacy based on treating Israel and the Palestinians roughly equally, rather than placing the burden of peacemaking mainly on the Palestinian side.

The road map, negotiated as a sop to the Europeans during the run-up to the war in Iraq and officially released after that war, is a rollback to the pre-June 24 model of peacemaking. It will therefore fail until President Bush again, as in his June 24 speech, does not try to place the burden of peace evenly on the victim and the aggressor.

Interesting Times: Unfinished Business
April 19, 2002

In his parting press conference, Secretary of State Colin Powell kept referring back to President George W. Bush's "enough is enough" speech as if it were a lifeline.

Powell clung desperately to that April 4 statement as if to say, "look, I'm not freelancing here, it is the president who sent me on this feckless mission." Powell is right to treat April 4 as a red-letter day for US policy toward the region, but it is red in the more ominous connotations of that color.

That was the day that Bush stumbled in the war on terrorism. On Wednesday, with his speech at the Virginia Military Institute [on the need for preemption], Bush began to pick himself up, but he still has not fully dusted himself off and found his bearings again.

April 4 was when Bush started pretending that there was a functional, if not moral, equivalence between Israel's fight against terrorism and terrorism itself. He defended Israel's right to self-defense, but he imposed arbitrary limits on the exercise of that right, which rendered his defense of it close to meaningless.

In doing this, Bush opened himself up to the charge of hypocrisy and of holding Israel to a double standard. But those who treat Bush's April 4 stumble as if it is mainly a question of treating Israel unfairly, or breaking a sort of campaign promise, miss its full significance. Likewise, the stakes in the war on terrorism itself are generally underestimated.

To call it the "war on terrorism" as Daniel Pipes has pointed out, is to pretend that this is a war against a tactic. What this war is really about is reshaping the world order as dramatically as did Western triumphs in World War II and the Cold War. More precisely, it is the unfinished business of America's Cold War and Gulf War victories.

Just over a decade ago, a wave of freedom swept over Central Europe and the former Soviet Union as 70 years of communist tyranny imploded. That wave stopped abruptly at the end of the Gulf War when the United States, having just liberated Kuwait in a spectacular fashion, stood by as Saddam Hussein crushed the popular revolt against him.

In 1991, the United States was not ready to say that freedom mattered in the Arab world. At that time, freedom and stability were seen to be in conflict, and stability won out.

It took September 11 to make America realize that what had passed for stability in the Middle East was not just an affront to American values, but a profound challenge to her security. While some may think that Bush is being melodramatic by railing against the "axis of evil," in some ways he has understated the magnitude of the threat.

To say this is merely a war against terrorism is like saying that World War II was a war against kamikazes and not the Japanese. It is a war against, as an editorial in the *National Review* succinctly put it, "the Baathist fascism of Iraq; the Shiite radicalism of Iran; and the Sunni radicalism of Saudi Arabia." Palestinian Authority Chairman Yasser Arafat, of course, is presiding over a mini-cauldron of all three of these allied ideologies.

These three forces, which can be lumped together as "militant Islam," are an enemy as ultimately dangerous as European and Japanese fascism and Soviet communism were.

Just because the threat does not come in the form of Panzer divisions or ICBM fields does not mean that it is less great. It does not take a great degree of imagination to see how terrorism, if allowed to spread and intensify, could force the West to sue for peace.

Bush instinctively understands this. Less consciously, he seems to understand that the real difference between before and after September 11 is two words: regime change.

As the Twin Towers fell, the idea that stability was the cornerstone of American security fell along with them. The cadets at VMI may have missed it, but it is no accident that Bush spoke of the Taliban as the "first" regime to fall in the war against terror.

On April 4, Bush decided for tactical reasons to blow a bubble around Israel and the Palestinians and declare this particular branch of the war a regime change-free zone.

There was and is no chance that this would work, because militant Islam immediately recognized that, by fiddling with the flames of terror and the smoke screen of peace plans, there was the possibility of expanding the bubble to include Iraq. An entire rogues' gallery is banking on Arafat to prove that harboring terrorism is not a crime punishable by regime change. Bush will get back on track when he realizes that saving Arafat, far from helping oust Saddam, is Saddam's last best hope.

◆ ◆ ◆

Jenin is one of the small cities in the West Bank that the Israeli army entered in Operation Defensive Shield of April 2002. It was the first major Israeli counter-offensive against the wave of terror that began in late September 2000. The offensive came after a particularly bad week of terror, including the "Passover Massacre" in the Park Hotel in Netanya, in which a suicide bomber detonated himself in the middle of a Passover seder, killing 29 Israelis.

Jenin, by this time, had developed a reputation as the "suicide capital" of the West Bank, since so many bombers had come from there. The terrorists were centered in what is called a "refugee camp," but is essentially an integral, if dense and poor, part of the city.

The terrorists had been corralled into a very small area, which most armies would have bombed from the air without warning, or warned civilians to leave first. Israeli forces, by contrast, went in on foot, and took heavy casualties as a result.

Palestinian officials claimed that Israel had massacred 500 people in Jenin, and much of the media coverage initially reported these claims uncritically. Peter Hansen, the director of the UN Relief and Works Agency, which is dedicated to supporting Palestinian refugees, toured Jenin and spoke of "wholesale obliteration," "a human catastrophe that has few parallels in recent history," "bodies...piling up" and "mass graves."

In August, a UN investigation found that 52 Palestinians had been killed, including both terrorists and the civilians they hid behind, compared to 23 killed among Israeli soldiers. There was no "massacre," only a battle in which Israelis took heavy losses in order to minimize civilian casualties on the Palestinian side – while the terrorists themselves deliberately hid in and booby-trapped civilian areas.

Interesting Times: The Real War Criminals
May 3, 2002

Israel has repeatedly claimed it has nothing to hide in Jenin, so why was it so keen on keeping the UN from investigating? The answer lies in the perversion of international humanitarian law, which has ramifications far beyond Israel's own situation.

The Palestinians, human rights groups, and the UN all stand ready to accuse Israel of war crimes, a category which is rightly reserved for some of the most terrible things human beings can do to each other. After all, for something to be a 'war crime' it must be so beyond the pale that even in war it is forbidden.

What defines a war crime is spelled out in great detail in international humanitarian law, but one fundamental is clear: the distinction between soldiers and civilians.

Terrorism, of course, turns the civilian-military distinction on its head: Civilians are the intended targets of the terrorist, not 'collateral damage.' Terrorists, according to international law, are unlawful combatants, meaning they are not entitled to the protections due prisoners of war.

The fact that terrorists are not considered soldiers, however, does not prevent them from being war criminals. A terrorist, for example, who chooses to hide in a hospital or a home – not to mention the Church of the Nativity – and shoots from behind civilians, is committing a war crime.

Accordingly, the real war criminals in Jenin were the Palestinians who booby-trapped a large civilian area and deliberately caused civilian

129

CONFRONTING JIHAD

casualties on their own side. The whole Palestinian 'military' strategy was to take advantage of the IDF's willingness to suffer casualties in a concrete test of the laws of war. As one Palestinian who fought there put it, seeing soldiers walking down the alleys of Jenin was "like a prize," in that they put themselves at an almost impossible disadvantage – for the sole purpose of protecting civilians.

Despite inevitable exceptions, in broad terms Israel's soldiers should have been considered heroes of humanitarian law, and the Palestinians who endangered their own people the villains. But the fact that the international community sees things in exact opposite terms is not just a problem for Israel. The real significance of the stampede to put Israel in the docket is that, if it was wrong to fight terror the way Israel fought it, then terror cannot be fought at all.

The way out of this predicament was shown by US President George W. Bush in another area of international law. In his 'axis of evil' speech to Congress, Bush declared, "The United States of America will not permit the world's most dangerous regimes to threaten us with the world's most destructive weapons." With this single master stroke, Bush brushed aside the most misguided premise of arms control, which pretended that no distinctions should be made between governments (aside from the five original nuclear powers) in the quest to prevent nuclear proliferation.

In just one sentence, Bush leapfrogged the existing lowest common denominator system, which acts as if Israel's Jericho missiles are as menacing as Saddam Hussein's weapons program, and put the focus where it belongs.

The refusal to make critical distinctions makes a mockery of international law and can lead to the opposite of what the law intended. Arms control is supposed to make the world safer, but Saddam had no trouble signing the Nuclear Non-Proliferation Treaty, because he knew that doing so would actually help him obtain high technology for his weapons program. By the same token, Palestinian terrorists hid out in a crowded warren of homes, because they knew the civilians endangered would be on Israel's head rather than their own.

The only antidote to the Orwellian abuse of international law is to speak the truth. The US, for starters, should not just protect Israel from what Daniel Patrick Moynihan once called the "jackals" at the UN, but should place credit and blame where it is due. America would also serve its own cause if it recognized the IDF soldiers who died fighting with such

130

courage and humanity in the battle against terrorism that both nations share.

◆ ◆ ◆

The Palestinians have done something that may be unique in history: indoctrinated their youth to kill themselves in order to kill others. The sociological significance of this is rarely discussed. This column raises the question of what happens the day after the Palestinians call off their attack, and wonders whether it will be as easy as people seem to assume to undo years of glorifying "martyrdom."

Interesting Times: Suicide is Not Painless
May 31, 2002

As an American, she might have aspired to be a nun. In Israel she would probably have poured her soul into community service. In would-be Palestine, Thauriya Hamamreh decided to become a suicide bomber.

David Rudge's interview with Hamamreh in yesterday's *Jerusalem Post* is a riveting document. One might assume that anyone so bent on mass murder that they would be willing to take their own life would be burning with hatred.

Hamamreh, who was so petite that there was not enough room to strap the standard bomb belt on her, said she had decided to become a martyr for "personal reasons." Anger at Israel was clearly a factor, but her underlying belief was the need for jihad to "create a just and equal, non-corrupt society by the spread and unification of Islam."

Palestinian society may be the first on earth to transform suicide and murder into a form of social work. Terrorist groups claim they try to weed out people who, like Hamamreh, are suicidal and want to harness their depression in the name of a grand cause. We can't have people who actually want to die killing themselves, goes this logic.

But Hamamreh's mixed motivations are probably much more typical than they are made out to be.

To the cynical masterminds who send young people out to die, suicide bombing is a 'military' tactic. Along the way, however, the

131

Palestinians have developed a culture of suicide that may not be so easily dismantled, even once they decide to try.

For a chilling preview, Palestinians had better look at what happened in an island paradise far away from their troubles.

In the early 1960s, suicide was almost unknown in Micronesia. By the end of the 1980s, there were more suicides in this sparse archipelago than anywhere else in the world. Teens began killing themselves for trivial reasons – being yelled at by a sibling, not having a graduation gown, or because a girlfriend had been seen with another boy.

Anthropologist Donald Rubinstein traced Micronesia's suicide epidemic and seems to have found its origins.

On the island of Ebeye in May 1966 – after a decade without a single suicide – an 18-year-old boy hanged himself in jail after his arrest for stealing a bicycle. Six months later, the well-known son of one of the island's wealthiest families hanged himself when he could not decide between his two girlfriends, having fathered a child with each. His lovers fainted on his grave, having met there for the first time.

Three days later, a 22-year old hanged himself over marital difficulties.

The epidemic was on. Other research, as Malcolm Gladwell noted in *The Tipping Point*, found that "suicide can be contagious." Studies in the US found that immediately after newspaper accounts of suicides, suicide rates jumped. Marilyn Monroe's suicide was followed by a temporary 12 percent increase in the national suicide rate.

In Micronesia, and elsewhere, of course, suicide can be contagious even when there is no support for it in the surrounding culture. Now imagine a situation in which suicide generates global – not just national – headlines, happens with dizzying frequency, is associated with a glorious struggle, and is rewarded with instant heroism rather than shame.

In such a culture Hamamreh's choice becomes rational. Why jump off a building in ignominy, when blowing up in a crowded cafe can secure your place in heaven, not to mention history?

Some have made the point that suicide bombing has little to do with desperation, but is the opposite – a macabre expression of hope in the future. Actually it is has become a mishmash of both, and something else: a fad.

Hamamreh became disillusioned when her handlers told her to blow herself up if she was caught, even if she was not in the middle of a crowd.

"I felt like they were playing a game with the blood of the martyrs," she explained.

It is more than the "martyrs'" blood these men are playing with. They have deliberately seeded a cultural suicide epidemic. Like their counterparts in nature, cultural epidemics are not easy to start, but they are even harder to control.

Even if word comes from the top that suicide bombing is no longer in the Palestinian interest, this does not really negate the cultural cues that have already been established. All other suicide epidemics, after all, started in places where suicide was already frowned upon.

Antidotes may be few, but one was recently demonstrated. When the Taliban were put out on their ears in Afghanistan, Osama bin Laden T-shirts suddenly became less popular in Peshawar. Bin Laden tried to start a terror epidemic and the US, through decisive military action, was able to stop it in its tracks, at least temporarily.

Operation Defensive Shield, though relatively effective, was essentially an aborted version of the US action, stopping far short of 'regime change.'

There is no precedent for the breadth of the suicide cult the Palestinians have created. What seems clear, however, is that the Palestinians will need a lot of help in snuffing it out.

◆　◆　◆

The process by which societies become inured to terrorism is perhaps the most dangerous one of all, because it constitutes the terrorists' only path to victory. The paradox is that a society's ability to withstand terror and not be defeated by it is a form of strength, but this same strength can turn into weakness if it produces a tolerance for higher and higher levels of terrorism.

Israel broke out of such a "tolerance cycle" in April 2002, when it launched a massive military operation to root out terrorists from Palestinian cities. About a year later (May 2003), after the fall of Saddam, we experienced a new wave of attacks – five suicide bombings in 48 hours – without responding with a significant change in tactics.

In June 2003, Abdel Aziz Rantisi, a senior Hamas leader and well-known spokesman, barely escaped an Israeli missile strike against his car: those in the front seat were killed, Rantisi managed to get away. This was the first such targeting of a Hamas "political" leader in recent times. President Bush responded by saying he was "troubled" by the action and believed it did not contribute to Israel's security.

The Israeli military and political echelons had hesitated to escalate the battle against Hamas in this fashion, because the diplomatic cost was estimated to be higher than the benefit of eliminating an easily replaceable leader. It is hard to see, however, why Israel should be made to pay a diplomatic price for killing Hamas leaders, whose relationship to terrorism is the same as Osama Bin Laden. No one ever distinguishes between the "political" and "military" wings of al-Qaida.

Interesting Times: Defining Terrorism Down
June 21, 2002

To someone in Washington or London, this week's suicide bombings happened on top of me. On their world maps, Israel is so small its name barely fits inside the country. Jerusalem is a speck, and I am inside that exploding speck.

Even within Israel, people in Tel Aviv call their friends and family in Jerusalem, concerned for their safety.

Here in Jerusalem itself, when a bomb goes off, the distance scale shifts again. For someone who lives in the south of the city, a bomb in the northern part of the city is far away. Once, a bomb went off in a parking lot a couple of blocks away from me, on a street I drive on daily, about 20 minutes after I passed by. But in my mind this was not a close call, because I didn't hear the bomb go off, and it didn't hurt anyone.

The protective armor of the mind grows closer, tighter. Even if I were to be caught close to an attack, my mind could create distance by arguing that I was lucky not to be wounded, or only to be wounded, as the case may be.

By a strange inversion, the farther one is from terrorism, the closer it seems to people you know; the closer one is, the better one gets at mental distancing. Craziness becomes relative. Americans think visiting Israel is crazy; Tel Avivians stay away from Jerusalem; Jerusalemites from Ariel; Ariel residents from Kiryat Arba; and Kiryat Arba people are probably a bit skittish when visiting Hebron. Just like 'fanatic' is defined as anyone who is more religiously observant than you are, 'dangerous' is the word for anywhere you don't go, whether or not there is objectively much difference.

A similar process occurs with the definition of a 'major' terrorist attack. In 1993, former US Senator Daniel Patrick Moynihan wrote a famous article titled, 'Defining Deviancy Down' – about how societies can become inured to increasing social decay. In an interview years later, he explained how he got the idea. Moynihan saw an item buried in the *New York Times* about seven people having been found dead in an apartment. The article noted that a mother had managed to hide her infant under a bed before she was shot. For the newspaper, the mother's desperate act "was sort of interesting," Moynihan wryly observed. "The fact that seven people had been shot in the back of the head was not interesting at all."

In 1929, when Al Capone gunned down seven competing mobsters, Moynihan remembered, it became an American legend dubbed the St. Valentine's Day Massacre. In the 1990s, it took a special twist on seven murders for it to even rate a story on page B14.

The same process has occurred with terrorism. When the PLO captured the Israeli Olympic team in Munich in 1972, German officials appealed to the terrorists to release their hostages because they were creating bad publicity for their own cause. It seemed unthinkable then that the Palestinians would simply murder the Israeli athletes, as they eventually did.

In domestic affairs, the process Moynihan identified happens without any directing hand. Crime rates, for example, do not go up because all the criminals get together and decide it is time to become more active. Terrorism is different – its whole purpose is to shock an entire public, or the world. Terrorists must by definition try to top themselves, in order to overcome the 'defining down' of what is considered a major, newsworthy attack.

In this instance, the normally healthy human ability to adapt to almost anything works against us. When we adapt to atrocities, we deny terrorism a victory in one sense, but encourage even more spectacular attacks in another.

So how does a society get out of a destructive spiral of 'defining deviancy down'? In the cases of crime and other social maladies, a reversal ultimately comes about when leaders go against the tide and begin to make the acceptable unacceptable.

We have not yet turned such a corner in the fight against terrorism. On the contrary, the level of terrorism that will trigger a given level of military response is continuing to slide upward.

It seems that we are waiting for terrorism to reach a level at which everyone in the world will understand that Yasser Arafat's regime must be replaced. This point may never be reached, however, precisely because the world becomes used to seeing Israel not react decisively to increasing levels of terrorism. Along the way, we are not only defining terrorism down for ourselves, but for the whole world.

◆ ◆ ◆

The horrible bombing at the Hebrew University cafeteria in Jerusalem came after a period of relative quiet, and some Israeli commentators were quick to link it to the army's targeted killing of a major Hamas terrorist, Salah Shehadeh. Such waves of internal second-guessing are not new; they seem to happen after every terrorist kingpin is removed. This argues that such recriminations make no sense and are actively harmful.

I also argue that Israel has actually been going beyond the letter of international law in its concern for not harming civilians who the terrorists surround themselves with, and that this concern, far from being rewarded, may incur a further price in both PR terms and in Israeli lives.

It All Started When He Hit Me Back
August 1, 2002

Before our dead have even been buried, recriminations are in the air. What if we had not killed Hamas megaterrorist Salah Shehadeh? Why did we bring upon ourselves a new wave of terrorism?

The more pertinent questions are quite different: Why do the terrorists, and the Palestinian leadership that does nothing to stop them, not ask itself similar questions before attacking Israelis? Why are patently justified and preventive Israeli actions considered provocative, while Palestinian "retaliation" is considered natural?

The idea that Hamas has some right to "retaliate" after Israel kills its terrorist mastermind is a form of the schoolyard logic, "it all started when he hit me back." Such a defense is absurd to the point of being comical, yet it is routinely applied to the current conflict, and even, perhaps unconsciously, internalized by many Israelis. Yesterday UN Secretary-General Kofi Annan reflected this mentality when he reflexively added to his condemnation of terrorism a call to "all concerned to end the cycle of violence, revenge, and retaliation."

The problem is that there is no "cycle of violence" and certainly no "cycle of terror," as a Palestinian Authority statement creatively put it. If anything, this latest gruesome bombing of a cafeteria in Jerusalem's Hebrew University accentuates how little reciprocity there is in this conflict.

Hamas, which has taken responsibility for the bombing, has been trying for almost two years to kill as many Israeli civilians as possible. Terrorism is by definition and design indiscriminate. In this case, the victims were as diverse as Hebrew University's community of students, which includes Jews, Arabs, and visitors from many countries.

In response, Israel would not for a moment dream of retaliating in kind. But Israel not only considers the targeting of civilians an anathema, but severely limits its actions against legitimate terrorist targets in order to minimize civilian casualties. After the relatively high civilian toll that accompanied the killing of Shehadeh, Israel revealed that the strike had been called off many times before because the terrorist was surrounded by civilians, such as his own family.

Given the nature of the war we are fighting, it is not clear that we should be so proud of this record. According to Part 3, Article 1, Section 28 of the Fourth Geneva Convention, "The presence of a protected person may not be used to render certain points or areas immune from military operations." Translated, this means that, under international law, combatants must not be allowed to protect themselves by hiding among civilians.

Indeed, the Geneva Convention goes further: "The party to the conflict in whose hands protected persons may be is responsible for the treatment accorded to them by its agents." In other words, if a terrorist hides among civilians, it is the terrorist who is responsible for their deaths in any military action.

That the Palestinians violate these provisions wholesale goes without saying. But Israel must also answer to its citizens for over-complying with international law. The question must be asked: How many Israeli civilians died because Israel refrained from killing Shehadeh and other terrorists because they were hiding among civilians?

The nations that condemned Israel for being "heavy-handed" (in the words of the United States) acted contrary to the letter and spirit of the Geneva Convention by blaming Israel rather than Shehadeh for Palestinian civilian deaths. The international community may well continue in this vein, no matter what Israel says or does. It has come to the point, however, when Israel should consider following, not going beyond, this basic principle of international law.

Israel must continue to attempt to minimize Palestinian civilian casualties, but not to the point that terrorist chieftains have effective immunity. The military pressure on Hamas and Islamic Jihad needs to be relentless. None of their leaders, including their "spiritual" leaders, should feel safe anywhere.

The irony is that, by going beyond the letter of the law, let alone how any other country would behave under such attack, Israel actually invites the world to apply a double standard. If Israel itself waives its rights and lets terrorists use their own families and neighbors as protection, why should the world not hold Israel to that standard? Excessive restraint fails in its own terms because no one gives us credit. It is also a false form of morality because, by prolonging this war, it increases the number of Israeli and Palestinian civilian casualties alike.

◆ ◆ ◆

It is difficult to see things from the inside, wars included. The amorphousness of the enemy in this case compounds the problem. In World War II, for example, it became clear that the war would be won when Germany and Japan had surrendered and their regimes replaced. This attempts to describe a concrete definition of victory in the war against the terror network.

The column was written more than eight months before the war in Iraq. At that time, the assumption was the war would come in a few months, and would remove the immunity that Yasser Arafat enjoyed, because the US did not want Israel to 'rock the boat' before that war.

Here I argue that Israel's pre-Iraq restraint is imposing a terrible price in terror, so that it is imperative for the Iraq war to happen as quickly as possible. I did not imagine then that the war would be delayed so long, and that in its aftermath, the appointment of Mahmoud Abbas (Abu Mazen) as prime minister would keep Arafat in place even longer.

Interesting Times: Hurry Up, We're Dying Here
August 2, 2002

Walking through the *Jerusalem Post* building yesterday, the morning after the terrible bombing at Hebrew University, was like going through an emotional minefield.

One staffer feared for the privacy of her friend, whose bloodied face was plastered over newspapers worldwide. Others wanted the story of stricken friends and acquaintances told, but were too distraught to write about it themselves.

The university, like this newspaper, has an international flavor, and the interconnectedness of the two communities was never more evident.

Also evident was the disconnect between the carnage we are facing and our national, not to mention the international, response to it.

Since President George W. Bush's landmark June 24 speech calling for a new Palestinian leadership, Israel's security services have been putting the terrorists under unprecedented and sustained military pressure, and have managed to prevent hundreds of attacks. What is more, this pressure, coupled with the dead end the Palestinians are facing on the diplomatic front, seems to have generated an internal Palestinian debate over the need for a unilateral 'cease-fire.'

Playing with cease-fires is an old game, so it is unclear that anything real was in the works before Israel killed Hamas arch-terrorist Salah Shehadeh. The significant thing is that for the first time since the Palestinians launched their offensive almost two years ago, it is beginning to sink in that terrorism and violence will not simply drive Israel out, as it seemed to have done in Lebanon.

But if the Palestinians have lost, or are at least modifying, their theory of victory, Israel does not seem to have one either. After every bombing, police chiefs and generals say that the nation cannot be hermetically sealed off.

This is obvious – particularly before the promised fence is built – but the question begged is rarely asked, let alone answered: If defensive measures cannot succeed, how can Israel defeat Palestinian terrorism through offensive and diplomatic action?

Somehow, it has been drummed into our heads that it is perfectly natural – even sophisticated – to have no theory of victory. The idea that there is a 'military solution' is denigrated at every turn, at the very

139

moment when the United States is rightly pursuing just such a solution to terrorism at the global level.

The diplomatic elements of the American effort do not contradict the fact that the goal is to defeat terrorists, not negotiate with them.

One telling example of this difference is the shameful fact that, hours before the slaughter at Hebrew University, Israel handed NIS 70 million (about $18 million) in withheld Palestinian tax revenues to the new PA finance minister. This is not parallel to the humanitarian aid that the US literally rained on the Afghan people during the fighting there - rather, it is as if the US had given money to the Taliban finance ministry.

Does anyone really believe that these funds will be hermetically sealed off from Yasser Arafat, or that the transfer will hasten his removal from power?

Based on Bush's speech, one might have expected that Israel and the US would vigorously pursue a two-pronged theory of victory: an all-out Israeli war against Hamas, Islamic Jihad and Arafat's own Fatah/Tanzim terrorists, coupled with the utter financial and diplomatic isolation of the current Palestinian leadership.

Instead, what we see is more or less the same holding pattern that existed before: Israel is 'allowed' to fight defensively but not decisively, and Yasser Arafat is slated for removal, but ambivalently and without any sense of urgency.

This is not to say that the Bush speech had no effect – far from it. Bush extricated the US from a trap, and set a goal for the future.

The trap was that Palestinian escalation had been granted a form of immunity because it was clear that the US did not want to confront Arafat before ousting Saddam. Since that immunity has ostensibly been removed, so has a great incentive for Palestinian terrorism.

Further, the demand for Palestinian democracy has shifted the burden for statehood onto the Palestinians themselves, again creating a reason to change paths.

What the Bush speech did not do – it is painfully evident now – is remove Israel from the pre-Iraq limbo it has been operating under for almost a year. All current diplomatic and military machinations aside, the order seems to be the same: First Saddam must go, then we will worry about Arafat.

This order is much preferable to what was the State Department's alternative – attempting to hammer out an Israeli-Palestinian peace agreement before dealing with Saddam. But it also leaves only two ways out of the current unacceptable situation: taking Bush at his word and speeding up Arafat's removal, or for the US to speed up its ouster of Saddam.

The outcome of this war is foreseen. The Palestinians have lost because, for all their sacrifices, they will have gained nothing that was not offered to them at Camp David two years ago.

Waiting for it to end, however, is a deadly business. The more quickly and decisively Arafat's offensive is defeated, the more Israeli and Palestinian lives will be saved, and the sooner we can move on.

◆ ◆ ◆

This column attempts to explore the strange combination of confidence and defeatism that affects both Americans and Israelis in the face of the threat of terror. The expectation that in the end the terrorists will not win is combined with an expectation that terrorism will not be eradicated either. My point is that the West's capabilities do not warrant such pessimism; that whether we live in a considerably safer world free of state-sponsored terror is a matter of the choices the West makes.

Interesting Times: What Should We Hope For?
August 8, 2002

My uncle just arrived here from New York for a visit, proving Woody Allen's observation that 90 percent of life is just showing up.

Since "the situation" began, Lewis has been visiting more than ever, without any particular occasion, just to be with his family in Israel for a few days. His quiet visits speak more loudly than much of the angst-ridden, what-can-we-do activity of American Jewry, as welcome as this heightened concern for Israel is.

His question to me was the same as practically everyone we met on a recent trip to the US: What is it like for you, living with terror?

My answer has been somewhat contradictory. First, our daily routine has not changed that much. Second, each attack hits us in the gut. And third, we protect ourselves with a certain numbness that does not let us feel the full force of these tragedies.

Hanging over all of these feelings, however, is the fundamental variable that allows anyone to survive almost anything: hope.

Terror is depressing in its own right, but if one does not see any end to it, the ability to grit teeth and move on is greatly reduced.

The question then becomes, what is the hope that keeps Israelis and, for that matter Americans, going after the devastating attacks both nations have suffered.

Here too, there are different levels. On the one hand, few Americans or Israelis imagine actually losing the war, in the sense that they cannot conceive of the US being subjugated by the Islamic world, or Israel being destroyed.

This is both a strength and a weakness, in that it shows confidence in the strength of the West, but also an innocence toward the enemy's threat.

On the other hand and without fully realizing it, many Americans and Israelis cannot imagine fully winning the war, either. They assume that the world will never go back to the way it was before September 11, and that the Arab enmity toward Israel is a fact of life. They see the war on terrorism as essentially a perpetual war.

Such underlying pessimism is also a strength and a weakness. It is healthy in that it motivates a level of vigilance that was missing before September 11, but damaging because it saps the confidence that makes democracies, particularly the US, great.

So what should we be hoping for? What is a realistic goal and – even more relevant to our collective mood – what should we expect?

The answer is that the West should be shooting for a world that is free of state-supported terrorism; that is, a world in which it is not safe for any nation to harbor a terrorist organization. Our goal should be not just returning to America's pre-September 11 sense of confidence and safety, but to something even better.

Before September 11, after all, the world was hardly free of state-supported terror. Al-Qaida itself had carried out devastating attacks on American embassies, and the terror war against Israel was in full bloom.

Western actions, however, do not project a sense that such a victory is possible, much less expected. In Israel, we are clamoring for a wall between us and the Palestinians. One can argue about how effective such a wall might be, but its premise would seem to be that Palestinian attacks will continue indefinitely.

In theory, a fence can be seen as a component of defeating terror, and even nations at peace are separated by fences. Psychologically, though, a fence is an expression of exasperation and the expectation of perpetual conflict.

In the US, this perpetual war syndrome is expressed in the debate over how to rebuild the site of the World Trade Center and the pall that remains over the US economy.

Will 100-story buildings be planned in the US? Or are architects, cities and corporations assuming that buildings must be designed to withstand aircraft transformed into human-guided missiles?

Does the American stock market believe that the war against terrorism will be won, or is the market discounting itself in light of an open-ended conflict?

This nagging sense that the war against terrorism will never be won, just not lost, should be resisted. It is true that it will never be won in the same way as it is true that there will always be crime and disease, and part of winning means never returning to a naive complacency. But the war can be won in the sense that the world will be considerably safer and freer than it was on September 10.

As President George W. Bush has hinted, this war is an opportunity to remake the Middle East, end the Arab-Israeli conflict by defeating radical Arab regimes, and rid the world of the threat of rogue regimes obtaining nuclear weapons (a development that previously seemed inevitable).

There is no inherent reason why the West must tolerate these threats to its own and international security. If we do, it will be essentially a matter of our own choosing, rather than a lack of capability to forge a different world.

◆　◆　◆

Much of the discussion of the war against terrorism's impact on the wider world order tends to focus on whether America has too much power, or is too unrestrained. Little attention has been paid to the impact a more outward-looking America could have on the global advance of democracy. Here I make the parallel between the unanticipated consequences of the Civil War and the current struggle against the terror network.

The War for Democracy
September 11, 2002

Neither party expected for the war the magnitude or the duration which it has already attained. Neither anticipated that the cause of the conflict might cease with or even before the conflict itself should cease. Each looked for an easier triumph, and a result less fundamental and astounding.
– Abraham Lincoln, Second Inaugural Address, March 4, 1865

On September 11, 2001, war was declared against the United States, and by extension, the Free World. Or more accurately, America joined a war launched against it by militant Islam, as Daniel Pipes argues on these pages, as early as the capture of the American Embassy in Teheran in 1979.

Many have drawn the analogy to Pearl Harbor, another attack that surprised America one clear day and forced the US to go to war. That war, too, had its transformative effects. But it is perhaps Lincoln's words summing up the Civil War that best touch on the nature of this conflict: one much broader than its protagonists expected, with ramifications even greater still.

What Lincoln was alluding to was not just the abolition of slavery, but that the Civil War transformed the US from an 'are' to 'is' – a single nation rather than a fractious federation of states. The current war is essentially one to transform the world from one in which freedom and democracy are the province of the lucky few to a world in which the concept of universal rights finally comes into its own.

Like the Union then, the US now may well be looking for "an easier triumph, and a result less fundamental and astounding." But President George W. Bush's June 24 speech on Palestinian democracy lays the intellectual groundwork for nothing less.

At this one-year mark, America can chalk up two fundamental accomplishments in the war so far: the liberation of Afghanistan and the breaking of the taboo that stability trumps democracy where the Arab world is concerned.

Bush's fundamental case on Iraq is that America's uncharacteristic worship of the false god of stability brought the ultimate instability: September 11. The Arab world, left to fester in its own despotism, was an unstable mixture that blew up in America's face.

Bush learned from this what America already knew but did not want to admit to itself: The only guarantor of true international stability and peace is some form of democracy, however imperfect. He is right, and the only real question now is whether America will look for an "easier triumph," or pursue its vision to its logical conclusion.

Yesterday Bush spoke at the Afghan Embassy in Washington, partly to quell talk that the US is not paying enough attention to winning the peace in Afghanistan, and partly to emphasize that there is a Muslim country that loves America and that America loves. Bush called Afghanistan an "emerging democracy." Despite the recent assassination attempt on President Hamid Karzai and despite the fact that the US may not be supporting democracy as deftly as it dispatched the dictatorship, Bush's characterization is a fair one.

The birth pangs of Afghan democracy do not negate the great deed of Afghanistan's liberation. Similarly, nurturing a democratic order in post-Saddam Iraq, or in a post-Arafat Palestinian Authority may not be easy or smooth. But where is it written that the best form of government is also the easiest one?

In an interview with this newspaper in April, eminent historian Bernard Lewis cautioned that "democracy is dangerous anywhere... We talk sometimes as if democracy were the natural human condition, as if any deviation from it is a crime to be punished or a disease to be cured. That is not true."

At the same time, Lewis's caution about democracy did not mean he advocated an alternative. Even in the Arab world, Lewis clearly saw the possibilities, provided one had "a realistic approach without illusions and saw democracy in terms of a gradual maturing that is possible, and has been done in many places."

One thing can be said about the challenge of promoting democracy: It is much preferable to the challenge of containing rogue dictatorships. This is the fundamental lesson that America has and should have drawn from September 11. It is the reason why removing Saddam is nearer to the beginning than to the end of this war. And it is the reason that this war should ultimately be seen as one for democracy even more than it is against terrorism, which is after all but a tool of the dictators who live by it.

◆　◆　◆

I have always admired the presidency of Harry S Truman, particularly so after reading David McCullough's fabulous biography, Truman. This column allowed me to dip back into that book, to give a flavor of the improbability of that presidency, which reminded me greatly of that of George W. Bush. The analogy between the two presidencies is striking, because it cuts across their political paths, style of governance, and the global challenges they faced.

Interesting Times: Unlikely Compatriots
October 4, 2002

When George W. Bush was elected, the first guess was he would be like his father, who also happened to be the previous Republican president. But Bush the father was a bureaucratic pragmatist who came to the presidency as if to the end of a natural sequence – it was practically the only significant job in government he had not held.

Bush the son surprised everyone by being much more like Ronald Reagan: a leader who had convictions strong enough to – at least sometimes – trump the pragmatic considerations that normally dominate politics.

Perhaps less noticed, however, is the convergence of the Bush presidency with that of a much earlier White House occupant from another party: Harry S Truman.

When Truman was sworn in hours after the death of the revered Franklin Roosevelt, the nation went into shock. As Truman biographer David McCullough put it, the news struck "like massive earth tremors... To many it was not just that the greatest of men had fallen, but that the least of men – or at any rate the least likely of men – had assumed his place."

Truman had only become vice president the summer before, having been a barely-known Senator from Missouri. Though he had gained a measure of respect for his conduct in the Senate, the charge that he was the "Senator from Pendergast" – a reference to the boss of a Midwest political machine – still dogged him with the reputation of an intellectual lightweight.

Nor did this unserious reputation leave him as president. When he ran for reelection three years later, my grandmother recalls that all the "good liberals" at the US Mission at the United Nations, where she

146

worked, were voting for Henry Wallace, a liberal Democrat who was running against the incumbent from his own party.

Remarkably, even after leading the nation through such momentous events as the Potsdam Conference, dropping the bomb on Japan, and the launching of the Marshall Plan to rebuild Europe, Truman was still dismissed by the intellectual elite of his own party as the "Senator from Pendergast."

Truman won that election almost as squeakily as Bush won his. But the similarities just begin there.

The first is that each had the personal sense of security to surround himself with heavyweights, despite the risk of being outshone by them. Truman appointed Dean Acheson and George Marshall, both considered senior statesmen of their day. Bush found Dick Cheney, Colin Powell, and Donald Rumsfeld – all of whom carried reputations somewhat weightier than his own.

Even more impressive, Truman and Bush showed they could go head-to-head with their mighty braintrusts and be right in the bargain. Truman did this most dramatically when he decided to recognize the State of Israel 11 minutes after it was declared, on May 14, 1948.

McCullough reports: "Some [US] delegates actually broke into laughter, thinking the announcement was somebody's idea of a joke... Marshall dispatched his head of UN affairs to New York to keep the whole delegation from resigning."

Marshall himself had opposed recognizing Israel so strongly that he told Truman to his face that he would vote against the president if he took that decision. In an eerie parallel with Bush's relationship with Powell, Marshall was appalled that "political" considerations could sway a foreign policy decision, while his own implied resignation threat became a central part of the political equation.

Bush, for his part, has twice overruled Powell in the most dramatic way: with his "axis of evil" speech that made regime change a centerpiece of US policy, and with his June 24 speech calling for a new Palestinian leadership. Bush may not have done something like firing General Douglas MacArthur (during the Korean War), but his takeover of the foreign policy arena – which he was expected to avoid out of ignorance – is no less stunning.

But the greatest similarity lies not in bureaucratic gutsiness but in an approach to a moment in history. As alluded to in the title of Dean Acheson's memoirs, *Present at the Creation*, Truman was the architect of the postwar era. It was Truman who charted the switch from the wartime alliance with "Uncle Joe" to the long resistance to Soviet adventurism. Truman's first decision as president was not to try and postpone the founding conference of the UN, which came just 12 days after Roosevelt's death.

Though the Cold War ended with the fall of the Soviet Union during his father's term, it is really Bush the son that is forging the' New World Order' proclaimed a decade ago. The vacuum produced by the Soviet collapse was filled by a great burst of freedom, but that burst did not spread as globally as expected.

Until now, our' new world' has been defined more by the absence of Soviet expansionism than by an American evangelism for democracy. The result of this complacency, it was belatedly discovered, was that a new menace – militant Islam – tempted to challenge the hegemony of the free world.

Bush, like Truman, is defining the architecture of the West's response to a global enemy it was slow to recognize. It is no coincidence that Bush has found himself challenging the UN to deliver or step aside. This is the stuff new orders are made of.

Bush's place in history will be determined by how boldly and comprehensively he grasps this task.

The Bush architecture begins, in a sense, where Truman left off. Truman's order was based on containment. Bush's discovery has been that, when facing an amorphous enemy with increasingly deadly gadgets and decreasing moral compunctions, containment is not enough. His new architecture, therefore, faces outward. As Bush's introduction to the US National Security Strategy put it, "We seek to create a balance of power that favors human freedom ....We will defend the peace by fighting terrorists and tyrants. ... We will extend the peace by encouraging free and open societies on every continent."

The difference between containing tyranny and expanding freedom is a sea change; if Bush sticks with it, his place in history is assured.

◆ ◆ ◆

This column refers to the death of the child Mohammed al-Dura, still the iconic image symbolizing for Palestinians the entire "second intifada." A subsequent article by James Fallows in The Atlantic Monthly *(June 2003,*

148

"Who Shot Mohammed al-Dura?") concludes that it was not possible that he was shot by Israeli forces, as I allude to below.

If al-Dura was deliberately murdered by Palestinians in order to tar Israel, then the humanity gap I write of here is even more pronounced. In any event, the point that Palestinian dehumanization of Israelis should be addressed before peace can be pursued would seem to be valid regardless of the al-Dura case.

Interesting Times: The Humanity Gap
November 15, 2002

On September 30, 2000, Muhammad al-Dura was shot to death while cowering behind his father during a firefight between Palestinians and IDF soldiers. The haunting images of the 12-year-old's death were broadcast around the world and have become the central icon in the Palestinian offensive against Israel.

On Sunday, Noam and Matan Ohayon, four and five, were shot point blank in their beds. Their mother, Revital, was also murdered while trying to protect them from the terrorist who had entered their home in Kibbutz Metzer.

Granted, Dura's death was caught on camera, and so it was not surprising that the searing pictures spread like wildfire. But every Israeli newspaper led for the next two days with pictures of Avi Ohayon, the father who had lost everything in an instant, collapsing in his children's room, and later on their graves.

Dura was initially assumed to have been killed inadvertently by IDF fire. The army apologized, and any Israeli with a heart was horrified by the tragedy. Further investigation, including a report that ran on German television, seemed to prove that he could not have been killed by the IDF. But this is not the point, because even if Dura was not, other Palestinian children have been inadvertently shot by Israeli forces.

Nor is the point that the orgy of coverage surrounding Dura's presumably accidental death dwarfs that of the deliberate murders of the Ohayon boys. The disproportion is so great that a search of the Web for a single picture of the boys or the funeral produced nothing. Since a search using their names drew a blank, I tried 'Israeli father' as keywords. Though no pictures of what was the Ohayon family popped up, two pictures of Dura's father did.

It is true, but banal, that the media has once again revealed its biases. What is more significant is what these particular murders, despite having come after so many others, reveal about the Palestinians.

This is, after all, a moment when Palestinians are reportedly reconsidering suicide bombings inside the Green Line as a tactic. Here was a perfect test for more moderate Palestinians: a particularly gruesome attack against a kibbutz, one that has been at the forefront of Jewish-Arab cooperation. Metzer even shared a soccer team with the Arab village next door. Would this act evince a peep of protest, shame, or misgiving, beyond the usual formal condemnations?

Here's how the official Palestinian Authority newspaper Al-Hayat al-Jadida headlined its coverage: 'Five Israelis killed in an attack on the settlement Metzer.' The report continued, 'A Palestinian infiltrated the settlement Metzer and opened fire on the settlers.' It is not well known that the Palestinian press frequently refers to towns in Israel, such as Holon and Kiryat Shmona, as 'settlements.' Besides implying that all of Israel is an illegitimate colonial outpost, such references clearly are brought to justify the killings and distinguish them from terrorism.

A survey of the Palestinian press by Palestinian Media Watch (www.pmw.org.il) found that the only critical reference to the attack came two days later. Salah Rifat, the secretary of the Democratic Union Party, the PA newspaper reported, sent a telegram to the secretary of an Israeli-Palestinian dialogue group and to Meretz expressing 'sincere condolences to the family of the victims... and to all the members of the kibbutz.'

PMW director Itamar Marcus says this is the first such condolence message he has seen in more than two years. Meanwhile, the official Fatah Web site published the announcement of the Aksa Martyrs Brigades confirming "our responsibility for the courageous, qualitative operation in the settlement of Metzer... killing and wounding several Zionist colonizers... We will continue to strike any place, targeting their children as well" (see www.fatehorg.org, translation by PMW).

It is here we get to the point: Palestinians feel freer to defend the murder of Israeli children than they do to condemn it. This state of affairs has profound implications not just for Israel, but for the Palestinians themselves.

In a fascinating interview in the November 4 *Weekly Standard*, Rawya Rashad Shawa, a member of the Palestinian Legislative Council who is highly critical of Yasser Arafat, states, "We all see the military strength of the Israelis... but we should also see the strengths of their political system... [just] because we cannot have a war machine like theirs does not mean we should not have democracy either."

I find myself rooting for Palestinians to close the democracy gap. But when asked if she approves of suicide bombings, Shawa launches into a long description of Israeli-imposed suffering and concludes, "You cannot drive human beings beyond the context of human life and still hold them to the highest ethical standard."

What Shawa does not seem to understand is that Palestinians cannot close the democracy gap before they close the humanity gap. Democracy is built on a fundamental respect for human dignity. It cannot coexist with the dehumanization of Israelis, which is what the justification of baby-killing is. Before Palestinians can recognize our right to exist as a nation, they must recognize the humanity of our children.

◆ ◆ ◆

The death of Abba Eban, Israel's iconic foreign minister during the Six Day War, was an occasion to remember some truths that, though often forgotten, are still relevant today.

The Best Representation
November 18, 2002

There was perhaps no man who was as synonymous with Israel's foreign policy, and for many, with Israel itself, as Abba Eban.

Just before the founding of the state, at the age of 31, David Ben-Gurion sent him to the United Nations as a liaison to the Special Committee on Palestine. He then became Israel's first ambassador to that body, then the only Israeli to serve simultaneously as ambassador both to the UN and to Washington.

In 1952, he was given a post that now seems unbelievable, that of vice president of the UN General Assembly. He went on to become a Knesset member, education minister, and finally the post he is most remembered for, foreign minister during the Six Day War.

Throughout and after his long diplomatic and political career, Eban continued to represent Israel through the numerous books that he wrote and through television documentaries. Eban was more than Israel's voice, as Ben- Gurion called him. He represented a time in which Israel's diplomatic prowess was valued and cultivated as much as its military skills.

Today we have many talented people in our foreign service who do not often receive the credit they deserve for the difficult job that they do. But the top posts – key ambassadorships and the foreign minister – have long ago become political playthings to be fobbed off in coalition negotiations.

Israel would never dream of appointing its generals, colonels, or its defense minister in the way it chooses its diplomatic leadership. Eban embodied the principle that Israel cannot afford anything less than the best representation the nation could muster.

His death is a reminder how far we have fallen in this regard, and how critical skills like Eban's are necessary today. Our diplomatic leadership was deliberately allowed to founder on the theory that the 'right policies' would make our case for us in the world. Now that those policies have fallen apart, and Israel has come under both military and diplomatic attack, it should be obvious that the battle for world opinion is at least as important as the battles on the ground.

In his later years, Eban became a defender of the Oslo Accords and became swept up, along with his party, with the idea that the right territorial concessions could bring peace. One can already predict that some will try to appropriate his memory to buttress failed policies that should not be resurrected. But the case that Eban presented to the world at the height of career, some 35 years ago, rings true and even bears important lessons for us today.

In March 1966, a few months after he was appointed foreign minister, Eban made a statement in the Knesset that is surprisingly relevant to our post-September 11 world: "Every country that maintains normal relations with Israel, that refuses to buckle to pressure and blackmail, that places its relations with Israel beyond the reach of the negative influence of our enemies – every such state brings the prospects of peace nearer by so doing. The more Arab enmity finds itself isolated, the weaker it will continue to become...On the other hand, every state that is deterred from openly and unequivocally establishing friendship with Israel for fear of what the Arabs will say is merely helping – even if unwittingly – to perpetuate and encourage Arab enmity ..."

Today as well, the key to peace will be to confront Arab rejectionism head on, and to recognize that peace does not come from how much land Israel is willing to relinquish, but whether the Arab world will accept Israel on any strip of land.

As Eban continued, "The whole subject of the dispute is the existence of Israel, no more and no less. As that is the essence of the argument, there is no one single key to resolve it. Discussions about the refugees, about 'gestures,' about declarations, and all the rest, are only of tactical influence, and do not get anywhere near the heart of the matter. If only Arab leadership were ready to reconcile itself to the simple fact of Israel's existence, then it would be disposed to accept the consequences of that existence."

It is for these views, which have once again become timely, that Eban should be remembered, and for his stirring belief in the Zionist project. In our darkest days, Eban stood for the idea that, as he put it, "Israel is not an interloper in the Middle East. Israel sprang from this region, Israel is returning to it ...There never was, there is not, and there cannot be a Middle East which is not illuminated by the influence of Israel." The days ahead are likely to be brighter ones, and all the more quickly if we more effectively remind the world of some of the truths Eban so eloquently put forth.

◆ ◆ ◆

In the election of 2003, incumbent Ariel Sharon trounced Labor's Amram Mitzna, a former general and mayor of Haifa. This election broke the pattern of the 1990s in which the incumbent party was booted out in each balloting. It also broke the rule that any prime minister who calls an early election ends up losing.

This piece examines why the Labor party, the party of David Ben-Gurion, Yitzhak Rabin, and Shimon Peres, which held a monopoly on power during the nation's first 29 years, not only lost the premiership but has shrunk to holding less than one-sixth of the seats in the Knesset and is now less than half the size of the Likud party.

Mitzna has since resigned as leader of the party, but blamed his failure on party infighting rather than his decision to roughly repeat the platform that produced Labor's defeat in the previous election. In June 2003, Shimon Peres, at age 80, was once again named leader of the party, ostensibly to revive it rather than to be its next candidate for prime minister.

Sect or Party?
January 30, 2003

The Labor Party has now suffered two major defeats in a row. It is still showing no sign that it understands why. To recover, Labor must decide whether it wants to be a religious sect or a political party.

In his concession speech, Amram Mitzna said, "We presented a clear, sharp and courageous position to the voter, that offers a path to hope. A path that will enable a confrontation with the harsh reality." While claiming to accept the results, he continued, "We will not stop until the public in Israel again has faith in us and I promise you friends, that this will be soon.... Our way is the right way.... We are one great camp, a camp of belief, a camp of hope, a camp of peace."

Listen closely to these words. Nothing in them suggests that Labor has made any mistakes, or that any fundamental course correction is necessary.

On the contrary, the sense given – and this is not unique to Mitzna but applies to the Left as a whole – is that the strategy is not to change or reassess, but to wait until the wheel of politics turns around again and dumps the public into its lap.

As Shimon Peres put it, "I don't see it as the end. In six years the government has changed four times, and there were elections. And I think that this time, too, there will not be stability, because it doesn't depend on the coalition, but rather on solutions. And I don't see the solutions." In other words, however the public votes, whatever happens, the solution remains the same and we have the monopoly on it.

On one level, there is something admirable about this stubbornness, because it bespeaks of a party that stands for something and does not simply blow with the electoral winds. But the job of a political party, unlike some religious sects, is not to preserve an ideology for its own sake but to know when it must adapt or die.

Meretz leader Yossi Sarid showed no signs that he was rethinking what his party represented, but at least he had the decency to resign. Yisrael B'Aliya leader Natan Sharansky, following the disappointing showing for his party, did both: resigned from the Knesset and committed himself to a complete reorientation of his party.

But Mitzna seems to be neither resigning nor rethinking. His plan is to not only wait for the government to fail, but push as hard as he can to hasten its demise.

To this, some may say, what could be more democratic? The Labor Party must rebuild itself, and it can only do so in the opposition.

The problem with this theory is that there is nothing restorative about being that opposition if the party deliberately refuses to draw any conclusions from its defeat. Ironically, Labor's strategy toward the voters mirrors its strategy toward the Palestinians that the voters have rejected: keep extending a hand in friendship, no matter how many times that gesture is met with a punch in the nose. Diplomatically, the public judges Labor's strategy as futile and dangerous; politically as insulting its intelligence.

But what about the idea that, just as Yasser Arafat single-handedly resurrected Ariel Sharon and the Right, outside circumstances will return the public to the Left's door?

This too is an illusion because it is built upon the notion that the Right is as incapable of responding to an opening for peace as the Left has been to a declaration of war. What is the precedent on which this fantasy is based? Was it not Menachem Begin who made the 'painful concessions' of his time in response to Anwar Sadat's overture? And if Ariel Sharon wants to avoid similar difficult choices, then why would he prefer Labor over the right-wing parties as his partner? Perhaps it is too much to ask that the Left admit that the Right actually has a better chance, and arguably a better record, of building a workable peace. But there is a difference between ideological capitulation and a healthy dose of pragmatism.

If the Labor Party wants to revive itself, whether it is in the government or opposition is much less important than whether it is willing to learn anything from its defeats. What it must learn is how to admit ideological, not just procedural, mistakes. So far, it shows no signs of doing so. Until it does, its decline will continue.

◆ ◆ ◆

This column surprised many, since it appeared at a time when Israel was preparing to be hit by a chemical attack from Iraq. As of this writing, 2003 is only about halfway through, but I still stand by this piece, including its title. But my terms need some explaining. I do not mean that the strategic changes that came in 2003 will come to full fruition this year. I certainly hope that when we look back a decade or two from now, we will see many better years.

My point is that, looking back, 2003 will be seen as a year in which Israel's strategic situation turned a positive corner, like 1979, the year a peace treaty was signed with Egypt.

What I did not anticipate here was that the appointment of Mahmoud Abbas as Palestinian prime minister would buy Yasser Arafat more time at the helm and allow him to weather the immediate aftermath of the war in Iraq. It remains to be seen how much time Arafat has bought.

This column also should not be read to rule out a significant economic downturn that will, if it happens, surely mark the year in Israeli eyes as one of the nation's worst years. But economic downturns are temporary, and do not erase the positive long-term effects of the strategic advance that I describe here.

Interesting Times: This Year Will Be Israel's Best Yet
January 24, 2003

Unemployment is rising, war looms, our child's kindergarten teacher has just handed out a note saying it is time to make "emergency preparations" beyond the armed guard who already stands outside. The idea that 2003 could be a good year, let alone a great one, doesn't seem to pass the laugh test.

But I am not just trying to grab your attention. And I don't think I am going out on a limb, betting that readers have short memories.

As a country that has been under attack since birth, a good year is when a major threat to our existence can be provisionally checked off the list. The first such year was 1979, the year we signed a peace treaty with Egypt (or perhaps 1977, when Anwar Sadat came to Jerusalem).

The peace with Egypt, so long as it remains more the exception than the Arab rule, cannot be considered irreversible. Yet it remains the single greatest leap forward in Israel's legitimization in the region. The 1994 peace treaty with Jordan was a ripple effect of peace with Egypt and the Oslo Accords.

Oslo itself was less of a strategic breakthrough then a false start at one. It is now clear that Yasser Arafat never intended to make peace with Israel and used Oslo to prepare for the war we are now experiencing.

Which brings me to this year. In the next few months (weeks?), Saddam Hussein will either flee or be impeached by US Special Forces. This fact alone is a strategic breakthrough at least as significant as the peace with Egypt.

We tend to bifurcate the threats against us into Palestinian terror on one hand, and big countries with missiles and armies on the other. Lately, what is considered to be the greater threat has changed somewhat. In October, for example, OC Intelligence Maj.-Gen. Aharon Ze'evi (Farkash) told the cabinet that Iraq, lacking nuclear weapons, was not an existential threat to Israel, but that terror was "a strategic threat to the world."

Regardless of which is a bigger threat, what is important is the usually neglected connection between them. Iraq is not just about missiles and potential nukes, but cash payments to the families of suicide bombers. Iran is not just tinkering with its latest Shihab missiles, but is funding Islamic Jihad and Hizbullah.

Each terrorist group that plagues us has a mother ship in either Teheran, Baghdad or Damascus. If any of those mother ships changes hands, severing the umbilical cord to its offspring, the terrorists will be substantially weakened.

But why do the Palestinians, who use cheap weapons like explosives and their own bodies, really need external help? Because it is not just a matter of direct financial assistance but the sense that they are not fighting alone, that they are representing the dreams of much of the Arab nation.

Terror alone has no military theory of victory. It is built on the idea that it will cause moral collapse within Israel, which in turn will tempt major states into provoking a regional war. Prime Minister Ariel Sharon's reelection will be an important blow to the theory of terrorism. Regime change in key radical states will be another sign that jihad is not the wave of the future.

This year, the mother ship in Baghdad will be destroyed. The one in Teheran, according to those who follow the region most closely, such as Bernard Lewis and Michael Ledeen, is likely to be deposed soon by the Iranian people. These two victories would – particularly since the successor governments are likely to be pro-Western – easily displace 1979 as a banner year in Israel's history.

But even if the mullahs manage to hold on a bit longer, Yasser Arafat probably will not. The consensus within the Israeli security establishment, Egypt, Jordan, and Europe has shifted over the last few months. Previously, it was believed that exile might strengthen Arafat. Now the belief is that he should be retired to some Arab country where he will no longer have veto power over Palestinian affairs.

Arafat's exile, the defeats for regional radicals, and general exhaustion will induce the Palestinians to cut their losses and make a deal. This prompts some to turn good news on its head and predict that we will have a lousy year because the pressure on Israel to make another questionable peace deal will be massive.

It is not clear that such pressure will emerge because there is increasing realization in Washington that previous administrations had it backwards: The Arab-Israeli peace process is not the key to stability in the region; rather, an improved regional climate makes peace possible. More broadly, the unexamined quest for stability is itself being recognized, in Mark Steyn's words, as "a fetish" that led to September 11.

The Bush Administration should understand that regime change in Baghdad, Teheran and Ramallah is the real peace process. Subsequent agreements would be the result of the Arab realization that the jihad against Israel had better be set aside indefinitely.

Unless Bush decides to abandon his June 24 vision for Palestinian democracy, Israel will not be pressured into a deal with another illegitimate, terror-ridden regime. If Israel and the US stick to this principle, the peace process could be transformed from a way of weakening Israel by nonmilitary means into a way of institutionalizing the defeat of Arab radicalism.

It may take some years for the fundamental changes wrought this year to produce their full effect. There is some danger that the progress made will not be followed up in Syria and Saudi Arabia, like when the US rested on its laurels at the end of the Cold War.

Even so, 2003 will be the year when, for the first time in our history, the tide turned, and real peace and stability became visible on the horizon.

This column follows up my first post 9/11 column (see "Design to Win," pages 71-74) where I suggest that a good goal for the war against terrorism is to win it by the time the new World Trade Center is rebuilt. Winning, in this case, would be defined by not having to design the new towers around the threat

of hijacked airplanes plowing into them, because people would no longer be concerned about such a threat.

The actual design chosen, by Daniel Libeskind, fits the test I suggested in terms of height, ambition, and fragility, but ultimately fudges the issue by not including any populated space at the higher levels. Perhaps another American city will have to pick up this gauntlet sometime in the future when America's victory over terror is further secured.

Interesting Times: Don't Design Around Terror
February 14, 2003

Though I was born in New York City, I never lived there. I feel connected to the city for much the same reason that it was attacked on September 11: because its vitality and spirit make it the symbol of America to the world.

Within New York, the soaring Twin Towers symbolized the vitality of the city that never sleeps, and of America as a whole. How they are rebuilt, then, is of importance not just to New Yorkers or Americans, but to the world.

The impulse to rebuild as a component of healing is overwhelming. The gargantuan task of removing the remnants of the Towers became a project of national urgency, and the competing architectural teams were given almost impossibly tight deadlines to submit their designs for a new complex.

On February 4, the Lower Manhattan Development Corporation (LMDC) announced that it had narrowed down the nine designs submitted in December to two finalists: those by Studio Daniel Libeskind and the THINK team of architects (see www.renewnyc.org).

The two designs are fascinating, even inspiring, for any architecture buff. It is a treat to watch the top firms apply their skills to what may be the highest-profile design competition the world has ever seen. But there is much more than architecture at stake here, and the winnowing-out process has reflected this.

The LMDC, for example, first unveiled six designs in July, which were immediately panned as lackluster. Though they might have been considered grand for any of other project, they all seemed to fall shy of the audacity of the original towers.

Just a month later, in response to the overwhelming public reaction, a new request for designs was issued whose first requirement was, "Distinctive Skyline: New York City lost a critical part of its identity when the World Trade Center towers were destroyed. A tall symbol or structure that would be recognized around the world is crucial to restoring the spirit of the city."

The architects and planners have heard the people's message. Each of the nine designs unveiled in December seemed loftier and more fantastic than the next. Though not chosen as a finalist, the most popular submission, by Norman Foster, featured angular towers soaring some 40 stories higher than the original twins. Libeskind proposes a spire 1,776 numerologically-correct feet tall, and the THINK team plans two lattice-like towers of a similar height.

As bold as these designs are, they still reflect a pronounced ambivalence, which is also found in the reactions to them. In *Newsday*, street reactions to building the world's tallest building ranged from "I don't think it's a bad idea. It will show bin Laden that we are not afraid and that we're coming back bigger and better than ever" to the seemingly pragmatic, "it just draws attention ... it will make al-Qaida want to prove once again that they can knock it down. They should have small buildings and a memorial."

Libeskind and THINK played to both sentiments by including dramatic skyline elements, but keeping their top halves largely empty. Both put elaborate gardens and tourist spots at levels where bond traders used to labor in the original WTC. Indeed, the new complexes keep the "world" part of the original WTC, but ditch the "trade" part in favor of ecological and cultural themes.

Some critics, understandably, question the idea of putting public parks some 100 stories up. It is hard to imagine the public strolling through such vertical theme parks. Speaking of Libeskind's "Gardens of the World," Anne Raver worries in the *New York Times*, "I'm afraid New Yorkers might go there only with Aunt Ethel, visiting from Des Moines."

The immediate problem with these designs is that they try to give the public the glory it wants without the guts of actually inhabiting the highest structures. The question must be asked, does a building really say "we are not afraid" if the top of it amounts to a treehouse?

The subtext here is that most people assume that no one will want to rent office space on triple-digit floors post-9/11. But this is the crux of the matter, and building high will not paper over that basic fear.

Even in the Foster proposal that had the highest real office space, that fear lurked. In his presentation, for example, Foster noted that his towers, "kiss at three points, creating public observation platforms, exhibits, cafes and other amenities. These links also have a safety benefit, as escape routes from one tower to the other." Since when are escape routes a major selling point?

There is evolution at work here. In July, the proposals were relatively staid and squat, and the public demanded more. In December, four proposals included the tallest buildings in the world, prompting one observer to note, "Six months ago, you never would have seen that."

The LMDC says they will choose between the two finalists this month. This is a mistake. Better to let the trend toward increased confidence continue for another six months, and then put out a no-rush request for more designs.

The last half year saw an evolution toward taller but 'unmanned' buildings. Once Saddam has been trounced in Iraq, predictions of doom have proved unfounded, and more dictators are on the run, watch how the idea of working on the 100th floor may not seem so crazy any more.

In the February 3 *New Republic*, Martin Filler called the impetus behind the latest proposals "a mad rush to create a new Tower of Babel." But it should not be considered hubris to plan for a day in which we do not build our lives around the possibility of hijacked aircraft being steered into tall buildings.

On a much smaller scale, the city of Jerusalem is building a light-rail system, seemingly oblivious to the fact that people are already afraid to go on the buses that have been the frequent target of suicide bombers. There is a lesson here for New York. Instead of designing around terrorism, we should plan to have beaten it.

◆　◆　◆

For all its pretensions that it is promoting Arab-Israeli peace, Europe is probably the single greatest factor blocking that eventuality. The reason is that Europe has been at the forefront of apologizing for and accepting Arab rejectionism, terrorism, and antisemitism. If European leaders were to boycott Yasser Arafat as has the United States, he could be safely shipped off to retirement in Tunisia or elsewhere, and Israelis and Palestinians could begin to dismantle the edifice of terror that he created.

This open letter is a plea to one prominent visiting European leader to reconsider Europe's course. Bret Stephens, our editor in chief, conceived and wrote a substantial part of this editorial.

To Joschka Fischer
April 8, 2003

Dear Joschka:

It is nice to have you here, because we appreciate the visit of every friend, and we see in you one of Israel's most credible and reliable friends in Europe.

Anyone who doubts this need only read the speech you gave on your last visit in May, when you received an honorary doctorate (your first degree, as you happily confessed) from the University of Haifa. You spoke candidly about German history and the hope that "through this unwavering solidarity of democratic Germany with Israel, trust and sometimes even friendship could develop between the survivors and the children of the victims on one side and the children of the perpetrators on the other side."

Since then much has happened. The government in which you serve has been re-elected, and your personal political position in it strengthened. That government openly and insistently opposed the American-led coalition to remove Saddam Hussein in Iraq, a position that raised eyebrows not only in Washington, but in Jerusalem.

Though Israel is much criticized in the West, we are a country that greatly appreciates the need for Western unity, particularly in NATO, and we see it as relevant over the long term to our security.

It is time, then, to have a look at our friendship in light of the wreckage – at least as many Israelis see it – of the Atlantic alliance. Coming as we do from a place that has suffered the blows of Iraqi missiles, the attacks of Iraqi armies, and Iraqi support for waves of suicide bombings, you no doubt will understand why Germany's position has been received here with some alarm.

We know that we have to be careful here. Israel, it is true, often misreads European politics and sometimes unfairly ascribes to it the darkest of motives. Then again, too often Europeans have failed to appreciate the seriousness of our predicament. Many of your colleagues take too lightly our real security concerns, thinking us a Goliath who can afford to be magnanimous when we see ourselves as a David fighting, time and again, against the odds.

Since we seem to be on the eve of a different Middle East, one in which Europe very much would like to have a role, it is worth speaking frankly, in the hopes that a new page can be opened. We must ask ourselves a question that you sometimes ask us – why do we so mistrust Europe? Why doesn't Europe count?

Despite what you may think, the first basis of mistrust is not Europe's wartime history. What we cannot forget is what has happened since, at times when the chips were down and Israel's very survival was at stake.

In 1967, when Israel was on the verge of being overrun and provisions for mass graves were being made, the French, our main arms provider, imposed an arms embargo, abandoning Israel to its fate.

In 1973, when Israel was under attack from all sides, no European country except Portugal – including, notoriously, Willy Brandt's Federal Republic of Germany – would grant the US overflight rights to rush to us emergency supplies.

These betrayals are fresh in our memories because they have not been obviously disavowed. Much fresher still, however, is perhaps the greatest betrayal of all, the one that continues at this moment.

In 2000, Israel finally did what Europe had been pressing for over three decades: it tabled an offer of Palestinian statehood over some 97 percent of the territories. The Palestinian counter-offer? A terrorist offensive that continues to this day.

As Israeli civilians were pounded by attack after grisly attack, Europe's media and political leadership did not rush to our defense. Nor were they particularly evenhanded. One might have expected a lonely European voice to ask the questions, "did Israel not do what we have asked? Is it right that Israel's outstretched hand was met with violence?"

Instead, as Paul Berman writes in his book *Terror and Liberalism*, "each new act of murder and suicide testified to how oppressive were the Israelis. Palestinian terror... was the measure of Israeli guilt." Your colleague Louis Michel of Belgium stood on the tarmac of the Brussels airport and sent the Palestinians supplies. Your colleague Chris Patten of the European Commission refused to countenance the idea that the *Karine A*, a smuggling ship laden with tons of explosives, might have something to do with Yasser Arafat. France's ambassador to London called us "that shitty little country." Leading European intellectuals came to Arafat's court to express their 'solidarity.' Jacques Chirac stood on the same platform with representatives from Hizbullah. And on and on.

Yes, Europeans expressed their condolences for our dead. They told us we had the right to self-defense. But it had to be 'proportional.' And what did that mean? When we imposed closures, blockades, curfews – this was 'punishing the innocent.' Fair enough. But when we pursued a policy of targeted killings against the worst of the worst, this was 'extrajudicial.' So just what did Europe mean by 'self-defense?'

To all this, of course, you have been an exception in that you did not join the anti-Israel chorus – a lonely exception, it seems. As we said at the beginning, this letter is written to a friend, a friend who has great influence with Messrs. Patten, Michel, Chirac, etc. So we would be grateful if you would tell them this:

Why does Europe not count for Israel? Why do we ignore its counsels? Because Europe has no money in its moral bank account. Because when our people are blown up in buses and cafes, when children are bludgeoned, when toddlers are shot in their beds, we expect something more than pro forma condemnations, condemnations often packaged with apologies for the perpetrators of these atrocities. Because when we make offers for peace, and those offers are rejected, we expect you to swing behind us, not make further demands on our 'reasonableness.' Because when Europeans tell us that, once we get out of the territories, Europe will 'guarantee' our security, we ask: with what political will and with what military means? Because when the US moves to remove one of the greatest existential threats to our security – namely, Saddam Hussein in Iraq – Europe vigorously opposes it. Because when the chips have been down for us in the past, it was always the US, and never Europe, that came to our rescue.

Joschka: When we have a true partner on the Palestinian side, you can depend on Israel to be 'reasonable.' Until then, we look to you to persuade your colleagues to be reasonable as well.

◆　◆　◆

This attempts to answer the question that many observers of the peace process may be asking: if the road map is a plan to implement Bush's June 24 speech about Palestinian democracy, why is the former so bad and the latter so good? It is unfortunate that Bush did not take the opportunity before the road map was released and before the June summits to steer the road map back in the right direction.

Ultimately, there is no substitute for applying the moral clarity that Bush has employed in the war against terrorism. Bush, in other words, should take Israel's side, with more than just general commitments to Israel's security.

Speak, Mr. President
April 14, 2003

The Quartet's 'road map' was widely seen as a place-holding exercise for what would come after the war in Iraq. Despite the work left to be done there, the day after Saddam's regime has, thankfully, arrived. It is time, therefore, to examine this exercise with a fresh eye, and determine how it measures up to the opportunities presented by a Saddam-free region.

To understand where we stand, we must step back a moment from the trees – the 15 clarifications that Prime Minister Ariel Sharon's emissary will reportedly request from the White House today – and look at the forest. The forest is determining what went wrong over three decades of Middle East diplomacy culminating in the Oslo Accords, and how to ensure that this round of 'peacemaking' will be different.

Peacemaking efforts to date have run aground on two related shoals: the belief that the Arab world was ready to live with Israel, and the belief that Israeli intransigence was therefore a primary obstacle to peace.

Viewed through this lens, it is possible to solve the mystery as to why Israel has such different reactions toward two supposedly linked documents: President George W. Bush's June 24 speech and the road map. The latter is supposed to be the implementation of the former, so why is the first so good and the second so bad?

The difference is that the June 24 speech, for the first time in America's post-1967 diplomacy, put the onus on the Palestinians to create the conditions for their own statehood. By calling for a new leadership and linking statehood to democracy, Bush required that the Palestinians choose between waging their war against Israel and their own independence. Statehood, which had been axiomatic, became conditioned on the Palestinians proving that they were not creating another terrorist state in the region.

The road map seems to follow the Bush speech because it has most of the same ingredients: ending terrorism, democratization, statehood, and for Israel, a settlement freeze. But the road map makes a subtle change that makes all the difference. Like Oslo and all the failed peace plans before it, the road map is built upon a moral equivalency between Israel and the Palestinians, whereby demands to 'both sides' are carefully matched.

For example, the latest draft of the road map (December 20) states explicitly that Israel and the Palestinians must implement the steps within each phase "in parallel." The document drips with equivalence, such as: "Palestinian leadership issues unequivocal statement... calling for an immediate and unconditional cease-fire to end armed activity and all acts of violence against Israelis everywhere. All official Palestinian institutions end incitement against Israel." This is paired with "Israeli leadership issues unequivocal statement... calling for an immediate end to violence against Palestinians everywhere. All official Israeli institutions end incitement against Palestinians."

This may not have been written by a UN bureaucrat, but it was certainly written not to offend the sensibilities of one. A reader of this document would have trouble determining which side is blowing up buses and which side is trying to prevent buses from blowing up.

The truth is that the road map is so obsessed with placing equal blame and making equal demands of both sides that it is hard to see how it can be satisfactorily amended. There is also little point in amending it, since that would mean going back for another lowest-common-denominator document from the UN and the Europeans, which would not turn out much better.

What should be done instead is to supplant the road map, just like the road map supplanted Bush's June 24 speech. Turnover is fair play. Bush, not the Quartet, is the ultimate interpreter of his own speech. And the essence of that speech was to place the primary burden of statehood and peace on the Palestinians, where it belongs.

The issues of blame and burden are not quibbles; they spell the difference between another failed round of 'peace' diplomacy and a viable attempt to end the Arab-Israeli conflict. Bush should say simply that he has confidence the people and government of Israel are ready for peace the moment the Palestinians and the Arab world demonstrate they are ready to live with Israel. This means ending incitement, cracking down on terrorism, and renouncing the demand (it is not a 'right') to flood Israel with Palestinians cynically kept by the Arab world as refugees.

If Bush wants the fruits of a new Middle East, he cannot get it using a failed diplomatic playbook.

Last June, Bush had the courage to rewrite that playbook and put the blame where it belongs. Now that Saddam is gone, and the road map has hopelessly confused matters, he has to do it again. If he does not have the courage to do so, it means that a new 'peace process' will go nowhere. This would be tragic not just for Israel and the Palestinians, but for the United States, because it would be taken for a sign of weakness at a moment of maximum strength.

◆　◆　◆

What goes here for Powell's visit, which produced no evident accomplishment, goes also for the Aqaba and Sharm summits that followed, attended by President Bush himself. The Palestinian offensive against Israel would not have been launched or sustained if the Palestinians knew that the world would consistently condemn them and take Israel's side.

If the Europeans, for example, told the Palestinian Authority they would cut off all funds until they cracked down on Hamas, the war would be over. Instead, the US and Europe continue to pepper their condemnations of terror with opposition to Israeli responses. Perhaps the Palestinians will tire of being pounded by Israel and stop attacking, but international diplomacy, so long as it is roughly evenhanded, won't have much to do with it.

Doomed Again?
April 28, 2003

It is spring, the war in Iraq is over, and US Secretary of State Colin Powell is heading for the region. It is clearly a time of opportunity, but how can the US ensure that this moment is not squandered?

A year ago, in an editorial that *New York Times* columnist Thomas Friedman called "hysterical," this newspaper predicted that Powell's last visit was "doomed to failure." Powell came as Israel was in the mopping-up phase of Operation Defensive Shield, in an attempt to browbeat Israel into curtailing that military action and the Palestinians into ending terrorism. Indeed, the trip, along with subsequent attempts to foster Palestinian-Israeli negotiations before the war in Iraq, failed.

These efforts failed because of the same compound misunderstanding that has plagued Middle East diplomacy for decades: the impulse to be 'evenhanded' and to put the Arab-Israeli cart before the regional climate horse.

Regarding the regional climate, the swift fall of Saddam is having the desired 'shock and awe' effect. The fact that the people did not fight for Saddam and the Iraqi glee at his downfall showed "how oppressed they were and what misery the regime inflicted upon them," as Gibran Tueni, editor of Lebanon's *Al-Nahar* newspaper explained.

Arab radicalism is having a crisis of confidence. A Palestinian cartoonist, reflecting the mindset of those who had been elated as the war seemed to be going badly for the US, compared Saddam's fall to the 'catastrophes' of 1948 and 1967.

Since peace is fundamentally a function of Arab decisions to end the war against Israel, Arab defeats have historically been fortuitous occasions for peacemaking. The stunning Arab defeat of 1967 brought UN Security Council Resolution 242, in which the Arab states were, for the first time, required to make peace with Israel. Egypt's defeat in 1973 led to a peace treaty with Israel six years later. The US defeat of Iraq in 1991 led to the Madrid Conference, and to the Oslo Accords two years later.

Now, once again, there is an improvement in the regional climate producing another chance for peacemaking. But again, peace will only come if we understand what it is made of: an Arab world in which the balance has tipped toward accepting Israel's right to live in peace as a Jewish state.

Until now it has been assumed that such Arab acceptance hinges on what Israel does - mainly, on how much land it will give up. It is generally forgotten that Israel, with or without what remains of the territories it acquired in 1967, is a but a drop in the Arab sea. Arab sympathy for the Palestinians is assumed to be the cause of Israel-hatred, rather than its symptom. Palestinians are the first to admit that the Arab world has little use for them except as a cudgel and a rallying point for repressive regimes.

That peace depends on Arab acceptance of us may sound obvious. What is less obvious is that Arab acceptance of Israel does not depend on our size or forthcoming behavior, but on the perception of our indestructibility. The elimination of Saddam, a major enemy of Israel, contributes to that sense of indestructibility, and therefore was a major advance toward peace. But the Arab world is now waiting to see whether the new strategic situation will affect American diplomacy in the Arab-Israeli conflict. Will diplomacy revert to the pre-Iraq mold, or will it reflect what one Hamas leader called "an earthquake" in the region?

There seems to be a substantial time lag between events and when their repercussions reach the Arab-Israeli conflict. It took from September 11, 2001 to June 24, 2002, for example, for US President George W. Bush to buck the previous 35 years of conventional wisdom and place the onus of Palestinian statehood on Palestinian leadership rather than Israeli concessions.

On June 24, Bush finally looked at the Palestinian-Israeli conflict with his post 9/11 glasses and saw, not a morally amorphous 'cycle of violence,' but a fellow democracy under terrorist attack. Bush's revolutionary idea was met by a fierce counterreaction from Europe, the State Department, and our own Labor and Meretz parties, resulting ultimately in the 'road map' we are about to see today. Now, we can again safely, if unfortunately, predict that Powell's upcoming trip to the region will fail, absent a major course correction by Bush.

Rather than bog down in the details of the road map, the overarching correction needed from Bush is to do something very 'unevenhanded' and say the truth: Israel is a democracy that wants peace, and it is the unconditional obligation of the Arab world to end its century of war against the only Jewish state. Until Bush returns the burden of realizing his two-state vision more starkly to Palestinian and other Arab shoulders, Powell might as well stay home.

◆ ◆ ◆

For all the interest in the Holocaust and the Western sensitivity toward any outbreak of antisemitism, it is amazing that antisemitism could run rampant in a group of nations in the 21st century without having any impact on those nations' diplomatic standing. This is one of the old rules of the game that should have changed after September 11, particularly in the context of attempts to revive a peace process, yet it has not.

This was written on Holocaust Remembrance Day, which coincided with the 60th anniversary of the Warsaw Ghetto uprising.

A Monument of Life
April 29, 2003

What's most important: The dream of my life has become a reality. I have lived to see Jewish resistance in the Ghetto in all its greatness and glory.
– Mordechai Anielewicz, 24, a leader of the Warsaw Ghetto uprising, in a letter written just before his death

Sixty years ago today, a few hundred Jews, already close to death from starvation and disease, took on the German Army in a fight to the death. The Warsaw Ghetto uprising was the first organized resistance from within German-occupied Europe. It took longer for the Germans to conquer the ghetto than it did to occupy most European countries.

In the current film *The Pianist*, the true story of Polish-Jewish pianist Wladyslaw Szpilman, he witnesses the uprising from his hiding place just outside the ghetto walls. When he expresses a sense of futility toward the Jews' last stand, his non-Jewish friend corrects him, arguing that the Poles themselves will now have the courage to rise up.

The Poles did rise up, and there were other heroic instances of Jewish resistance, including even in the concentration camps. But what is the purpose of clinging to these events today?

The first purpose is to fulfill our obligation to those who sacrificed and lost their lives, and whose only hope was that someone would remember them and learn from their suffering. The State of Israel is itself the ultimate testament to the memory, and fulfillment of what could scarcely be dreamed of in the ashes of Europe.

At the opening ceremony last night, Prime Minister Ariel Sharon reiterated another lesson that has coursed through the veins of every Israeli leader, but particularly his own: "The Jewish people arose from the abyss of the Holocaust severely wounded, but still breathing and wiser. Never again will Jews be unprotected and homeless. Never again will we place our security in the hands of strangers, nor rely on the kindness of others."

Sharon continued with a note of reassurance to those who fear he has lost his bearings: "We will not be led astray by illusions, nor underestimate those who wish us harm. We shall be strong, determined, and steadfast in defending ourselves and will cut off any hand raised against Jews anywhere. We seek peace with all our hearts, but we have learned this lesson: It is not in weakness, nor with faint heart, that we will achieve security and peace; rather with boldness, courage, and a willingness to guard that which is most precious and vital to our future."

A sense of vigilance and independence, however, is not the only contemporary lesson we take with us from events of the last century. Antisemitism, the hatred that fueled the Holocaust in the first place, far from being conquered, has reared its head again. Antisemitic attacks have increased over the past year, in tandem with the wave of terrorism against Israel and the opposition to Israeli efforts to defend itself. It is no coincidence that extremists on the Left and the Right display three shared characteristics: antisemitism, hatred of Israel, and opposition to the war against terrorism.

It is often said that Jews are like the canary in the coal mine. This was certainly true in Europe, where Jew-hatred was an early harbinger for the threat that Nazism posed to all free peoples. But this is especially evident in the post-9/11 world, in which the terror campaign against Israel preceded the globalization of the struggle against terrorism.

But if antisemitism is the warning sign, the main place this warning is being ignored is not Europe, where sensitivities are justifiably high, but in the Arab world, where antisemitism is seen to be natural and acceptable.

In Austria, hints of sympathy for a Nazi past was taken with understandable seriousness, leading to European-wide boycotts of an elected leader. In Egypt, Saudi Arabia, Syria, and among Palestinians, antisemitism that is much more open, pervasive, and virulent passes almost without comment, and has no impact on relations with the West.

The only explanation for the relative tolerance for Arab antisemitism is that it is, if not justified, understandable in light of the Arab-Israeli conflict. This is a terrible mistake on both a factual and pragmatic basis. In fact, antisemitism preceded, caused, and continues to fuel hatred of Israel. Only a virulent racism could lead a sea of Arabs to a oppose with such vehemence a sliver of Jewish presence in their midst.

In pragmatic terms, giving the Arabs a pass on their antisemitism leads inexorably to tolerance for Arab rejection of the Jewish right to self-determination in the only land we have ever known as our own. If the Arabs' Jew-hatred is understandable, how can their desire to destroy Israel not be?

It is possible to oppose Israeli policies without being antisemitic, but it is not possible to be anti-Semitic without being anti-Israel. Israel's

171

critics must not be indiscriminately tarred with the charge of antisemitism, but by the same token, opposition to Israel must not be allowed to cloak antisemitism.

Israel and the Jewish fate are inextricably linked. The thread between us and the fighters of the Warsaw Ghetto is as unmistakable as it is unbreakable. As the poet Haim Gouri wrote,

From this fire, which enveloped your tortured and burnt bodies
We ignited a torch for our souls,
In which we lit the blaze of freedom,
And with which we marched into battle for our land.
We have avenged your bitter and lonely deaths
With our fist, heavy and warm;
To the burnt ghetto we built here a monument,
A monument of life – a life which shall never be forsaken.

◆ ◆ ◆

The parallel between Palestinian prime minister Mahmoud Abbas (Abu Mazen) and Mikhail Gorbachev will likely, for better and for worse, prove an apt one. For worse because he will fail to fulfill the expectations being attached to him; for better because he will be a transition figure whose rise presages the full collapse of the regime he is trying to save.

Don't Stop Fighting Terror
May 1, 2003

Yasser Arafat and Mahmoud Abbas walked into the meeting of the Palestinian legislature together, sat next to each other, and were otherwise as inseparable as their long histories as comrades in arms. Now the latter, also known as Abu Mazen, has been forced on the former as prime minister, a powerless position in most Arab regimes.

The international community, including the United States, has accepted the notion that Abbas should be given a chance. He has, after all, for some time been calling amorphously for an end to the 'military' attacks against Israel, on the grounds that they have become counterproductive.

172

The order of the day has become to help Abbas in his power struggle with Arafat, so that Abbas can end the Palestinian offensive that has taken so many Israeli and Palestinian lives with so little result. But the drive to 'help Abu Mazen' only makes sense if that help will produce a positive result, rather than wasting further time and lives on propping up what is essentially a facade for real change.

Let us work backwards for a moment and see whether Abbas's appointment fits the goal. The immediate objective, Israel and the international community generally agree, is either that all Palestinian organizations end their terrorist offensive on their own, or the Palestinian Authority forces an end to terrorism against Israel.

Let's further take the Hamas and Islamic Jihad at their word that they will not voluntarily lay down their arms, let alone give them into to the Palestinian Authority. Why should they? Neither Arafat, nor Abbas, nor Muhammad Dahlan – who some think might implement a crackdown – have given any indication that they intend to confront Hamas, Islamic Jihad, or even Fatah (which took responsibility for the suicide bombing in Tel Aviv yesterday morning) by force.

On the contrary, the widespread expectation is that Abbas and Dahlan plan to reopen the failed inter-Palestinian talks that began in Cairo. It seems unlikely that such talks will yield any agreement, but if they did, it would be to suspend suicide bombings within Israel while continuing terrorist attacks beyond the Green Line. Obviously, no diplomatic process can begin while such attacks continue. Further, even if the terrorism ceased, all the terrorist organizations would remain armed and intact, waiting for the 'cease-fire' to fall apart.

There is a reason that even the 'best case' scenarios under the circumstances turn out to be dead ends. Call it the Gorbachev or Khatami syndrome. Just before the Soviet Union collapsed, Mikhail Gorbachev was hailed as a great reformer who must be helped. In retrospect, it is clear that Gorbachev was trying to save the system, not destroy it, that the system was unreformable, and that only after complete collapse could real change begin.

In Iran, Muhammad Khatami was also hailed as a reformer, and the West was thrilled by his talk of a 'dialogue of civilizations.' After years of experience, it is now clear that Khatami supports Iran's terrorist foreign policy and, despite his popularity and title of 'president,' that domestically he is powerless to implement real reform and that the only solution in Iran is regime change.

Another example, from a different angle, is Iraq, where even after Saddam has lost power, the lack of proof that he is dead and gone could complicate the formation of an new, constructive Iraqi government.

The point of all these examples is that in dictatorships, particularly those long dominated by a single, untouchable leader, half-way regime changes don't really exist and certainly don't work.

So let's be generous and say this is a transition period to real, full regime change. What's the problem with that?

The problem is that this transition period, assuming it is one, will not be benign, but a period of continuing and perhaps increased terrorism. Over seven days during the recent Pessah (Passover) holiday, seven suicide bombers attempted attacks, including the one who did blow up at the Kfar Saba Train Station, murdering the security guard who stopped him. Yesterday's suicide bombing at a Tel Aviv night spot killed three and wounded 26.

Further, Israel is now under pressure to 'help Abu Mazen,' which is taken to mean easing up on its military operations. If Israel unilaterally eases up on its constant pursuit of terrorists, the result will be to give those much depleted organizations a chance to recover, as Chief of General Staff Lt.-Gen. Moshe Ya'alon just told a Knesset committee. Ya'alon, incidentally, also said this would be the result if Hamas and Islamic Jihad did agree to a temporary cease-fire.

The objective of Israel and the US, therefore, should not be to 'help Abu Mazen,' unless what is meant by that is to hold him to the only effective standard, which is the complete dismantling of all terrorist organizations.

In the meantime, the US has no moral right to request, nor Israel to accede to, any diminution in the IDF campaign to protect Israelis from Palestinian terrorism.

◆ ◆ ◆

The Palestinians have been waging a jihad against Israel no less virulent than that of Osama bin Laden against the United States. The products of diplomacy, such as the Oslo Accords and the road map, are built on the idea that the conflict is essentially one of borders, not of Israel's existence. But pretending it is not so does not change reality. Ultimately the reality of Palestinian rejectionism must be recognized and defeated for any diplomatic solution can work.

174

This was written just after the war in Iraq and the appointment of Abu Mazen, but before the road map had been officially unveiled.

Interesting Times: Peace and the God of Martyrdom
May 2, 2003

Since roughly 1967, the West has seen solving the Palestinian problem as the key to peace and stability in this region. The war in Iraq was partly an implicit admission that this paradigm has failed and is in need of reversal: The road to peace lay through defeating Arab radicalism, therefore it ran through Baghdad.

It would seem natural, then, that post-Saddam US diplomacy would begin with the welcoming of Mahmoud Abbas (Abu Mazen) as Palestinian Authority prime minister and the presentation of the Quartet's road map to the parties.

So why are the Palestinians and Europe happy, while Israel seems worried and nervous? Why does Israel seem to feel threatened when a major strategic enemy has been wiped out and there is a fresh opportunity to pursue peace?

For those trained to believe that Israeli land-hunger is the perennial obstacle to peace, jitters in Jerusalem make perfect sense. But this standard picture of Israel avoiding and the Palestinians pursuing a land-for-peace deal is a misreading of the situation.

Think of it this way. Let's say the heart of a deal is statehood for peace.

When Yitzhak Rabin and Yasser Arafat shook hands at Oslo's signing on the White House lawn a decade ago, the idea of Palestinian statehood was not only an anathema to Israelis, but had just a few years before been ruled out by US secretary of state George Shultz.

Over the following decade, on the Israeli side, the prospect of a Palestinian state went through a sea change from an unutterable taboo to something approaching a consensus. Remarkably, this consensus has remained largely intact despite the collapse of the 2000 Camp David summit and the brutal terrorism of the past 30 months.

In 1993, if an independent Palestine was unthinkable for Israelis, peace with Israel was, despite the rhetoric of Oslo, unthinkable for the Palestinians. Before Oslo, the PLO was formally dedicated to destroying

175

Israel and the symbol of the homes Palestinian refugees left in Israel encapsulated the ethos of the 'right of return.' Oslo was built on the theory that while Israelis got used to the idea of a Palestinian state, Palestinians would part with the idea that they could return to Israel (most Palestinians have never lived in Israel).

No one thought this would be easy. When Oslo was signed the right of return – more accurately described as the demand of Palestinians to move to Israel – was as unacceptable to Israelis across the political spectrum as it was axiomatic to Palestinians.

Oslo's fundamental failure was that the Israeli evolution toward the Palestinian position was not reciprocated. Throughout the past decade, even in Oslo's heyday, there was no Palestinian effort to prepare themselves to limit their demands to their own state and abandon the idea of moving into Israel.

House keys remain a potent symbol of Palestinian propaganda and mythology to this day. Having built up the notion of return, there is no way it can be turned off in an instant, and there is little indication that Abu Mazen, let alone Arafat, is prepared to try.

Further, if the shooting stopped tomorrow, we would not be back to the square one of 1993, or of 2000, but to a situation more difficult than when Oslo was signed. For the last 30 months, the Palestinians have been glorifying terrorism on an almost hourly basis.

It is a measure of how deeply the ethos of 'martyrdom' has penetrated that even Abu Mazen's speech, hailed for its moderation, was permeated with it.

Much attention was paid to Abu Mazen's denouncing of "terrorism by any party and in all its shapes and forms both because of our religious and moral traditions and because such methods do not lend support to a just cause like ours, but rather destroy it." But Arab states routinely distinguish between terror, which they are against, and attacking Israelis, which is called 'armed resistance.'

In almost the same breath as Abu Mazen condemned terror, he praised the "courageous uprising against Israel's aggression" and claimed that Palestinians had "fought with honor." How would a Palestinian learn from this that suicide bombings or shooting children in their beds is wrong rather than heroic? Why didn't Abu Mazen simply condemn suicide bombings, which would have gone far to remove this ambiguity?

If Abu Mazen is unable to speak clearly against terrorism it is hard to see how he can act clearly against it.

176

At the same time as Israelis were drumming into themselves that there are no military solutions and that a Palestinian state was not only safe, but necessary to preserve Israel as a democratic and Jewish state, the Palestinians have compounded the myth of return with the god of martyrdom.

How are the Palestinians to deprogram themselves of ideas that are incompatible with peace? Hard to say. But we do know the task can't be done until it is begun. And once begun, its seems naive to believe it can happen overnight.

The conclusion is that the Palestinians have a lot of catching up to do to reach the point where they can really accept that the Jewish people has a right to national self-determination in this land. There is not much Israel can do to hasten this process, except to block all the alternatives. The fall of Saddam Hussein was a massive psychological shock in the right direction.

The fall of Arafat, whenever it happens, will be another. At this point, until further notice, fighting terror and its sponsors is the greatest educational tool, and therefore the most effective peace process.

◆ ◆ ◆

With the ascent of the Israeli-Palestinian track to the center of American post-Saddam diplomacy, the Syrian regime does, for the moment, seem to be receiving scant attention from the United States despite its clear adjunct membership in the axis of evil. Syria's leader was not present at the June 2003 summits with President Bush in Sharm and Aqaba to launch the diplomatic "road map." And after four Israeli soldiers were killed in a joint attack by Fatah, Hamas, and Islamic Jihad, Bashar Assad himself responded that the Palestinians have the "right to defend themselves."

End Plausible Deniability
May 5, 2003

In a classic Yiddish folktale, a rabbi advises a poor man who complains of overcrowding to bring his goat inside the house. Though puzzled, he goes along with bringing animal after animal inside. The

177

rabbi's logic is finally revealed when he tells the man to remove all the animals, leaving a seemingly spacious house behind.

Perhaps there is an Arabic version of this story, because Syrian President Bashar Assad seems to know it well. For years, Syria's strategy has been simple, foisting on the West as many 'goats' as possible, so that when the international community complains, one can be removed and the diplomatic pressure along with it.

The list of Syrian misdeeds is so long it is hard to know where to begin: occupying Lebanon, dealing in drugs, providing a weapons gateway for Hizbullah, hosting Palestinian terrorists, and crushing domestic dissidents. In the context of the war on Iraq, Assad threw in a few more goats: opening a sanctions-busting pipeline for Iraqi oil and, during and after the war, hiding Iraqi regime figures and, perhaps, Saddam Hussein's weapons of mass destruction.

So when US Secretary of State Colin Powell arrived in Damascus this weekend, Assad had a choice of goats to offer his visitor. On leaving, Powell noted with satisfaction that Assad had been forthcoming, and news reports indicate that he was promised that the Damascus offices of Hamas, Islamic Jihad, and other groups would be closed.

As of yesterday, the British newspaper *Telegraph* reported that all these offices were open as usual. As one man armed with an assault rifle at Hamas headquarters put it, "We are working as normal." Making and breaking promises to Americans is business as usual for Syria, which committed to Powell two years ago to shut down the oil pipeline to Iraq and did not.

There is also a history of Syria opening and closing terrorist offices, and making symbolic withdrawals from Lebanon, as needed to release momentary diplomatic pressure.

So none of this is surprising, except that Powell, by going to Damascus in the first place, is not showing signs that the rules of the game have really changed.

For years, Syria has been a master of the game that all the rogue states of the region, including Iraq, Iran, and Libya, had played: the game of plausible deniability. According to the old rules of the game, these nations could support terrorism with the ample knowledge that the world, and the State Department, could list them as 'terrorist-supporting states,' but little would come of it as long as the regimes denied what they were doing.

The whole idea of the war against the terror network was to change the rules of this game. US President George W. Bush once again laid out the new rules in his excellent speech aboard the USS *Abraham Lincoln*: "Any person, organization, or government that supports, protects, or harbors terrorists is complicit in the murder of the innocent, and equally guilty of terrorist crimes. Any outlaw regime that has ties to terrorist groups and seeks or possesses weapons of mass destruction is a grave danger to the civilized world – and will be confronted."

The significance of Bush throwing down the gauntlet again in this fashion, after the liberation of Iraq, should not be minimized. These words, combined with the actions in Afghanistan and Iraq, themselves change the context of the game. But each rogue leader must now ask himself, 'Will the US really apply these new rules to me, or can I just throw out a goat or two and be left alone?'

Before 9/11, the US played along with the plausible deniability game, because it knew that if it fully exposed the terror network, it would have to confront the rogue states. Bush has clearly ended this coyness, which cost America so dearly.

But now that the US has changed the rules both declaratively and with concrete actions, a separate danger has arisen: maintaining credibility. Bush has rightly set the standard very high, but if countries like Syria do not come into line, all the rogues will take notice.

Syria must now do much more than close a few offices and boot out a few wanted Iraqis – that's playing by the old rules. Now, if US credibility is not to be eroded, Syria must shut down its support for terrorism entirely, including the planeloads of weapons that flow to Hizbullah via Damascus, and the blocking of the overdue deployment of the Lebanese army on Israel's border, in order to displace Hizbullah.

Even a total end to support for terror would only begin to ameliorate Syria's sins. Lebanon would still be occupied and the Syrian people still oppressed. But it would be a start. It would also be no more than what Turkey demanded and received regarding the PKK terrorists that tormented Ankara, following the massing of the Turkish army on the Syrian border.

There is little doubt that Damascus has taken note of the American divisions in Iraq, not to mention their mobility. The only question is whether Syria can continue its rogue behavior without being paid a visit.

◆ ◆ ◆

Our first post-Saddam Independence Day was an occasion to note that, despite the difficulties of the moment, a great thing had been accomplished. In fact, it was a time when optimism for the long term was more appropriate than it had been when peace had seemed imminent.

Israel at 55
May 6, 2003

Today we remember our fallen; tonight we celebrate the freedom and independence that they fought for. In addition to the traditional outdoor barbecue, it is a time to take stock as a nation.

How things look depend largely on how far one looks. In the short term, there is no denying that once again we will be celebrating under the threat of terrorism, and that simply carrying on with a degree of normality is a triumph of its own. Unemployment is high and many are suffering from the effects of a prolonged economic downturn, with little relief visible on the immediate horizon.

But a longer view is also in order. On Israel's founding 55 years ago, our population stood at 806,000. It is now 6.7 million – an eight-fold increase. Three million people have immigrated to Israel since 1948, including a million since 1990 and, perhaps most remarkably, 31,000 in the past year.

Judging by these figures, we have made steady progress toward a goal that most nations take for granted – establishing our permanence as a state. On another level, progress on this basic objective has not been, or at least not seemed, steady.

The Oslo Accords, signed almost a decade ago, were built on the assumption that the Arab world in general, and the Palestinians in particular, had reconciled themselves to our existence – all that was left was to negotiate borders with a Palestinian state.

During Oslo's heyday it seemed to many that the Arab-Israeli conflict was behind us. Typifying the mindset of the time, the *Middle East Quarterly* (September 1996) published a debate centered on an article titled 'The Arab-Israel Conflict is Over.' "The critical development," this article argued, "was a PLO able to redefine its goal from destroying Israel to building a state alongside Israel." Few imagined at this time that just a few years later Yasser Arafat would reject a state over 97 percent of the disputed territories and launch a terrorist offensive against Israel to boot.

The viciousness of the war against us these past 30 months, in which over 760 Israelis have died – over 520 of them civilians – has set back our views regarding Arab intentions to those held during the early years of the state. At that time, there was no question that the bulk of the Arab world would wipe us off the map if given half a chance.

But if our belief in the Arab readiness for peace was premature, realizing this can hardly be seen as a step backwards in Israel's objective situation. If anything, our moments of greatest danger have been when we were caught in the throes of an illusion. Our new realism, however disconcerting, should be seen as a step forward toward a peace that will last.

Even more important than our improved perceptions is the great advancement in our strategic position that has just occurred. Not since Egypt made peace with Israel have we been able to shift a major Arab nation off the list of states that pose an immediate strategic threat. Iraq's immediate future remains uncertain, but Saddam Hussein is permanently gone from power, and there is reason to believe that the next Iraqi government will not be a threat to its neighbors, including Israel.

Another great and dangerous illusion has been substantially dispelled is that terrorism against Israel is an isolated phenomenon, without strategic implications for the West as a whole. The latest revelations, such as the capture of Palestinian arch-terrorist Abu Abbas in Iraq and reports that the suicide bombers at Mike's Place in Tel Aviv last week were tied to Iran, only accentuate what we have long known: there is only one Islamist terror network and it is targeting the US and Israel simultaneously.

America's war against the terrorism network is a war against our enemies, and our war against terrorism is part of the global struggle led by the United States. We are no longer alone in this struggle, either as victims or as combatants fighting back.

The road map, a throwback to the pre-9/11 paradigm that still dominates European and UN thinking, is a harmful distraction, but it does not change the fundamental reality: The greatest and most powerful nation in the world is now in the trenches with us in a way it never has been before.

It would, of course, be better on this anniversary if we did not have to fight, and if the euphoria of the mid-90s had been more related to reality.

It would be better if, as we remember our fallen and celebrate our independence, we would no longer have to guard our kindergartens, coffee houses, and malls. It would be better if the US and Israel had more support from other democracies, given that we have been attacked and are fighting back. But it is better to be in a fight that has a chance of bringing lasting peace than in a 'peace' built on denial, leading only to war.

◆ ◆ ◆

One might think that the experience with Oslo was bad enough that, upon restarting the peace process, one might want to try to do things differently. This would be true even if 9/11 had not happened and the US did not see itself in a global war with militant Islam. A primary lesson from the Oslo experience is that it cannot be assumed that the Palestinians are willing to give up their demand to move to Israel (the "right of return") in exchange for a state.

Interesting Times: Breaking Oslo's Spell
May 9, 2003

In a classic move of political jujitsu, Prime Minister Ariel Sharon has just paired two significant, seemingly contradictory steps. This week Sharon said he would meet with Palestinian Authority Prime Minister Mahmoud Abbas (Abu Mazen), but that negotiations would begin only once the Palestinians had given up their demand to 'return' to Israel itself.

When White House spokesman Ari Fleischer was asked about Sharon's new condition, he responded with an ominous "all parties have responsibilities" line – what you say to kids fighting in the back seat when you want them to sort it out or equally feel the consequences.

Missed here is the significance of what Sharon has done, which could well have a more lasting impact than Abbas's appointment. The issue of refugees was defined by Oslo as a 'final status' issue and was left to the final stage of Oslo's new incarnation, the 'road map,' as well. What right does Sharon have to move it up to the front, as a precondition for talks?

First a reality check. Now that Saddam is gone, winning the peace in Iraq is rightly uppermost on Bush's foreign policy agenda, contending

182

with Syria and Iran next, and making a run at Arab-Israeli peace third. Bush, like Sharon, does not believe much will come of the Abbas/Yasser Arafat combination, but the road map is something that can be used to fend off accusations that the US has no post-Iraq peace policy.

This situation produces two camps: those appalled that Bush is not pushing the road map hard enough, which they equate with the prospects for peace; and those happy that the road map will become hopelessly entangled, since it cannot lead to peace in any case.

I find myself in neither camp. My concern is not so much that the Palestinians, Europe, and the State Department will succeed in using the road map to turn the screws on Israel, but that an opportunity for creating a new paradigm for peacemaking is being at least delayed and perhaps missed.

It is in this context that I find Sharon's new negotiating condition encouraging. It is the first real innovation since Bush postulated, in his June 24 speech, that it was the Palestinian leadership that was the principal obstacle to peace.

Sharon has put his finger on a critical truth that anyone who is serious about peace should embrace: If the Palestinians are not willing to give up 'returning' to Israel, there's nothing to talk about.

Those who claim that it is cheating for Sharon to front-load a final-status issue should take a closer look at the road map itself. Right at the beginning, at the outset of Phase I, the plan sets out supposedly parallel demands. The Palestinians are supposed to reiterate Israel's right to exist, call for an end to "armed activity," and end incitement against Israel.

Israel, at this same stage, is required to issue an "unequivocal statement affirming its commitment to the two-state vision of an independent, viable, sovereign Palestinian state living in peace and security alongside Israel." There should not be any real problem with asking Israel to say up front that it is committed to living alongside a peaceful Palestinian state, despite the fact this is a final-status issue. Sharon has said as much already.

But the parallel step is not for the Palestinians to once again promise to end terrorism and recognize Israel, promises that have proven worthless. Now that the Palestinian commitment in Oslo to the peaceful resolution of disputes has become a cruel joke, remaking the same promises will impress no one. What would be significant is if the Palestinians say up front they agree to solving the refugee problem outside, and only outside, of Israel.

Such a statement would not take the issue of refugees off the final-status table. There is much to be discussed regarding how to resolve a problem that the Arab world has carefully cultivated all these years. But unless the idea of a 'right' of Palestinians to move to Israel is dropped, talk of recognizing Israel's right to exist is meaningless.

Rather than acting piqued, the White House should endorse and amplify Sharon's new precondition. This is where the Arab world should come in.

Bush, to his credit, always mentions the responsibility Arab states have in advancing peace. But he does not say what those responsibilities are, except for not supporting terrorism.

The Arab states could, at US insistence, take the lead in saying that they will help solve the refugee problem, and agree that it can be solved outside of Israel. This may sound unrealistic. But it is more unrealistic to expect Israel to embark on serious negotiations before such a step is taken.

The simplest way for Bush to get the ball rolling is for him to point out the obvious inconsistency of claiming to recognize Israel on the one hand, and flood it with refugees on the other. Either the Palestinians believe in two separate states or they do not. Israelis do not imagine they would have a right to move to a Palestinian state; no Palestinian should have a right to move to Israel. If Washington is unwilling to reiterate this, why should Arab capitals?

It took a while, but the Americans and Israelis became used to saying that there will be a Palestinian state. Americans and Arabs must become equally used to speaking of the 'right of return' as an obsolete concept, abandoned in favor of creating two states for two peoples. Until this happens, the spell of failure cast by Oslo will not have been broken, and a peace process worthy of the name cannot begin.

◆ ◆ ◆

I wish Bush were not so alone on the issue of promoting freedom and democratization in the Arab world. His own State Department does not believe in this, nor does any other world leader. Even Israel is not particularly interested in this cause, with the exception of Natan Sharansky, who played an important role in convincing Vice President Richard Cheney and Bush that Western security was intimately tied to the nature of Arab regimes.

184

Freeing the Middle East
May 11, 2003

In case you missed it, US President George W. Bush gave a pathbreaking speech at the University of South Carolina on Friday, a speech that should not be obscured by the minutiae of Secretary of State Colin Powell's visit here today. Let's look at it with the care it deserves.

"In an age of global terror and weapons of mass destruction, what happens in the Middle East greatly matters to America. The bitterness of that region can bring violence and suffering to our own cities. The advance of freedom and peace in the Middle East would drain this bitterness and increase our own security...."

This may be Bush's clearest statement yet linking the Middle East's political dysfunctionality with American security. Note that the word "freedom" comes before "peace." Bush seems to have realized that it is the lack of freedom in the region that fuels radicalism, which in turn produces the hatred both of Israel and America. The Arab-Israeli conflict is an element of the problem; tyranny is its facilitator and root cause.

"A time of historic opportunity has arrived. A dictator in Iraq has been removed from power.... Reformers in the Middle East are gaining influence, and the momentum of freedom is growing. We have reached a moment of tremendous promise, and the United States will seize this moment for the sake of peace.... The future of peace requires the defeat of terror."

Yes, it turns out that fighting the terrorist network is the key to peace. It should be obvious that the more body blows the network receives, the more the forces of moderation will emerge, and the greater the opportunities for peacemaking. For years, diplomacy has been confused with peacemaking.

Actually, diplomacy can only reap the harvest produced by defeating the forces opposed to peace, in this case militant Islamism.

"Some believe that democracy in the Middle East is unlikely, if not impossible.... These same arguments have been heard before in other times, about other people.... In each of these cases – in Germany, in Japan, in Eastern Europe, and in Russia – the skeptics doubted, then history replied. Every milestone of liberty over the last 60 years was declared impossible until the very moment it happened. The history of the modern world offers a lesson for the skeptics: Do not bet against the success of freedom."

Bush is right, but he has not yet enforced his views on his own administration. Right now, neighboring Arab governments, along with their friends in the State Department and Europe, still believe that Iraq needs a 'strongman' from the Sunni minority to dominate the country. Bush, unfortunately, has not yet clearly weighed in against these forces, and told his own diplomats to solidly back the pluralist vision of Iraqi leaders such as Ahmad Chalabi and Kenan Makiya.

Bush continued with praise for the "hopeful signs of change" in the Muslim world, mentioned that half of all Muslims "live under democratic rule in nations from Turkey to Indonesia," and noted elections or movement toward reform in Bahrain, Morocco, Jordan, Qatar, and Saudi Arabia.

Such praise for progress is understandable, but we need to hear a lot more of the frank talk that followed:

"And in Iran, the desire for freedom is stirring. In the face of harsh repression, Iranians are courageously speaking out for democracy and the rule of law and human rights. And the United States strongly supports their aspirations for freedom."

This statement should be just the beginning of a comprehensive campaign to support dissidents struggling against the region's worst regimes, particularly in Iran and Syria. We have yet to see Bush's concrete actions to support the people in these countries risking their lives for freedom, and to more systematically isolate their oppressors.

"The combined GDP of all Arab countries is smaller than that of Spain.... The Arab world has a great cultural tradition, but is largely missing out on the economic progress of our time.... I propose the establishment of a US-Middle East free-trade area within a decade, to bring the Middle East into an expanding circle of opportunity."

This proposal, which garnered most of the attention paid to the speech, seems to be an interesting twist on previous efforts to promote normalization with Israel. The fine print here is that, before any Arab state can join the free trade area it must join the World Trade Organization, and before it can do that it must drop all boycotts, including of Israel.

We see the attraction of this subtle approach, but subtlety alone is rarely enough in this region. The ethos of Arab rejectionism that includes open antisemitism in the Arab state-controlled press and prevents any contact with Israelis needs to be confronted by name. This rejectionism is so pervasive that it extended to Kuwait at the onset of the war in Iraq, where international reporters embedded with American troops were banned from filing news reports to Israel.

Finally, we cannot fail to comment on the 'all sides... have duties' section of the speech, in which Israel was exhorted to "stop settlement activity" and the Arab nations to "fight terror in all forms, and recognize and state the obvious once and for all: Israel has a right to exist as a Jewish state at peace with its neighbors." The juxtaposition of terror and settlements is as odious as it is commonplace, but attention should be paid to a significant new formulation here: "as a Jewish state."

Bush, in other words, is on to what Bill Clinton discovered at Camp David: getting Arabs to say they accept Israel is relatively easy; getting them to accept it as a Jewish state has been next to impossible.

This is a subtle hint that should be made more explicit. The Arabs have to drop the ruse of recognizing Israel with one hand, and attempting to demographically transform it into yet another Arab state by flooding it with "refugees" with the other. The simple way for Bush to press this point would be to back Prime Minister Ariel Sharon's demand that the Palestinians be required to renounce the 'right of return' to Israel at the beginning of the process, just as Israel is being asked to commit to establishing a Palestinian state.

◆　◆　◆

About three weeks after this appeared, Israel did take the course advocated here and attempted to kill Rantisi, a senior Hamas leader who is often interviewed by the international media. Unfortunately, the first missile hit the engine of his car, and by the time the second missile came in he had jumped out and escaped with only light injuries.

A Change in Tactics
May 20, 2003

As the victims of Sunday's bus bombing in Jerusalem were being buried, another suicide bomber struck in Afula yesterday, the fifth in three days.

The special cabinet meeting Sunday night produced little more than business as usual. It is time for a change in tactics.

The cabinet decided to refuse to meet with foreign leaders who met with Yasser Arafat, to revoke all the measures taken to ease pressure on the Palestinians leading up to the visit of US Secretary of State Colin Powell, and to once again pursue the 'deportation' of the families of suicide bombers to the Gaza Strip.

In other words, this wave of murderous attacks, the first since the fall of Baghdad, is being met with a 'stay the course' approach. But what is the course we are on?

We continue to build a fence, to demolish the homes of terrorists, to kill and capture them when we can, and to toy with expelling the families of suicide bombers, but only when the direct connection of the family to terror can be demonstrated. All of these measures arguably have played a role in stopping hundreds of attempted attacks.

But for all the sense that we are doing everything we can, we tend to rule out the one thing we have not tried: going after not just the 'troops' of terror but its leadership. The leaders are not just those directly involved in planning specific attacks, but the 'political' leaders who encourage, justify, and fund the terrorists. These leaders are well known to the security forces and indeed to the international press, and some of them operate more or less in the open.

Before the fall of Saddam Hussein, targeting such leaders presumably was avoided so as not to complicate US plans to eliminate a major strategic threat to Israel. Perhaps this was wise then, but it obviously can no longer be argued now.

Another argument often heard against attacking terrorist leaders is that to do so would be an 'escalation' that would provoke further attacks. Such arguments were made even after Israel killed top terrorist operatives, such as Salah Shehadeh and Yihye Ayash (the Engineer).

Finally, it is argued by some, such as our own Labor Party and British Foreign Secretary Jack Straw, that to fight back too hard simply plays into the hands of the terrorists, whose goal is to 'kill the peace.' Even US President George W. Bush said after the Afula bombing, "There are terrorists who want to disrupt [Prime Minister Ariel Sharon's planned] visit by bombing and killing. It's clear there are people there that still cannot stand the thought of peace." Yes, they hate peace with Israel, but no, they are not motivated by this or that visit, and we do not fight them by going through the motions of a 'peace process' when bombs are going off.

188

The answer to all these arguments is to apply a bit less psychology and a bit more elbow grease. The terrorists are throwing all they can at us, all the time, regardless of diplomatic visits and initiatives. Attempted attacks have not gone up; 'successful' ones have since we eased its pressure on the Palestinians slightly in honor of Powell's visit.

In Afghanistan, the US toppled the Taliban because that was the only way to evict al-Qaida. In Iraq, the US toppled Saddam, partly because that was the only way to prevent him from obtaining more effective weapons of mass destruction, but mainly to send a signal to all radical regimes that they must fall into line or just fall.

With the Palestinian Authority, we are sending a very different signal: You can continue to preside over a hotbed of terrorism, the terrorists can continue to show disdain for your meaningless condemnations, and we will fight terror for you, as if you are not accountable.

To the leaders of Hamas and Islamic Jihad, we send a similar signal: As long as you do not personally handle mortars, bombs, and bullets, we will not kill or capture you, because to touch 'political' leaders would be to escalate.

This must change. If Sharon, understandably, does not want to part ways with the US, he should say to Bush that Israel, like the US, must fight terror at its source, from the top down, rather than letting more of us die to test the intentions of leaders he has already said must be removed. Bush will understand, and even if he does not, further restraint will only serve to legitimate the terror against us.

◆ ◆ ◆

The only way to tell if the Arab world in general and the Palestinians in particular are really giving up the goal of destroying Israel is if they can bring themselves to say the words "Jewish state." If they can't, we know that they are still harboring the dream of flooding Israel with Palestinians, so that it no longer has a clear Jewish majority. Islam, after all, has no problem with Jews living under Muslims, only with Jews exercising their own sovereignty.

The Sharm summit was attended by the leaders of Saudi Arabia, Egypt, Jordan, the United States, and for the Palestinians, Mahmoud Abbas. The Aqaba summit the next day included Bush, Sharon, Abbas, and King Abdullah of Jordan.

Interesting Times: Build Our Confidence
June 5, 2003

In 1975, Ahmed Jbarra placed a refrigerator filled with explosives in Jerusalem's busiest square. The explosion killed 14 Israelis and wounded 60. This week he was released from an Israeli prison, and received a hero's welcome in Ramallah, including a personal audience with Yasser Arafat.

Shlomo Bezem, whose brother was killed by Jbarra's bomb, told this newspaper, "His release isn't worth it, even if it brings peace." Yet this mass-murderer is not being let free as part of a final peace agreement, but as part of a package of "confidence-building measures." We are probably the only people in the world that anyone would dare even ask to build the confidence of the people who have been showering us with terrorism for over two years. The idea that we have to build Palestinian confidence is essentially an admission that lack of such confidence is a reason for terrorism. It's a bit like handing over a few bills to a gangster who is breaking your knees, while promising to pay everything he claims you owe him.

Prime Minister Ariel Sharon has decided there is no point in trying to rewrite the rules of the game, as stacked against us as they are. You say the Palestinians need convincing of our good intentions, figures Sharon, I'll convince everyone I'm sincere, thereby tossing the ball back into their court.

This strategy seems to be working so far, but there is a major catch. Regardless of the skewed logic applied to this conflict, it is Israel's confidence that must be built, not just so we will take risks, but for peace to be possible at all.

Which brings us to the Aqaba summit. The main purpose of the summit was to provide the backdrop for the paired declarations required by Phase I of the road map: Israel pledges support for an "independent, viable, sovereign Palestinian state;" the Palestinians pledge to end terrorism, incitement, and "all acts of violence against Israelis anywhere" and reaffirm Israel's "unequivocal" right to exist in peace and security.

This is what happened in Aqaba. The problem, as Israel pointed out about the road map before its release, is that this initial declaratory phase was too easy on the Palestinians. It let them continue the dodge of recognizing Israel, while pressing the demand to 'return' to Israel and overwhelm it, thereby negating this recognition.

The Palestinians respond to this concern by saying that the matter of refugees is a final-status issue. The United States agrees, according to remarks by Secretary of State Colin Powell after the Sharm summit this week. But this wisdom received from the Oslo era must be reexamined.

The truth is that the refugee matter is an amalgam. On one hand, there are legitimate topics for negotiation in final-status talks, such as compensation and resettlement. On the other hand, there is the claim of a 'right' of Palestinians to move to Israel itself, which is a negation of Israel's sovereignty, legitimacy, and right to exist.

The Palestinian leadership has argued that in order for them to confront, one way or another, groups that do not want to give up terrorism, they have Israel's commitment to a Palestinian state up front. Fair enough. They got it. In fact they had it back at the 2000 Camp David summit when Ehud Barak offered them a state on a silver platter, without the war they chose to bring upon both peoples.

But if the Palestinians need to know the end point before they move forward, Israel needs to know even more so. If the Palestinians cannot drop the idea that they have a right, not only to evict all Jews from Palestine, but to move to Israel, there is nothing to talk about it, and no point in Israel making any concessions.

The need to build Israeli confidence goes further. There is no country or people who wants to destroy the Palestinians or deny them a state. Israel, by contrast, is surrounded by peoples who believe that Israel's existence blocks any just solution to the Palestinian problem.

The just-released poll of Pew Global Attitudes Project (http://people-press.org/) found that 80 percent or more of Palestinians, Jordanians, and Moroccans believe there is 'no way' for Israeli and Palestinian rights to coexist. Smaller but significant majorities believe the same in Indonesia, Pakistan, Lebanon, and Kuwait.

The same poll, taken after the war in Iraq, asked people in a range of Western and Muslim countries which of eight leaders they trusted most to 'do the right thing.' People in non-Muslim countries rated Vladimir Putin, Gerhard Schroeder, Jacques Chirac, and Tony Blair more highly than they did George Bush. But this finding pales beside the results in Muslim countries.

In four countries surveyed – Pakistan, Morocco, Jordan, and Indonesia (after Bali!) – Osama bin Laden came in second or third. And in one place bin Laden came in first: the Palestinian Authority.

This poll sharpens the absurdity that Palestinian confidence must be earned and Israeli confidence can be assumed. We are being asked to hand over a state to a people that still believes Israel's existence is incompatible with its own rights, that lionizes the world's most prominent terrorist, and that has been systematically indoctrinating its children to give their own lives to murder Israeli civilians.

It should not be surprising, then, that we find it a tad disturbing that even the reformist Palestinian prime minister cannot bring himself to utter the words "Jewish state." Chances are, unfortunately, that Mahmoud Abbas is missing either the strength or the will to fulfill his pledges to end terrorism and disarm Hamas and Islamic Jihad. But even if he did, we cannot afford to create even a provisional state before the asterisk is removed from Palestinian recognition of Israel. That recognition will only begin to look "unequivocal," as the road map states, when the demand of Palestinians to settle in Israel is abandoned.

◆ ◆ ◆

Since he became prime minister, Sharon's behavior has mystified many people. Some believe his moderate front is a facade, others that his right-wing past was the facade and now we are seeing the "real" Sharon. Which is the real Sharon, the political patron of the settlements, or the Sharon who helped Menachem Begin dismantle the settlement of Yamit in order to give the Sinai back to Egypt? The one who will not shake hands with Arafat, or the one who lectures his own party about the need to "end the occupation?"

Here I argue that the attempt to fit Sharon into one side or the other of the usual land-for-peace dichotomy misses the point about Sharon, and arguably about the peace process as a whole. The choice, it seems, is not between war and peace, but between pursuing a stable but partial cold peace, or the full end-of-the-conflict that Oslo envisioned and Ehud Barak tried to culminate at Camp David.

In this view, Sharon's goal is neither to stonewall nor to achieve a comprehensive peace but something in the middle: a long-term interim solution in which the Palestinians do not get their full state and Israel does not get its full peace. Before the American-led war against terror, this was a much riskier bet, because the radical states of the region were getting stronger, not weaker.

Now the Palestinians increasingly look like a spearhead that is losing its spear – a group of anti-Western dictatorships that might be rallied to attack

Israel. Saddam is already gone, and the Iranian mullahs may be next, leaving backward and isolated Syria as the main radical state in the region.

The pursuit of a comprehensive, end-of-conflict deal, which I too favored in the past, seems to have cost both Israel and the Palestinians dearly and actually reduced the prospects for peace. Now that time may have come over to Israel's side, the gradualist school may be right.

Interesting Times: Sharon's Not-So-Secret Plan
June 13, 2003

As another mass murder seems to snuff out the Aqaba summit's ray of hope, the unavoidable question screams out: When will this ever stop? At first glance, the road map now looks like a sick joke, a pathetic attempt to impose order on a conflict that has no end.

Yet within this chaos, a new structure is emerging that could well determine the sequence of events in the years to come, and their ultimate outcome for Israel. This structure is etched in invisible ink on the road map. Once described, it can be seen out in the open, but in practice it is Bush's and Sharon's secret plan.

Much attention has been paid to the flawed details of the road map: its obsessive evenhandedness between the aggressor and the victim, its vague demands of the Palestinians and concrete demands of Israel, the short shrift played to Palestinian democratization, and so on. But the most fundamental component of the road map, one that is staring us in the face, is barely mentioned: the creation of a provisional Palestinian state before final-status talks.

In style, the road map repeats all the mistakes of Oslo. In structure it makes one critical change: In Oslo, Palestinian statehood was to be the end result; in the road map, the state comes in the middle.

What difference does this make? In essence, it means a choice has been made between the gradualist and the 'big bang' schools. The gradualists believe the Arab-Israeli struggle may never be resolved, because the Arab world will never accept the Jewish people's right to its own state, only to Israel's de facto existence.

As David Ben-Gurion put it in 1919, "Everybody sees the problem in the relations between the Jews and the [Palestinian] Arabs. But not

193

everybody sees that there's no solution to it. There is no solution! ... I don't know any Arabs who would agree to Palestine being ours – even if we learn Arabic... and I have no need to learn Arabic. On the other hand, I don't see why 'Mustafa' should learn Hebrew.... There's a national question here. We want the country to be ours. The Arabs want the country to be theirs."

Ariel Sharon is a disciple of Ben-Gurion and sees the conflict in roughly these terms. This does not mean that Sharon is being dishonest when he talks about peace. It means that the peace Sharon is talking about is not a full 'solution' to the conflict, but a form of livable cold war.

The 'big bang' school, by contrast, believes the Arab world has fundamentally decided to accept Israel, and therefore a peace agreement simply awaits granting the Palestinians the right terms. The Oslo agreement was built according to this paradigm. Ehud Barak and Bill Clinton were its ultimate practitioners, in that they believed the Palestinians could be induced to drop all further claims and make a full peace with Israel.

It is fashionable on the Right to claim that the road map is worse than Oslo. What is meant by this is that, under the road map, the Palestinians get a state first, before they have to make peace with Israel. In this view, the road map is the latest, most serious step in Israel's serial capitulation to terrorism. "The only consistent element in the Israeli position has been the constant retreat from its stated positions on issues that are critical to the country's future. Evidently, terrorism works," writes reclusive Likud scion Binyamin Begin.

Begin is largely right. Terrorism is what brought Yasser Arafat to power and is bringing the Palestinians a state. But here's the secret. For Sharon, the road map's "independent Palestinian state with provisional borders' is not at the bottom of the slippery slope, but a brake that prevents precisely the slide that Begin fears.

The deal Sharon is offering the Palestinians is a partial state in exchange for a partial peace. You don't want to renounce the 'right of return' and accept Israel as a Jewish state? Fine, says Sharon, but for that all you get is a truncated state whose borders are controlled by Israel.

Why would the Palestinians accept such a deal? Because they know that the only alternatives are the status quo, in which both sides bleed indefinitely, or making a full peace, neither of which they want.

Sharon's real objective is to get to the middle phase of the road map and park there until the Arab world is ready for peace, which may or may

194

not ever happen. It is a reasonably comfortable place for a gradualist to be.

Palestine may choose to be belligerent, but Israel will have a provisional border to defend and a state to hold accountable.

The risk of this plan is that statehood will be no more of a firewall against pressure to fulfill Palestinian demands than all the other agreements that the Palestinians sign and the world ignores. Eventually, the Palestinians will use terror again to force their next objective: a full Israeli unilateral withdrawal, without having to concede the demand of 'return' to Israel.

The protections against this dangerous scenario are Israeli will and the trust of the United States. Sharon feels that he and Bush can be trusted to ensure that the dates in the road map do not mean that Israel will be forced to fill out Palestine's borders even if it turns out to be a terrorist state. Whether future Israeli and American leaders can be so trusted is another question.

As a good gradualist, Sharon is not troubled by the fact that a full peace is not obtainable in the near future. In 1938, Ben-Gurion said, "The conflict had lasted 30 years, and is liable to continue for perhaps hundreds more." But Ben-Gurion could never have imagined that US divisions would role into Baghdad and topple an Iraqi despot, and that other radical regimes would be in the sites of an American president.

While Israel is betting on rolling regime changes, the Palestinians are betting on demography. As long as America and Israel don't abandon their own interests, Sharon has the better bet.

◆ ◆ ◆

During the war that has raged for almost three years, Europe more or less has taken the Palestinian side, and the United States has been roughly neutral. My contention all along has been that if the US and Europe could have been counted on to reject the Palestinian resort to violence and back Israel, this war would not have started, and certainly would not have continued for so long. Even today, the refusal to label the Palestinians as the aggressors of the conflict makes it almost impossible to end it and builds in an incentive to restart hostilities when talks break down.

Interesting Times: 'No Fault' Doesn't Work Here
June 20, 2003

I am usually a great believer in trusting the common sense of the American people. Since 1997, for example, Gallup polls have shown that Americans do not believe there ever will be Arab-Israeli peace by a margin of roughly 60 to 40 percent. Twice in this period Americans became slightly more optimistic, splitting about 50-50 on this question: during the 2000 Camp David summit, and just before the Aqaba summit.

The fact that even the media euphoria around peace summits leaves half of Americans cold shows a high degree of healthy skepticism, in contrast with the very American notion that all conflicts are solvable. Most people assume that the Middle East will always be dominated by hostile despotisms.

I don't, but I agree that if the US does not succeed in changing the balance in favor of more democratic and pro-Western governments, the prospects for peace will not be good.

Americans also, by large margins, tend to side with Israel over the Palestinians and Arabs generally. A McLaughlin poll taken one month after September 11 found that 72 percent of Americans wanted continued support for Israel, and thought, by a 4-to-1 margin, that the Arab world still sought Israel's destruction.

Yet on one critical tactical question, I believe that Americans misunderstand the situation. When asked in the June Gallup poll whether the US should take sides in the conflict, a negligible number said to take the Palestinian side, 18 percent said to take Israel's side, and a whopping 74 percent advised taking neither side.

If Americans support Israel and want their government to reflect that support, why would they not want the US to 'take Israel's side' in the conflict? The only explanation I can see is that Americans believe that, if the US wants to help broker peace agreements, it must project some degree of neutrality between the parties.

This instinct is, at first blush, entirely natural. Most people don't understand conflicts they are not a part of. Even Bill Clinton, no simpleton, said of his own mediation efforts, according to Sidney Blumenthal's new book, 'Sometimes I wish I was a psychologist. It's just not rational.'

But if there are two boys in the schoolyard who are always fighting, and you want to do something about it, you need to know: are they both bullies, or is one of them the instigator and the other basically a good kid?

Sometimes you can't know who starts what, or for institutional reasons you can't be bothered to find out. So you just try to set a 'no fighting' rule and then enforce it. Being impartial often seems not only simpler, but necessary. How else can you maintain your credibility with everyone?

There is a problem, however, with the neutral approach: It favors bullies.

If you are the bully, the more neutral the mediator, the more you can diffuse the blame for your actions. If you're lucky, you might even be able to stick the blame on your victim. This is easier if you happen to be smaller and weaker than the kid you are picking on.

And if the bully regularly succeeds in tagging the blame on others, it gets worse – far from being deterred by the mediator, he has incentive to continue making trouble.

International relations has a term for bullying: It's called aggression. The whole purpose of the international system is to police it. International law is not built like 'no fault' car insurance – rather, aggressors are to be sanctioned, victims protected.

This is not a matter of sentimentality or even justice. It is purely pragmatic. Everyone knows that if you want less aggression, you should deter it rather than reward it. But it's less widely recognized that misplaced neutrality violates this cardinal rule. It therefore does not advance peace efforts; it cripples them.

The notion of an honest broker needs to be refined. When Israel and the Palestinians were at Camp David, an honest broker was needed to craft an agreement that met the needs, if not all the dreams, of both parties. But when one side refused to negotiate, turned over the table, and (a few months later) started shooting, being honest required crying foul.

For all the progress that has been made since then, the US still has not fully done that. Crying foul does not just mean condemning terrorism, it means acting in a temporarily lopsided way, putting full blame on the aggressor, and fully backing the victim's efforts to fight back.

When fighting is going on the instinct to be neutral must be turned on its head: The more the blame is focused, rather than shared, the sooner aggression will become counterproductive, the sooner it will stop, and the sooner negotiations can begin.

There is nothing more demoralizing for Israel, and more encouraging for Hamas and other terrorist groups, than for the United States, Israel's best friend, to say you can fight, but don't touch their leaders. No one in al-Qaida has immunity, from Osama bin Laden on down; Hamas should be treated the same way. Yet US President George W. Bush even went so far as to say that attempting to kill senior Hamas leader Abdel Aziz Rantisi was not in Israel's security interests.

It is hard to overstate the damage caused by the knowledge that our only ally is setting limits on how we can fight back, and if we go beyond those limits then the blame for the conflict will shift to our shoulders. The current attempt to induce a Palestinian crackdown against terrorism is publicly limited to withholding a carrot – Palestinian statehood – without brandishing the real stick – giving Israel full backing to fight.

As a result of the post-Aqaba wave of attacks, the US now reportedly dropped its objection to targeted killings, which it continues to officially oppose, in any area where the Palestinians are not actively working to prevent attacks. But the fact that having limited permission to hit Hamas is considered progress shows how far the US has been from fully backing Israel's right to self-defense. Americans are right to want their country to act as an honest broker, but being honest does not mean being blind.

◆ ◆ ◆

The goal of physically dismantling Hamas may be an elusive and somewhat overrated one. Even if most of its leaders were dead or in prison and thousands of weapons were confiscated, Hamas or something like it could be relatively quickly reconstituted if its ideological infrastructure remained intact.

In New York City, Mayor Rudolph Giuliani showed how cracking down on supposedly incidental crimes, like graffiti and subway fare-beating, was the key to changing the climate, which brought serious crime down drastically. Similarly, ending Palestinian incitement may be at least as important as confiscating weapons.

Interesting Times: The Softer Side Has the Bigger Kick
June 27, 2003

President George W. Bush deserves credit for sticking to his guns. When asked about the hudna (temporary cease-fire) reportedly in the works, Bush repeatedly brushed aside the idea and kept the focus where it should be. 'The true test for Hamas and terrorist organizations is the complete dismantlement of their terrorist networks, their capacity to blow up the peace process... In order for there to be peace, Hamas must be dismantled.'

The questions are, who will do the dismantling and what happens if they don't? Though a cease-fire is being billed as a chance for the Palestinian Authority to build up strength to take on Hamas and Islamic Jihad, there are major problems with this theory.

First, Mahmoud Abbas and Muhammad Dahlan are presumably leading the charge, and they say there will be no confrontation with presumed Palestinian rivals, only dialogue. Second, if they will not crack down now, when there are dozens of warnings of terrorist attacks (a suicide bomber was caught 10 minutes before his bomb went off this week), why would they do so when there is a cease-fire and there seems to be no need?

Third, the same cease-fire allows everyone to regroup and strengthen, especially the terrorist organizations. More fundamentally, the Palestinians throughout the Oslo period and contrary to that agreement, believed that the threat of terrorism should be kept on the side for use at the appropriate moment. So a crackdown would not only contradict the PA glorification of 'martyrdom' over the past 1000 days, but would be giving up the 'good cop/bad cop' game that Yasser Arafat has played for so long.

What is more, how would we know that a crackdown is actually taking place? It is easy to imagine the PA making a show of some arrests or collecting some weapons, similar to past actions. Perhaps there would be some real confrontations, and Israel and the US could let it be known that progress was being made against the infrastructure of terrorism, but the reality would be that Hamas had lived to fight another day.

There is much to be said under such circumstances for the distrustful stance of the US and Israel, which demand to see actions rather than more promises and shell games. But the emphasis on the more concrete side is certainly insufficient and possibly misplaced.

By now there is much more understanding than there was that ending Palestinian incitement against Israel is necessary, and that goal is featured in the road map. Secretary of State Colin Powell just mentioned it among the steps being demanded of the PA.

Less appreciated, however, is that what seem to be 'soft' issues, may actually be more important than the supposedly more real benchmarks that are given most of the attention.

Collecting guns and arresting terrorists are considered real and measurable steps, and sometimes they are. Just as often, such steps are reminiscent of the classic order issued by the Vichy captain in Casablanca after he witnessed Rick (Humphrey Bogart) shoot a Nazi officer, 'Round up the usual suspects!' In some ways, it is harder to take back a word than an action.

Prime Minister Ariel Sharon, for example, later downplayed his dressing down of his own Likud faction, saying it was time to 'end the occupation.' But once those words were uttered both friend and foe looked at him differently.

The Palestinians seem to understand the power of words better than we do. Regarding the 'right of return' (itself a brilliant way to frame the demand to demographically wipe Israel off the map), the Palestinians have always been happy to negotiate over numbers, which they care less about, provided the principle is recognized. Similarly, many Israelis seem more willing than are Palestinians to give on the issue of the Temple Mount, though it is Judaism's holiest site and symbolic of our entire connection to this land. Incitement is also seen as a 'soft,' symbolic issue. Actually, Yigal Carmon of MEMRI (www.memri.org) is on to something when he calls incitement the 'ideological infrastructure' of terrorism. Dismantling this infrastructure may be even more important than its physical counterpart.

Imagine, for example, if the PA did make a wave of arrests, but continued to broadcast and print images of Israelis as merciless killers of Palestinian children, who should be eager to die for their cause, the elimination of Israel. And what would happen if, on the contrary, the PA began to say it sees a place to fulfill both Jewish and Palestinian national aspirations in this land.

It is striking that the peace movement is at the forefront of efforts to dialogue and 'educate for peace,' and yet these same activists tend to dismiss Palestinian radicalism and hate-sowing as understandable 'rhetoric.'

Again, many now recognize that not paying attention to incitement was a mistake during the Oslo years, but the same mistake continues to be made.

In general, if they want the road map to fare better than Oslo, the US and Israel have to decide on a point where they willing to stop the process if the PA does not comply. Bush's unwillingness to be satisfied with a hudna is a promising sign that this time the Palestinians will be held to some kind of standard. But the red line should not just be measured in arrests and weapons confiscations, but in the reversal of PA positions that lay the groundwork for terrorism just as surely as any physical infrastructure.

As Itamar Marcus of Palestinian Media Watch documented on these pages (June 20), the Palestinian media is as bloodcurdlingly anti-Israel as ever. A new Palestinian video clip that has been broadcast regularly since January, and continuing after the Aqaba summit, includes a portrayal of a girl laughing on a swing, who is then engulfed by an Israeli firebomb. Next, children are shown playing football, until a bomb hidden by Israel inside the ball explodes when a child kicks it. Then a father reads his young son a section from the Koran that calls for fighting enemies, and hands him a stone to throw. Actors then depict Israeli soldiers murdering an elderly man by shooting him in the head. This is followed by a mother and her infant being blown up by Israeli soldiers.

The PA can claim, without much credibility, that it is powerless to confront Hamas. It cannot claim that it is powerless to stop its own incitement. The road map should be frozen until the Palestinians start educating for peace rather than for terrorism.

◆ ◆ ◆

One of the more surprising aspects of this conflict, to many people, is that Israel has been attempting to defend itself against terrorism with less of a barrier between it and the Palestinians than there is between the U.S. and Canada. The reason is that there is no agreed-upon place to put such a border, and there is no easy way to draw it without seeming to claim or give up territory, or writing off people on the other side of it.

Over time, however, the need to create a physical barrier has overwhelmed the political-diplomatic difficulties in doing so. The fence was first constructed in areas where the was little controversy where it should run, but as the project has preceded, more difficult choices have emerged. Here I argue that the Palestinians' diplomatic concerns over the fence may be a chief argument for continuing to build it, since there is otherwise little or no diplomatic cost being imposed on the Palestinians for violating their own renunciation of terrorism. In any case, whether Israel should build it and what the U.S position should be regarding Israel's decision should be separate questions.

Who's Building the Fence?
June 30, 2003

The surprise Israeli-US controversy during National Security Advisor Condoleeza Rice's visit to the region was over the security fence. President George W. Bush's close adviser asked us to stop building it, because even if it is not meant to be a political border, it looks like one. Rice's admonition came after she received an earful on this issue from the Palestinian side. Prime Minister Mahmoud Abbas reportedly claimed that the fence was a way to create "facts on the ground" and that it undermined his authority by breaking up Palestinian areas and disturbing daily life.

Abbas is not the only one who is steamed. In the current issue of *The Atlantic Monthly*, analysts from the Rand Corporation were asked to rate the top ten underattended international problems in the world today. Topping the list was Israel's security fence, which "will profoundly change the geographical and political landscape of the Israeli-Palestinian conflict." This alone may sound alarming, but the thinkers at Rand were just getting started.

"The wall could also deepen Palestinian rage and enmity, of course, prompting escalated mortar and ground-to-ground missile attacks against targets inside Israel," they counseled. "The wall could also prompt further attacks on Israelis overseas, like the suicide bombing last November of a Mombasa hotel filled with Israeli tourists and the accompanying attempt to shoot down an Israeli chartered plane."

Let's get this straight. For the last thousand days, Israel is pummeled by a panoply of terrorist groups competing over who can kill the most Jews. After much delay, and much too slowly according to most of the public, Israel finally starts building a fence to protect its entirely open non-border with the West Bank. Now we are told that fence itself will provoke more attacks.

Is this really the logic to which Bush wishes to subscribe? Is he really telling us, like the analysts at Rand, that if we build a fence we have no one but ourselves to blame for all the missiles that will be shot over it and the bombs that will blow up around it? We would be the last to argue that the fence is a panacea. The fence, in fact, is arguably a dangerous concession to the idea that terror must be lived with, rather than wiped out. The United States understands that, for all the billions it is investing in homeland security, its own fence, the only real security lies in crushing terrorism, not redesigning your country around it.

But whether the fence is a good idea or not for Israel's security should be our decision, not a subject for scolding from the United States.

There is no law that any problem the Palestinians complain about should be dutifully dropped by visiting mediators on our doorstep. Rice, normally a straight-talking and straight-thinking interlocutor, should have told the Palestinians what any fair-minded observer would have automatically responded: You don't like the fence? Produce security for Israel and there will be no need for a fence.

Israel is not building the fence, the Palestinians are. It took thousands of attacks and dozens of dead before Israel began to contemplate building it, and even now it is being built reluctantly. Those who believe that a full peace is possible don't like it, and neither do those who abhor any concession to terrorism. But the voices from the security community who say it will make their job easier have won the day.

The US should not echo this Palestinian complaint for two other reasons.

First, it is not possible to claim to support Israel's right to self-defense while opposing targeted killings and the fence. What are Israelis supposed to do, if they cannot actively or passively defend themselves?

Second, when the Palestinian Authority is concerned that the fence might have territorial implications, what they really are saying is that they should not have to pay a territorial price for their terror war. Is this the lesson the US wants to teach? The current diplomatic process is an elaborate attempt to find a workable alternative to the type of decisive victories won over Germany and Japan and, more recently, in Afghanistan and Iraq. It is one thing to avoid the unmistakable defeat of an enemy, as is being attempted now.

It is quite another to avoid imposing even a cost for years of one of the more unprovoked, illegal, and barbaric spasms of aggression that the world has seen. If the fence happens to impose a political-diplomatic cost on the Palestinians for the jihad they chose to launch, the US should be explaining to the Palestinians that this is the consequence of their actions, not a problem for Israel to solve.

4. The Battle is Joined

From the period before, during, and after the US war in Iraq.

Listening to the debate before the war in Iraq in 2003, one might have thought President George W. Bush invented the threat, or picked Saddam for toppling out of a hat. This piece, written almost two years before September 11 and Bush's "axis of evil" speech, singles out the same three countries that Bush did—Iraq, Iran, and North Korea. It indicates that September 11 did not create the need to remove Saddam, and that Bush and Tony Blair did not invent the concern over weapons of mass destruction.

The Clinton administration, before 9/11, shared the same concerns. Despite this, years were wasted, under both Clinton and Bush, that could have been used to bolster the Iraqi opposition, as a bipartisan majority in the US Congress was suggesting.

The US and the Rogues
October 25, 1999

The regional sweep of US Secretary of Defense William Cohen, who arrives here today, has a surrealistic air. In Egypt, he viewed Operation Bright Star, billed as the world's largest military exercise. In Kuwait yesterday, Cohen pledged that the US would upgrade three military bases there, at a cost of $193 million. In short, the conventional business of defending the world proceeds apace, blissfully removed from the unconventional threats that are growing daily.

Before UNSCOM, the United Nations inspection agency, was forced to suspend its activities in Iraq a year ago, it estimated that an Iraq unfettered by inspections was still capable of producing 350 liters of weapons-grade anthrax each week, enough to fill two missile warheads or four aerial bombs.

In August this year, the White House reported to Congress that "We are concerned by activity at Iraqi sites known to be capable of producing weapons of mass destruction and long-range ballistic missiles." A bipartisan letter that month from six prominent senators to President Bill Clinton, decrying the lack of a coherent US policy, was more blunt: "There is considerable evidence that Iraq continues to seek and develop weapons of mass destruction."

It stands to reason that the concern of US senators pales in comparison with that of Cohen's recent hosts, the Kuwaitis. Yet Cohen reported on his meeting with Emir Sheikh Jaber al-Ahmad al-Sabah, stating, "We agreed that the current British-Dutch draft resolution offers an effective way to enable the UN to resume its inspection program, while continuing to expand humanitarian assistance to the Iraqi people." From this we are to understand that the leader of a nation that was entirely overrun, largely destroyed, and that is still missing thousands of its citizens, is looking forward to the resumption of something less than the now-defunct UNSCOM inspection regime.

Perhaps sensing that UNSCOM-light was not actually what the Kuwaitis had in mind, Cohen did assure them that the US would "continue to contain Saddam Hussein... until such time when the Iraqi people have an opportunity to have new leadership. We hope that will be sooner rather than later." When asked directly by a journalist in Doha, Qatar – another concerned nation – whether the United States would give military assistance to the Iraqi opposition, Cohen's response reflected the self-limited nature of US policy: "The support we have given so far to the Iraqi opposition is political in nature. But we believe that, ultimately, the change of the regime must come from the Iraqi people, from within Iraq itself."

US policy, then, is in a cul-de-sac. It admits that the danger from Saddam Hussein is growing, and will not necessarily be detected in time from the outside. It admits that the only solution is 'regime change,' but the thrust of US policy – the creation of an UNSCOM-light – has nothing to do with removing Saddam. And it states that Saddam must be removed by his own people – but so far, this is an idea mainly on paper. The basis of this tortured policy is hinted at by Cohen and other US officials, namely that the Iraqi opposition is a collection of ineffective exiles, with no chance of overthrowing Saddam.

This skepticism is legitimate, given that the dissidents have a limited track record and, absent Western willingness to provide air cover, there is a possibility that Saddam may slaughter them. Similar wariness about the dissidents dominates the top echelons of the Israeli security establishment, as well. Yet there may be a logic to train the dissidents, even if they are not being prepared to fight immediately or march on to Baghdad. As a fighting force, they could be crushed. However, such training should be seen as a contingency plan in the event that, one day, the below-surface anger of the Iraqi public spills over into mass action.

As Patrick Clawson, of the Washington Institute for Near East Policy, writes in the October 11 *New Republic*: "To be sure, the opposition is unlikely to defeat Saddam's forces in the field. But that is largely irrelevant. The issue is what must be done to crack the aura of invincibility around Saddam and his repressive apparatus." Clawson continues, "If Saddam's security organizations are spending their time worrying about the country's internal opposition, they will have fewer resources to repress outbreaks of the now-seething popular discontent. If emboldened protesters began to act on a wide scale, an active opposition could catalyze and coordinate an uprising, turning what would otherwise be a riot into a regime-threatening rebellion." A recent letter signed by prominent Democratic Senators Joseph Lieberman and Robert Kerrey reflects the widespread congressional support for such logic.

The senators pushed for provision of "lethal training and lethal weapons," as opposed to the fax machines, desks, and computers offered to the opposition by the Clinton administration.

The picture with respect to the two other most dangerous rogue regimes, Iran and North Korea, is not more heartening. The most recent Clinton administration deal with North Korea is particularly worrisome, because it does not explicitly prohibit exports of its missiles to third countries. By all accounts, Russian technical assistance to Iran's missile program is continuing, while massive US financial leverage on Russia remains unexercised.

Secretary Cohen oversees the most powerful military apparatus known to man, yet it is hard to escape that structure's impotence with respect to proliferation challenges posed by Iraq, Iran, and North Korea. When one or more of these states confronts the West with some form of nuclear blackmail, no amount of military might will make up for the unpalatable nature of the choices facing the US and its allies. Dangerous deals in North Korea, a refusal to use sufficient economic sanctions to staunch the technology flow to Iran, and resistance to congressional calls to aid the Iraqi opposition, amount to an inadequate response to growing threats.

◆ ◆ ◆

This piece made two predictions, one of which has already come true; regarding the other it is too soon tell. The first was that the fall of Baghdad would reveal the jubilation of Iraqis to be rid of Saddam, like the fall of Kabul in Afghanistan. It did, to the surprise of many who just days before the allied victory thought that Iraqis did not support the war.

The second prediction was that pacifism itself will be dealt a serious blow once it was revealed that the protesters were the last line of defense for an indefensible regime. It is hard to know if this has happened because there has not yet been another case of Western military action against a tyranny. But my guess is that it will be difficult for the pacifists on the extreme left to repeat something like the anti-Iraq war protests for a long time.

Interesting Times: The Fall of Pacifism
February 21, 2003

Men can only be happy when they do not assume that the object of life is happiness.
– George Orwell, *Animal Farm*, 1945

These are words to live by, if there ever were. But they are equally true regarding peace as they are about happiness. Peace, in a way, is a form of happiness; a positive state of being that paradoxically becomes more remote the more it is set up as an absolute.

There is a related paradox. The masterfully synchronized demonstrations last weekend seemed, particularly after the floundering of the anti-globalization movement, to be a show of strength for the 'peace movement.' In reality, this dramatic attempt to prevent the liberation of Iraq could end up being the greatest blow to pacifism since World War II.

Pacifism has a long and distinguished history. "The Spirit of Christ ... will never move us to fight war against any man with outward weapons," declared the Quakers' Peace Testimony in 1661. The Society for the Promotion of Permanent and Universal Peace was founded in London in 1816, in response to mass conscription during the Napoleonic Wars.

Pre-20th century peace activists were true pioneers in an uphill struggle against the positive, almost ecstatic, elite attitudes towards war. Rudolf Euken, a German laureate of Nobel Prize for Literature, wrote of the pro-war 'Spirit of 1914' in his country: "An exultation took place, a transformation of an ethical nature... We experienced a powerful upswing in our souls... everything stale was swept away, new fountains of life opened themselves up."

The subsequent wholesale slaughter of World War I gave war a bad name and pacifism its first break toward respectability. But while that war was about defending indefensible monarchies, in the next world war, pacifism itself became indefensible in the face of Nazi tyranny and the Holocaust.

To this day, the overwhelming justice of the fight to defeat Nazism remains the most powerful proof-text against pacifism. The pendulum swung around again due to the Vietnam War, which, like World War I, boosted pacifism because it was portrayed as a futile war in defense of a corrupt tyranny.

But as generals tend to fight the last war, so do pacifists. World War I pacifism made no sense in the face of Hitler; Vietnam-era pacifism rings equally hollow in the face of Saddam. Pacifism is about to be discredited more thoroughly than it has been for over half a century.

The liberation of Baghdad will make the jubilation at the fall of the Taliban pale by comparison. Since the Soviet bloc collapsed, those who ridiculed Ronald Reagan's characterization of the "evil empire" have themselves been discredited. It will be difficult to disassociate the horrors revealed in Saddam's wake from the Western masses who, intentionally or not, helped protect his rule at such a critical moment.

Indeed, we can only hope that the fall of Baghdad will do to pacifism what the fall of the Soviet Union did to socialism. Today those who cling to socialism, with the tautological claim that wherever it has failed it has been misapplied, sound somewhat pathetic.

Socialism is down for the count and pacifism may follow. Yet, so far, the champions of freedom have failed to capture the vacated high moral ground.

The pursuit of freedom, like pacifism, can become whacky or dangerous when turned into an absolute. But the absence of a 'freedom movement' analogous to the 'peace movement' is a telling sign that it is the remnants of the leftist zeitgeist that still holds moral sway.

The ethos of pacifism deserves credit for the fact that today, unlike in 1914, the reluctance to go to war is, fortunately, almost universal. Those who care about freedom feel as Abraham Lincoln described the North's attitude toward the Civil War: "Both parties deprecated war, but one of them would make war rather than let the nation survive, and the other would accept war rather than let it perish, and the war came." It is good that war has been discredited and that the burden of proof lies on those who would wage it. What is missing is for tyranny to be as abhorrent as war, and for the burden of proof to be on those who defend tyrants.

Now, both parties deprecate tyranny, but one would rather block a war and let tyranny survive, and the other would rather accept war to ensure that tyranny perishes.

The world is still recovering or suffering from the follies of pacifism and socialism. The key to human well-being, including the desired victory over war and poverty that those ideologies claimed they would deliver, lies in the ascent of the value of freedom. When we see more rallies demanding freedom than demanding peace, the world will be on a better track, and we will have more of both.

◆　◆　◆

The run-up to the war in Iraq includes a dramatic presentation by Secretary of State Colin Powell, complete with satellite photos of suspected chemical and biological weapons facilities. A strange controversy over this evidence arose after the war, in which the US and Britain were accused of lying because little evidence of Iraqi weapons programs has been found. This is strange because even the Europeans did not doubt that Iraq had such capabilities; their argument was with the urgency of the problem and how to deal with it.

The main point of this piece, however, is that the UN Security Council has become a corrupt police department that is more of an obstacle to fighting organized crime – in this case, international aggression – than it is part of the solution.

I wonder how France would have voted, its threats to impose a veto notwithstanding, if the matter had been put to a vote, as I erroneously predicted.

Interesting Times: Eliot Ness Meets the Security Council
February 7, 2003

Iraq's efforts at obfuscation are so blatant that they border on comical. So why did US Secretary of State Colin Powell have to reveal precious intelligence capabilities to convince the Security Council of the painfully obvious?

For those who were truly confused by the chorus demanding evidence against Saddam, Powell's presentation was a useful exercise. Saddam could be testing his germ-ready unmanned aircraft over the Champs Elysees before the French found the evidence convincing. Evidently a master of understatement, French Foreign Minister Dominique De Villepin's reaction to Powell was "[Iraq's] cooperation still contains some gray areas." So let's admit that the effort was not really about convincing recalcitrant countries of the facts, as if they cared. The more interesting question is, do we even want them to be convinced?

If I had to bet, there will be a Security Council resolution authorizing the use of force in Iraq and France will support it. The effect of this, as De Villepin said Wednesday, will be to "affirm at each stage the central role of the Security Council." This may please the French, but should the rest of us be happy about it?

Either the US goes in without further UN authorization, as Condoleeza Rice just stated it has the full right to do, or the UN blesses military action first. It is usually assumed that the second is preferable.

In a narrow sense, this is true. A UN stamp of approval allows the US to share responsibility for the aftermath of the war, and provides cover if something goes wrong. But it is not clear that it advances the bigger picture of which ousting Saddam should be but one part.

Saddam is a problem, but he is not the problem. The problem is architectural: the opportunity to fix Cold War distortions was squandered in the decade following the Soviet collapse.

For almost half a century, the world got used to a lot of bad behavior. Terrorism and other forms of international aggression were allowed to rise under the rubric of 'liberation struggles.' Human rights were systematically quashed within the Soviet bloc, and the West lowered standards for its allies in blocking the expansion of communism. International organizations were bastardized beyond recognition by the Soviet/Arab bloc and its 'non- aligned' allies. Non-proliferation treaties became a cover for rogue regimes building bombs.

September 11 was a product of this neglect. It was as if the West came to realize only after 9/11 that the mess outside its own neighborhood needed to be cleaned up. But wiping the graffiti off the walls and collecting the garbage is a somewhat fruitless struggle if the gangs that ruined the neighborhood are still running loose.

Currently, the UN acts more as a protector of international criminality than as the enforcer of the world order envisioned by its charter. The Security Council, if not quite in cahoots with the gang leaders, is like a police force that has long ago given up imposing something close to the rule of law.

In this context, the American decision to go to the Security Council for authorization was a bit of a non-sequitur: the collision of the order the US is creating with the old order.

The war in Iraq is about smashing a particular gang, which will send a powerful message to the other gangs that the US is no longer going to tolerate gang rule. If the US is Eliot Ness, out to take on organized crime with a select band of Untouchables, the Security Council is the corrupt police establishment that can only look bad if America succeeds.

Ness knew that, as big a prize as Al Capone was, the larger objective was to break the police corruption that allowed crime to flourish. And that is what he did, moving on to become chief of police in Cleveland, where he busted open a system riddled with cops on the take.

According to a history of Ness's exploits, "The honest men on the police force took courage from Ness's relentless pursuit of corruption" and started going after criminals themselves.

The American strategy, therefore, should not be so much to shame the Security Council members with the truth, but with actions that fly in the face of their capitulation to gang rule.

211

If this is the objective, it is not clear that Security Council authorization is a step in the right direction, because it places a veneer of legitimacy over a fundamentally corrupted system.

During the Korean War, as Max Abrahms noted in these pages, President Harry Truman had the same problem. When North Korea barreled across the 38th parallel on June 25, 1950, Truman brought the issue before the Security Council, which quickly passed a resolution calling for the aggressors to withdraw. But it took Truman's unilateral decision to move US forces into the area to shock the council into passing a much stronger resolution, putting the threat of force behind its words.

The Truman case was a positive example of how the Security Council can be shamed into action, but also a negative example of what happens when nothing is done to change the corruption of the international system. In fact, periodically doing the right thing arguably preserves the rotten system rather than reforming it.

The only way to break this cycle is to break out of it. A complete break would have been not to go for UN authorization in the first place, as happened in the instance of Afghanistan in 2001. It is too late for that, but it is not too late to at least deliberately skip a re-reauthorization that the US has already said it does not need. A side benefit would be to deprive the French of a chance for a death-bed conversion to the allied cause. That alone is worth a smidgen of unilateralism.

◆ ◆ ◆

On the evening of March 19, Washington time, a hail of missiles destroyed a building where the US believed Saddam Hussein was holding a meeting. It was the official beginning of the war in Iraq. Three weeks later, Baghdad fell, and the war was essentially over.

I thought of calling this column, "The anti-9/11." In strategic terms, the ousting of Saddam was America's answer to 9/11 more than anything that had happened before that, including the war in Afghanistan, and despite the fact that 9/11 was barely mentioned as a justification for the war.

212

Interesting Times: The Meaning of March 19
March 21, 2003

September 11, 2001 was a day history parted into before and after. On March 19, 2003, the day the war to oust Saddam Hussein began, history parted again.

This may sound a bit sweeping. Does not the swift toppling of the Taliban in Afghanistan count for anything? Or the steady victories against al-Qaida, culminating in the capture of Osama bin Laden's No. 2?

The difference is that nothing in the war on terrorism until now truly broke the mold, the way 9/11 itself broke the mold in the opposite direction. It is sometimes possible to kill as many or more people with conventional weapons (or knives, for that matter, as in Rwanda) as it is with nuclear weapons. But this fact does not eliminate the qualitative, psychological distinction between conventional and non-conventional weapons.

Almost everything done before March 19 in the war against terrorism fell into the 'conventional' category. The regime change accomplished in Afghanistan, though edging into the unconventional realm, could have been dismissed as a unique spasm, not a harbinger of new rules of the game.

For over a year some of us have been convinced that US President George W. Bush would oust Saddam, come hell or high water. But the dictators of the region have not exactly been quaking in their boots in response to becoming charter or alternate members of the axis of evil.

Bold rhetoric, even when surrounded by a sense of inevitability that action will follow, has not caused nations to abandon terror and close down their weapons programs. The question has been, what will the West do about it?

As Tony Blair put it in his latest brilliant pitch in the House of Commons, "September 11 has changed the psychology of America. It should have changed the psychology of the world. Of course Iraq is not the only part of this threat. But it is the test of whether we treat the threat seriously."

September 11 and March 19 were both about changing the psychology of the world: the former to pound it into fear and submission, the latter to inculcate the same dread into the terror network itself.

213

It is, of course, jarring to compare the two actions, as if there were any moral similarity between them. The crowd that views Bush as a greater threat than Saddam would have little compunction in lumping them together as twin acts of aggression.

Pairing the two, however, would be worse than equating Hitler's invasion of France and the Allied landing at Normandy. They are similar only in the use of force – but in essence, one act was taken to reverse the other.

Indeed, March 19 is a sort of D-Day in the war against terrorism. This comparison is not quite fair to the heroes of that time, who charged beaches on foot under a hail of machine-gun and artillery fire. Over 4,000 of them died.

March 19 cannot hold a candle to D-Day in its sheer physical audacity and scope. But D-Day did not break new ground in the order of the world; it was a classic battle in a classic war. The significance of the war in Iraq is not in the formidability of the enemy, but in the groundbreaking justification for bringing him down.

The beach that was stormed on March 19 was the idea that the United States must wait helplessly to be attacked again as its enemies hid behind the skirts of, of all countries, France, the nation so many Americans died to liberate.

Until March 19, the leaders in Baghdad, Teheran, Damascus, and elsewhere knew that Bush wanted to make supporting terrorism a crime punishable by regime change, but they had reason to believe he would be unable to do so. After all, these governments had attacked their neighbors (sometimes through terrorist proxies), oppressed their peoples, and built their arsenals with nary a peep from the Security Council. They could not only violate international law with impunity, but do so knowing the same law would protect them from any consequences.

The meaning of March 19 is that the United States is willing to defy an interpretation of international law that protects rogue regimes at the expense of their victims. Terrorism has been a way for these regimes to go under the radar screen of international law, with the purpose of overturning the world order. America has just lowered this radar screen and said: We will not let you overturn our order, we will overturn yours.

The risk America is taking is to replace one kind of unruliness, one that accepts terror, with another that accepts preemptive attack. There is little alternative, however, in a world in which so many Western nations steadfastly refuse to use effective non-military sanctions against rogue states. Perhaps this will change now if the choice is no longer between economic sanctions and doing nothing, but between military and economic measures.

The American, British, and Australian troops now entering Iraq may not face a war machine as formidable as Nazi Germany's, but the stakes they are fighting for are as great. Speaking to the troops on D-Day, General Dwight Eisenhower said, "The eyes of the world are upon you. The hope and prayers of liberty-loving people everywhere are with you." Amen.

◆ ◆ ◆

I asked here, rhetorically, why would anyone be rooting for Saddam Hussein to win. A global poll later found out that there were plenty of such people. The Pew Global Attitudes Project asked people in a range of countries whether they were "happy" or "disappointed" at the lack of resistance to the US forces in Baghdad. In Morocco and Jordan, over 90 percent, and in Turkey, Indonesia, and the Palestinian Authority over 80 percent were "disappointed." France was the most ambivalent Western country, with 59 percent happy and 30 percent disappointed.

Interesting Times: Not in Their Name
March 28, 2003

Iraqis have not exactly been showering American troops with flowers. Iraqi divisions are not dancing in the streets. I admit to being among those who expected the regime to be more fragile than it is. But the reasons these expectations have been dashed serve to strengthen, not weaken, the case for the war.

In six days, coalition forces charged across Iraq to within spitting distance of Baghdad, without being engaged frontally by a single regular Iraqi division. Yet no matter how successful coalition forces are, they can never beat the expectations of zero resistance that have been widely applied to this effort.

One might think that it would be unnecessary for coalition spokesmen to constantly repeat how well the war is going militarily, given that, after almost a week of supposedly serious resistance, aside from those

215

captured and killed in accidents, exactly three coalition soldiers were killed in fights with Iraqi forces.

But the key moral question relates less to how the war is going militarily than to how the Iraqi people are responding. There have been nice pictures of people waving at convoys and shaking hands with soldiers, there have also been scenes of Iraqis seemingly rejoicing over a downed helicopter, and civilians who tell reporters the Americans are 'criminals.' What gives?

Two stories tell us what is really going on. In Basra, Iraq's second largest city, a muddled picture is emerging of irregular forces attacking the coalition, and the population rising up against Saddam's secret police. According to Brig. Gen. Vince Brooks, Saddam's thugs have been seizing children and telling fathers "they must fight" or the children "will all face execution." Even with coalition forces ringing the city, rising up against Saddam in Basra means taking your life into your hands. It is hard for most of us, having never lived in a Stalinist police state, to fully appreciate how such regimes produce thousands of loyalists who have nothing to lose.

Saddam's apparatus knows how much the people hates them, and what will happen to them the day he falls. They also may think, encouraged by global antiwar protests, that if only the regime can create enough humanitarian tragedies, the US might be forced to withdraw.

It is certainly understandable that the people of Basra, having already been betrayed by the United States in 1991 when it failed to come to their aid when they rose up then, do not know whether the coalition can be trusted now. Yet despite the danger, they reportedly have rebelled. Now the coalition has to decide whether to take over the city, with all the mopping-up difficulties that entails, or simply lob artillery shells from outside.

The other story is a related one, concerning the few troops that are engaging coalition forces. "Up and down the 320-kilometer stretch of desert where American and British forces have advanced," the New York Times reported yesterday, "one Iraqi prisoner after another has told a similar tale: Many Iraqi soldiers are fighting at gunpoint, threatened with death by hard-core loyalists of President Saddam Hussein." One soldier said, "The officers threatened to shoot us unless we fought. They took out their guns and pointed them and told us to fight." Another lay dying in the American hospital with a small-caliber bullet in the back of his head, probably from an Iraqi officer.

In other words, the "resistance" and the lack of more spontaneous demonstrations in support of the invasion are hardly evidence that Iraqis do not want to be liberated, but the opposite: a regime so totalitarian and pervasive that even in its death throes it is able to terrorize its people.

The fact that antiwar protests are continuing, and seem to be encouraged by the troubles the coalition has been having in winning the war of expectations, just accentuates how little these supposed humanitarians care about the Iraqi people. Why would anyone with a shred of human caring want Saddam to win this war, or to prolong it by a single day? What other possible effect could such protests have?

One wonders whether the protest movement that is now giving Saddam comfort, but has not a single word to say about the brutalities of his regime, will have some pangs of conscience when Saddam's torture chambers are revealed, and when the Iraqi people are free to say what they will about their years of suffering. When every totalitarian dictatorship falls, such as the Soviet Union and someday China, there are those who are surprised to discover that, if anything, those who called them evil understated the situation.

Former Soviet dissidents, such as Natan Sharansky, poignantly describe how those under a dictator's thumb, particularly those in his prisons, cherished any scrap of news of opposition to their oppressors. Sharansky was in a Siberian prison cell when he was shown the headline in Pravda condemning Ronald Reagan for calling the Soviet Union an "evil empire." "Tapping on walls and talking through toilets, prisoners quickly spread the word of Reagan's 'provocation' throughout the prison," Sharansky wrote of the moment. "The dissidents were ecstatic. Finally, the leader of the free world had spoken the truth."

Now Iraqis are divided in two: the thousands who will stop at nothing to support Saddam and save their lives, and the imprisoned millions who cheer the coalition – now in their hearts and soon in the streets. The antiwar protest movement, "Not In Our Name" is aptly titled. If there is anyone fighting in the name of the Iraqi people, it is the American-led coalition.

◆ ◆ ◆

As time goes on, it will be increasingly understood that the cause of freedom was central to the war in Iraq, not just a happy consequence. It is striking that the quest for freedom still has to be hidden, as if it is illegitimate.

The idea of the West tends to be associated with McDonalds and Hollywood, but it has more to do with the notion of freedom that Judaism and Christianity have introduced to the world.

Interesting Times: Jesus in Baghdad
April 4, 2003

The two related raps on the war so far are not enough troops, not enough flowers. The *New York Times*, in its editorial on Thursday, began to concede the former, hinting that militarily the plan may prove itself. But "the big failure," according to the *Times*, "has been in political assessment, and the expectation that southern Iraq would welcome US troops." There was a mistaken assessment, but there are two possible explanations for it: either Saddam's grip was stronger than expected, or the people genuinely opposed, or at least did not support, the American-led action.

The evidence is already in that once Saddam's gangs are dispatched the people's true feelings do emerge. The *Times* editorialists may have missed the item in their own paper the same day from the first fully liberated Iraqi town of Najaf. "People rushed to greet [US troops]," the *Times* reports, "crying out repeatedly, 'Thank you, this is beautiful.'" It will become increasingly obvious that Iraqis are jubilant and grateful to be rid of Saddam, but this is not the most telling part. What is striking is how so many people are ready to believe that it what is holding Iraqis back is not the gun to their head but their opposition, or at least ambivalence, to being liberated.

This nagging doubt also existed during the Cold War. Yet throughout that struggle, there was never really an ideological battle over the desirability of freedom. Even communists called their government's "people's democracies." Communists never argued for tyranny, they always claimed that they were providing a better form of freedom.

Even Saddam had a need to show how popular he was. Why else have an "election" with only one candidate to show that you can rake in 99 percent of the vote?

Despite the fact that even tyrants won't intellectually defend tyranny, free people often quietly doubt the superiority of freedom. Behind the doubt that we are in fact liberators lurks a doubt in liberty itself.

To confront this doubt in its full force, we should consider the question we tend to avoid: whether people are meant to be free. In Dostoevsky's classic story of the Grand Inquisitor, Jesus himself shows up in 16th-century Seville and proceeds to heal the sick and revive the dead. He is immediately thrown in jail by the cardinal, who berates him for interfering with his Inquisition, which had just executed 100 heretics.

"You are the wickedest of all heretics," the cardinal tells Jesus in his cell without a hint of irony. "For 1,500 years we were pestered by [your] notion of freedom, but in the end we succeeded in getting rid of it." Gaining steam, the inquisitor continues, "It is only now that it has become possible to think of men's happiness."

To him, freedom only benefits the strong, while the weak majority is only too happy to hand a burden they are "too frightened to face." This is radical stuff – not just a defense of a benign dictatorship, but of dictatorship as an ideal. Nor can it be automatically dismissed. We must remember that millions of Russians remember the Stalin era as something of a high point in their history. Even today, many in the West, including much of the Israeli establishment, believe that Arabs are culturally incapable of democracy and prefer a 'strong leader' – an idea that Saddam's popularity among Arabs tends to support.

We see Iraqis returning from Jordan to fight against the American invaders and wonder, is it our conceit to assume that everyone wants to be free?

When Americans talk about this as a fight for their own freedom, this is usually taken as a shorthand for security, which is certainly an aspect of freedom. No one means Iraqis are about to take over America.

In another sense, though, this really is about the future of freedom. Iraq has become a test case not just for the notion of Arab democracy, but for whether the desire for freedom really is as strong and universal as we assume it to be.

Freedom can be less than universally embraced for it to be legitimate and worth defending. But a world in which freedom is just one legitimate option is a very different from one in which tyranny, ipso facto, is increasingly illegitimate.

Iraq is not just a critical cog in the terror network, it symbolizes a dictatorial model that is prevalent to one degree or another throughout the Arab world and elsewhere. Bin Ladenism is normally thought of as a separate phenomenon, but he too is peddling dictatorship as a form of liberation.

The ideological component of this global war is between Western democracy and militant Islam. But it is also more broadly between freedom and tyranny in a way that could have an impact on non-Arab dictatorships in Asia and Africa.

Americans and Iraqis, now ostensibly at war, will soon share a burden much greater than themselves: to prove that freedom can be planted in what had been the heart of darkness, and therefore can and should thrive anywhere.

I was worried at this time about America losing the post-war battle for Iraq's future to Iran and Syria. As of June 2003, I am still worried, but less so. Jay Garner has been replaced with Paul Bremer, who seems to be a better administrator. There have also been encouraging signs that the US has not forgotten about Iran, such as a statement from the June 2003 G8 summit in Evian leaving open "other measures" to prevent Iran from going nuclear if sanctions fail. But Syria is being largely ignored and the US is using only a small fraction of the tools at its disposal to isolate these regimes and help the people topple them.

Interesting Times: Back to the Revolution
April 25, 2003

When the Chicken Littles were saying the sky is falling before the war in Iraq, I was in the 'don't worry' school. But now that the doomsayers are hoping that everyone forgets their predictions of a difficult war, it is I who am beginning to worry.

My worry is not that the post-war focus will be to pressure Israel to make a deal with a largely unreformed Palestinian Authority. There is such a danger but, roughly speaking, Israel and the US are agreed that the days of talking and fighting are over: Either the Palestinians deliver against terrorism or there will be no real negotiations or Israeli concessions.

My concern is more immediate: that the US will discover too late that it is in a race with Iran and Syria over which will be destabilized first – their own regimes or the post-Saddam order the US is trying to create in Iraq.

Iran and Syria may not know much about football, but they do seem to have absorbed what Americans are supposed to have learned from that game – that the best defense is a good offense. Iran is so far outspending and out-hustling the US within the Iraqi Shi'ite majority.

On Wednesday, White House spokesman Ari Fleischer said, "I want to stress that people should not overinterpret the capability of the Shia Iranians to influence the Shia Iraqis." Not only is he right, but the influence could flow in the other direction: rather than Iranian-exported hatred infecting Iraq, pro-American Iraqi Shi'ism could help destabilize Iran.

But for that to happen, the US has to flex some old and unused muscles, not of military might but of old-fashioned political action. As of this writing, the Iraq-Iran border has been left largely open to Iranian penetration. Top Iraqi Shi'ite clerics who want to be aligned with the US have apparently not been contacted, let alone wooed and supported, by the White House, State Department, or by retired general Jay Garner's new administration.

In its military campaign, the US accomplished the unprecedented: the destruction of a regime while preserving most of the national infrastructure, killing a minimum number of Iraqi civilians, and losing a minimum number of its own soldiers. Now the US seems to be trying the equivalent political feat: to win the post-war struggle for Iraq's future with the lightest possible touch, without taking sides, and saying at every moment how eager it is to leave.

While touring Kurdish areas this week, Garner said that, "The majority of people realize we are only going to stay here long enough to start a democratic government for them. We're only going to stay here long enough to get their economy going." Once that is grasped, according to Garner, "In a very short order you'll see a change in the attitudes and the will of the people themselves."

Garner is talking as if his main audience were Iranian-backed Shi'ite fundamentalists and European Bush-bashers, neither of which wanted the war in the first place. In reality, America's challenge is not to convince Iraqis that it will leave quickly enough, but that it will not abandon them to outside infiltrators.

Iraqi Shi'ite leaders now have to bet on who will be ahead over the longer term – Americans who come and go, or Iran, which is vigorously supporting its allies and will always be there? It is perhaps understandable that the US is at pains to show that it is not imposing its will. But the outcome of the current more subtle struggle should be considered integral to the military campaign to oust Saddam. American objectives

221

will not have been fulfilled if it is not safe to be a pro-American Shi'ite leader in Iraq, because Iran has been given a free hand to fund, arm, and organize its allies.

Regime change, after all, comes in many shapes and sizes. Over a decade ago, the West was spoiled by the seemingly effortless revolutions in central Europe, as each regime fell like ripe fruit in tight succession. This is the ideal model for regime change, but it was not possible in Iraq, where Saddam's control was so tight that people were afraid to rise up even with American marines surrounding their cities.

We should not be confused by recent history into thinking that, between spontaneous people power at one extreme and the 82nd Airborne at the other, there are no other alternatives. In between, there is the detail-laden, patience-trying task of fomenting change from within dictatorial regimes.

The Iranian revolution calcified long ago in Iran, and is vulnerable to democratic revolutionaries who now seek to topple it. The US must now draw upon its own revolutionary tradition, both to prevent Iran and Syria from hijacking the peace in Iraq, and to free the peoples living under those regimes.

It is ironic that the Iranian regime, as sclerotic as it is, seems to understand better than America that there is no equilibrium between revolutionary Islamism and revolutionary democracy. One will advance at the expense of the other.

The deck is stacked in America's favor. Iraqis, including the Shi'ites, don't want to be in Iran's orbit, much less live under a new Islamic dictatorship. Syrians would be as happy to be rid of their Ba'athist regime as were Iraqis. But the people cannot free themselves without help.

They need simple things, such as for dissidents to be invited to the White House, for US President George W. Bush to highlight the abuses of their regimes, including Syria's occupation of Lebanon. High-level meetings should end, and concerted effort to increase the economic isolation of both regimes should begin. Opposition radio stations should be amply funded.

The liberation of Iraq was a great and necessary example of America's will and power. But, unlike in Afghanistan, the Iraqis were largely bystanders in the fighting. The next regime changes will be led by peoples, not armies. If America is to win the peace in Iraq and the next battles elsewhere, it must engage on behalf of its friends and potential friends by tapping into its own revolutionary roots.

5. The Other Israel

Israeli society, the economy, and general issues concerned with the
Jewish world.

*The issue of Jewish religious extremists who put their own messianic
ideology above democracy and the rule of law may well reappear if Israel ever
reaches a final status agreement with the Palestinians. But it is hard to believe
that since a "religious" Jew murdered Yitzhak Rabin, that the atmosphere of
fratricidal violence preceding that murder will return.*

Religious Denial
January 7, 1997

This week a cartoon appeared in *Yediot Aharonot* depicting Noam
Friedman, the kippa-wearing soldier arrested for shooting into a crowd
of Arabs in Hebron, in the strange sitting position he chose to commit
his barbaric act. The cartoon is captioned "From yeshiva to yeshiva;"
"yeshiva" is the Hebrew word for a place of Jewish study and also the word
for sitting.

The cartoon's implication, that it was Friedman's Jewish studies that
led him to attempt a massacre of innocent people, would have been
termed antisemitic if it had appeared in an Egyptian or other foreign
newspaper.

223

The problem is that, in an Israeli context, the cartoon highlights a deeply disturbing fact: that in recent times political violence has come from the religious extreme right.

Baruch Goldstein [massacred Arabs in Hebron], Yigal Amir [assassin of Yitzhak Rabin], and Noam Friedman all studied in religious schools and considered themselves religious Jews. The vast majority of the religious public here is horrified by what these people did, and believes that the murderers' Judaism is so deeply perverted that it bears little relationship to the peaceful, ethical religion that most observant Jews aspire to practice.

It is understandable, therefore, that religious institutions, be they educational or political, have rejected attempts to blame the entire religious community for the extremists in their midst. The phenomenon of violent Jewish extremism is a tragedy for all Israelis, but most of all for religious Jews who feel that an entire educational system and way of life has been defamed.

It is hard, for example, not to feel for the mother and grandmother of Friedman, who spoke in bewilderment and horror at his actions. "This wasn't what he learned at home, not what he learned from his family, not from his mother or his father, not from his sisters, not from school," his grandmother, a Holocaust survivor said.

Every community has its disturbed and extreme people. Religious nationalists must not be blamed as a movement or a group, but neither is this community absolved from doing all it can to rout out and reject violent people and the ideas that motivate them.

It is encouraging that in the wake of this recent attack, leaders of the nationalist religious camp are not just condemning the act, but calling for action within their own community. Education Minister Zevulun Hammer (NRP) said there must be soul-searching within the religious sector, and admitted that the religious educational establishment has been extremely cautious in addressing the murder of Yitzhak Rabin. Efrat resident and Third Way MK Alex Lubotsky said, "We, the religious and residents of Judea and Samaria, must denounce violence and exorcise the bad from among us. Such acts are a moral crime which are a stain on all of us."

Religious Zionists, with some justification, have always considered themselves to be among the most self-sacrificing, patriotic, and loyal members of Israeli society. It is not surprising that a community that produces some of the best of Israel would be in a sense of denial that it had also produced the worst.

It is unclear whether the national religious community is really emerging from this state of denial, born of the sense of contradiction between the vision of the Zionist ideal and the horror of that same ideal when taken to extremes.

The fact that an ideal can be perverted, however, does not reflect on the merits of the ideal. There should be no contradiction between fostering the pioneering spirit and sense of religious mission that religious Zionism is proudest of, while instilling the values of tolerance, democracy, and human dignity.

The value of retaining possession of the biblical land of Israel cannot be treated as an absolute. It must be balanced against values such as democracy, peace, and the sanctity of human life. Such a balance does not minimize any of these values; in fact moderation and balance is in itself a Jewish value.

After the murder of Yitzhak Rabin, the Ministry of Education increased efforts to develop programs to foster education toward such democratic values in the curriculum of the national religious schools. Unfortunately, most of these programs still are in the development phase and have not been introduced into the schools.

It will take a substantial and sustained push from the top to accelerate the implementation of these programs, and to overcome the natural resistance of educators to enter very subjective, controversial areas.

Special care must be taken to ensure that 'values education' maintain a delicate balance. It cannot become the province of one camp or another. Teaching values is a tricky business, but the difficulties must be addressed, because the nation cannot afford a vacuum in this area.

That said, the responsibility does not lie solely with the schools. Political and religious leaders, particularly in the national religious camp, must work systematically to strengthen the complementary values of democracy, rule of law, and the long-term need to build lives with our Arab neighbors. Historically, these values have had a place in religious Zionism; they must be brought back into the fold.

◆ ◆ ◆

The challenge of integrating Israeli Arabs has been greatly complicated by the radicalization of their leadership in conjunction with the Palestinian war that began in late September 2000. A terrible watershed came at the beginning of that conflict, when Israeli Arabs joined in the rioting against Ariel Sharon's visit to the Temple Mount, and a number of Israeli Arab citizens were killed by Israeli police. These deaths were investigated by a high-level commission, before which Prime Minister Ehud Barak and many other officials were required to testify.

The overall balance on this issue, however, remains the same: Israel needs to minimize discrimination and open opportunities; Israeli Arabs must be loyal to the state they are citizens of, not to those attacking Israel. It is also important to remember that Israeli Arabs already have much more freedom and prosperity than Arabs in surrounding countries, not to mention the Palestinian Authority, and most would not like to be ruled by Yasser Arafat.

Equal Rights, Equal Responsibilities
July 15, 1999

The latest historical 'first' in Israel – the appointment of MK Hashem Mahameed as the first Arab member of the Knesset Foreign Affairs and Defense Committee – and the debate surrounding it, highlights the need to clarify our attitudes as a society toward the participation of minorities in public life.

The full participation of all citizens with equal rights – in the Knesset as well as in other spheres – is a commendable goal. At the same time, the process must be a two-way street, in which those benefiting from the rights and protections the country affords them also participate positively in society.

It is safe to say that there is a solid majority of Israelis who wish the state to remain both 'Jewish and democratic.' What this means is open to different interpretations, but it is mostly understood as implying a state with Jewish national symbols that continues to serve as a haven for Jews from abroad, while at the same time guaranteeing full civil and democratic rights to all of its citizens equally. It is with regard to the latter point that Israeli democracy has fallen far short of the ideal, leaving much room for improvement.

It is no secret that Arab Israelis face constant discrimination, either open or institutional, in virtually all walks of life. Although they constitute nearly one-fifth of the population, their representation in many publicly or privately owned corporations, such as the Israel Electric Corporation or Bezeq, is minuscule – and non-existent when it comes to top management. The same can be said with respect to government ministries. Whenever this fact is pointed out, various non-convincing excuses are trotted out, such as El Al's defending its lack of a single Arab flight attendant with the claim that no suitable candidate has ever applied.

The patterns of discrimination are apparent at the sectoral level as well. The low level of infrastructure investment in Arab towns and villages is immediately apparent. Government budget allocations to the non-Jewish sectors are pitifully small. As just one example, the amount the Religious Affairs Ministry spends annually to support Jewish religious institutions as compared to Moslem and Christian ones is out of all demographic proportion.

The roots of these phenomena are historical, given the formation of the state and its existential struggle through wars and against terrorism. Change will not come easily. In fact, the era of peace agreements with neighboring countries, while accelerating catalysts for change in society, also brings with it complications that cannot be ignored.

The government and state proclaimed by David Ben-Gurion in May 1948 did not grow out of a vacuum. They were an extension of the institutions of the pre-state Jewish yishuv, which by definition strived for the betterment of the Jewish population under the British Mandate. Just as significantly, the multiple wars and state of enmity that were the constant lot of Israel in its early years caused its Arab sector to be viewed with suspicion and as a potential fifth column for invading Arab armies – leading to the imposition of martial law that was not lifted until the 1960s. At the same time, Ben-Gurion was intent on forging a 'melting pot' from the Jewish immigrants who were pouring in from dozens of cultures and countries. That pot had no room for Arabs. All of these factors combined to create the infrastructure for discrimination.

With Israel now moving away from the old melting pot ideal to one in which different cultural heritages are respected and individual rights are protected, the Arab sector can also move toward greater participation in society. This implies granting Israeli Arabs opportunities in a wide range of career tracks, from industry to the Foreign Ministry to the Knesset. The fact that in the new Knesset, three Arab MKs – Mahmeed, Taleb a-Sana'a, and Ahmed Tibi – have been selected to parliamentary positions is a reflection of these new opportunities.

At the same time, as noted above, this must be a two-way street. The existence of an autonomous Palestinian Authority has initiated no small amount of confusion and blurring of identities among Arab Israelis and their leadership. It would be intolerable, however, for an Israeli public employee or office holder to serve two separate entities – no country in the world accepts foreign agents in its government.

The Arab parliamentarians swear an oath of loyalty to the state, just as every other MK does in accepting the responsibility of public office. They are expected to work positively for the benefit of the state and country, and gimmicks such as attempting to represent Israeli Arabs in the Arab League – as part of the PLO delegation, no less – or talk about a future secession of the Galilee can only cause harm. Those who see themselves as belonging to the PA have the option of establishing their lives and careers there. Those who choose to work within the Israeli democratic system need to be committed to it.

The time has also come to begin seriously discussing some form of national service for young Arab Israelis, reflecting the fact that rights and responsibilities come together as one package. In the end, having Israeli Arabs, as individuals and as a sector, fully involved in society and contributing to it, can only further strengthen Israel as a democratic country.

◆ ◆ ◆

The chance to reflect over an entire century and millennium was a challenge and a treat. In retrospect, I mistakenly assumed that Israel's own battle for existence was drawing to a happy close. But setting Israel aside, the title of this editorial is apt: the 20th century was one of both extreme progress and extreme depredation. The suspicion that this is no coincidence might be taken as a powerful case against modernity. The previous centuries, however, are hardly ideal models for the future.

The Best and Worst of Centuries
December 31, 1999

Though the week, month, year, decade, century, and millennium are ending tonight according to the Christian calendar, the act of separating moments in the seamlessness of time is something with which the Jewish people can identify. By separating out every seventh day from what was an undifferentiated stream of time, Judaism gave the world the concept that time, not just people and places, could be holy. As a historically minded people, Jews should also welcome the opportunity to reflect upon chunks of time that stretch far beyond our own lives or generation.

As it happens, the 20th century neatly straddles one of the most significant events in Jewish history, the creation of the State of Israel. From this perspective, the century began in 1896 with the publication of Theodor Herzl's pamphlet *The Jewish State*, centered upon the founding of the state in 1948, and can be tentatively drawn to a close when, for the first time, Israel settles upon mutually recognized borders with all of its neighbors.

The success of Zionism, in contrast to the demise of the '-isms' that made this century such a bloody one – Nazism, fascism, and communism – is cause for satisfaction. The bloodiest phenomenon of this century was not war, though wars killed 60 million people. An additional 80 million were murdered by governments in the name of ideologies born and defeated in this century. The Holocaust was perhaps the most systematic of these slaughters, and the only one targeting an entire people for extermination based on pure hatred, rather than a struggle for power.

The most striking thing about this century, however, was not the enlarged scale of man's age-old capacity for evil but the changes that it wrought in the most basic aspects of human life. During the first eight or nine centuries of this millennium, most people lived their entire short lives in a small village and tilled the soil. In just the last century or so, life expectancy has doubled and world population has tripled – a transition that was and could remain unique in history.

As physicist Steven Hawkins writes in *Time* magazine, "The world has changed far more in the past 100 years than in any other century in history. The reason is not political or economic, but technological – technologies that flowed directly from advances in basic science." Toward the end of this century, the pace of technological change has accelerated beyond belief. As late as 1943, the chief of IBM predicted that "there is a world market for about five computers." Twenty years ago a fax machine was a novelty. Ten years ago the Internet was an arcane academic preserve. It took four years to register the first one million domain names on the World Wide Web; the increase from four to five million domain names took three months.

This technological explosion would not have been possible, however, without a parallel and synergistic expansion in human freedom. Future generations will probably be unable to untangle the twin legacies of the 20th century: the triumph of democracy and free markets and the dramatic take-off of technological advance.

Though it is tempting to assume that totalitarian regimes were doomed by the advance of the global economy and the tentacles of the information superhighway, it could have been otherwise. In the 1930s and early 1940s, many in the West viewed the democracies as weak and vacillating and looked admiringly at Hitler's Germany and Stalin's Russia. Without leaders such as Churchill, Roosevelt, and Truman, World War II could have been lost, and without decades of bipartisan and President Ronald Reagan's culminating push, the Cold War might not have ended so decisively with the Soviet Union's collapse.

This century marked the transition from a world in which most people lived short lives in poverty under oppressive regimes, to a world in which freedom, health, wealth, and technology have an unstoppable momentum. Israel's creation and development is among the more striking examples and beneficiaries of this transition. The challenges of the next century will have been created by the success of this one, such as finding meaning in a world in which the struggles for freedom and prosperity – and in Israel's case, existence – are largely won.

◆ ◆ ◆

There are arguably three watershed election victories in Israeli politics: Menachem Begin's in 1977 (first Likud prime minister), Yitzhak Rabin's in 1992 (Labor's comeback), and Ariel Sharon's in 2001. The last symbolized the public's intense desire to end the ideological see-saw between left and right that began with Rabin and Peres, flipped to Binyamin Netanyahu, back again to Ehud Barak, and finally landed with Ariel Sharon.

The election of the right-wing icon Sharon by a landslide, when just half a year before Israel seemed about to sign a final status deal with the Palestinians, is testimony to the tectonic shift caused by the Palestinian's post-Camp David terror offensive.

Interesting Times: Answering Ilil
January 26, 2001

At the risk of being deluged with junk mail and unsolicited phone calls, I hereby reveal that I am a precious commodity: a swing voter. More accurately than a walking Blich High School, my vote predicts elections. I voted for the last two winners in Israel and a string of winners in the US before moving here.

True to my predictive form, I'm leaning toward Ariel Sharon, along with many who, a short time ago, could not have imagined voting for him. But I felt my sensitive swing sensors detecting the crowd shifting slightly towards Ehud Barak when articulate teenager Ilil Komai stood up and coolly recited her 'J'accuse' against Sharon.

Opposition cynics aside, she clearly believed that Sharon was responsible for the suffering of her father, who returned shell-shocked from the Lebanon War.

If Barak manages to pull an upset in this election, Komai's speech will be marked as the turning point where, despite all odds, the incumbent managed to make the challenger the issue in the campaign. But without diminishing the suffering of Komai and her family, I have trouble accepting the attempt to brand a particular camp, let alone an individual, with the mark of Cain over the Lebanon War.

Though I did not intend to introduce my own loss into this context, I cannot help but consider my own feelings as someone who lost a brother in Lebanon.

For starters, I tend to avoid thinking through who is to blame for my brother's death because to do so just adds impotent anger to the pain.

The loss is difficult enough to live with, without adding the corrosive effect of a quest for revenge. But if I had to draw up a list of who was responsible, Sharon would not be on it.

My brother Alex was killed on September 15, 1987, his 25th birthday, while attempting to save his commander on a rocky hilltop near Har Dov in southern Lebanon. The men who killed him were, based on captured documents, Syrian-backed terrorists who were planning to cross the border and kill Israeli citizens. I blame the men who shot Alex and the leaders who sent them for his death.

The people who sent Alex, Komai's father, and thousands of other Israelis into Lebanon, by contrast, were successive Israeli governments starting with Yitzhak Rabin in 1975 until Barak's unilateral withdrawal early last year.

Throughout these many years, Israel's governments may have acted with lesser or greater wisdom, but always with the legitimacy granted by our democratic system. At every level, from the prime minister to the generals to the platoon commander in the field, difficult choices had to be made between risking the lives of soldiers and those of civilians, and how to minimize Israel's losses while maximizing its security.

The distinction between a 'war of choice' and 'war of existence' that is often bandied about to delegitimize the Lebanon War is a uniquely Israeli one. While the concept of a 'just war' is valid, only in Israel is the right of self-defense unilaterally limited to threats to national survival.

No other country would flagellate itself for taking military action against a terrorist state-within-a-state that was murdering its citizens with impunity.

The attempt to paint Israel's 'tragedy' (as Barak calls it) in Lebanon as the personal adventure of presumably bloodthirsty Israeli leaders is unfair, divisive, anti-democratic, and – perhaps worst of all – demeans the sacrifice of those who died there.

Neither Barak nor Sharon have a monopoly on war or on peace. The choice between them is between flawed leaders, each of whom has disqualified himself for the premiership in the eyes of much of the public. Israel's choice, ironically, is between two leaders whose penchant for reckless audacity is both their strength and their weakness. Though the press has made much of Sharon's lack of a diplomatic plan, we have little idea what either leader would do the day after elections, or whether they would show more respect for democratic mores than they have in the past.

Meretz has cleverly plastered the spaces that normally tout the latest films with the message 'War and Sharon: We've already been through that movie.' Actually, the more relevant movie we have been through is the Left and the Right toppling each other's governments in quick succession.

It is this process of self-destruction that carries with it the greatest risk of war. The campaign's descent into demonization is exactly the wrong preparation for the day after that campaign is over.

One of the remarkable, if unsettling, things about Israel is that it is perhaps the only state in the world whose right to exist, over half a century after its founding, is still a matter of debate. Ruth Gavison is one of the few Israeli scholars who has addressed this question on the terms of those who challenge our right to be here, namely in terms of moral legitimacy and human rights.

The lecture to which I refer remains unpublished, but a related article called "The Jews' Right to Statehood: A Defense" appears in the Summer 2003 issue of Azure.

Interesting Times: Back to the Future
March 2, 2001

I went shopping for a typewriter this week. Typewriters, if you remember, were those devices that would put ink directly on paper with a clackety-clack noise, and some would make a satisfying wrrrr as the finished product was yanked off the platten.

The person I was shopping with was tired of dealing with computer breakdowns, so I had suggested going back to something more basic that works.

It doesn't happen that often, but there are times when it makes sense to go back to something that we thought we had moved beyond, never to return. At this challenging and troubling time, it is perhaps no coincidence that the keys to the kingdom have been handed over to a supplanted generation, that of Ariel Sharon and Shimon Peres. The sense, however, that Israel must reopen finished business was most powerfully put forth in a recent lecture by Hebrew University professor Ruth Gavison.

Gavison's speech, given in memory of philanthropist Zalman Bernstein and sponsored by the Shalem Center, deserves to be cherished and studied as an intellectual watershed, like Alexander Solzhenitsyn's famous speech at Harvard.

Gavison made three seminal points: Israel must make the case for its legitimacy as a Jewish state, that this case can and should be built upon universal (not just religious) values, and that the same actions that are necessary to strengthen Israel's legitimacy are also critical to maintaining our social fabric.

If your hackles have already been raised by the idea that Israel's legitimacy must be defended, bear with me. Without using this analogy, Gavison recognized that to seriously respond to attacks on Israel's legitimacy might be seen as akin to debating Holocaust deniers – why help give such people a platform? Why should Israel have to defend its right to exist any more than France or Syria?

This was Gavison's own view for some time, but what tipped the scales for her was the realization that almost no one among the Israeli Arab leadership, let alone among the Palestinians, is willing to accept the moral right of a Jewish state to be here, as opposed to its de facto presence.

However unacceptable, a view that is held by roughly one-fifth of the citizenry, which wins sympathy from significant Jewish circles, and which many Israelis would have trouble coherently rebutting, must, argues Gavison, be addressed head on.

The Arab view which Gavison seeks to refute is straightforward: that Israel is a form of colonialism imposed by force on the local population, and therefore by right should be expelled. Gavison's answer is twofold: that the Jewish people returned to and did not colonize the Land of Israel, and that a Jewish state fulfills universal criteria for a people to demand a state.

Unlike real colonists, the Jews did not come to subject another people, to plunder a land, or to extend the power of another nation. They did not come to find their fortune, freedom, or a nice place to hang their hat. The land they came to was barren, malaria-infested, and fraught with dangers, but for a Jew it was coming home. As importantly, they came, as Gavison put it, "like Abraham, not Joshua" – buying stakes in the land rather than conquering it.

According to Gavison, the right of self-determination belongs to all peoples, but not necessarily in the form of an independent state. For a people to claim the right to a state, she argues, they must be a majority in a particular place, and must have concrete needs for a state that outweigh the costs that state imposes on the minorities in its midst.

The ancient and continuous Jewish connection to this land did not alone justify forming a state here, but it did give the Jews the right to try. In 1900, Gavison admits, "Jews did not have a right to establish a Jewish state in Zion," but by 1948 that right had been demographically established.

Moreover, even if Israel were to concede that it had been 'born in sin' – which Gavison does not – today's 80 percent Jewish majority firmly anchors Israel's right to demand that other nations recognize its legitimacy.

But Gavison's lecture should not just be memorized within the Foreign Ministry; she also posed a critical challenge to Israeli society. Perhaps her most powerful point was that Israel must ensure that its Arab minority feels included and fairly treated, not just to be enlightened, but because Israel's legitimacy rests in part on the non-Jewish minority not paying too high a price for the Jewishness of the state.

To some, thinking seriously about what makes Israel legitimate may seem like a step backward, but Gavison draws important lessons for how not only Jews and Arabs, but different Jewish groups, should live here together in the future.

◆ ◆ ◆

Demography is usually used in the Israeli political debate as the ultimate proof of the necessity of a Palestinian state, because there is no way Israel can absorb the Palestinian population of the territories and retain its Jewish and democratic character. There is a lot of truth to this, but the argument tends to assume that the Palestinian population will grow by leaps and bounds, while Israel's days of substantial immigration are behind her.

This is only true if we are short-sighted enough to make it so. There are two impediments to substantial immigration to Israel: our sclerotic economy and the general demographic crisis of the Jewish people. Here I set out the general demographic issues. In "Stocks and Bombs," pages 237-240, I elaborate on the economic side, and in "What Good are Jews," pages 278-281, I argue that our goal should be for the Jewish people as a whole, not just Israel, to grow dramatically.

Interesting Times: Counting Babies
March 16, 2001

We have three kids. Demographers have a word for this; we have 'replaced' ourselves in the treadmill of population growth. At our house, particularly at bedtime, the word that more readily comes to mind is 'outnumbered.' It is not easy juggling work and three small children.

235

We are in awe of those who have four or more, just as friends who have only one cannot fathom how we get through the week. The idea of deliberately helping them outnumber us two-to-one often seems, to put it delicately, counter-intuitive.

I wanted to ask the haredi woman who was next to my wife in the maternity ward last time whether 10 children – her current brood – seemed about right or whether her concept of the ideal family had no limits. On the other end, I find it a bit hard to comprehend that in wealthier countries around the world, populations are headed for a nosedive because most people have only one or two kids.

In places as diverse as Italy and Japan, Australia and Russia, fertility rates have dropped to below replacement level. The United Nations now estimates that even if developed countries absorb two million immigrants a year, their population will be lower in 2050 than it is today. Russia is particularly hard hit by population collapse: Russian women average only 1.14 births in their lifetime, so by 2050 Russia will be smaller than Vietnam or Iran.

Around the world, in every culture, the pattern has been repeated: as people become wealthier, they have fewer children. The drop in fertility has been most dramatic in poorer countries – from six children per woman in 1970 to three today.

The upshot is that the world's population will not double again - it is set to peak at about 10 billion this century – but its composition will be radically different. Today what we call the West numbers less than one-fifth of the world; in 2050 the same countries will be around one-ninth.

Globally, you can forget about the 'baby boom' – it is the over-60 set who will grow at three times the general growth rate. And if you think kids are pampered now, imagine Europe in 2050, when the median age is just below 50 and every third person is a grandparent.

How does Israel stack up in the more Asian, 'bubbefied' world of the future?

Numbers were never our strong suit; this won't change. Iran, Iraq, Syria and Egypt currently have 30 times our population; in 2050 they will have 32 times as many people. Closer to home, however, the UN projects a more pronounced change: the population of what the UN helpfully calls 'Occupied Palestinian Territories' will almost quadruple by 2050.

The UN, however, is counting babies when what has driven Israel's population is immigration. Israel's population leaped five times in the last 50 years, mostly through aliya. Over the next half century, Israel hopes to absorb millions more, while the Palestinians expect to throw open their doors to millions from their diaspora. With both sides racing to collect immigrants, the UN estimate of 21 million people west of the Jordan river by 2050 could be on the low side.

The conclusion from this peek into the future is not that we should throttle back our aspirations for immigration – if anything aliya is as necessary as ever for Israel to hold its own. The question is how much stability we can expect if 11 million Palestinians will squeeze into an area less than one-third of the size of Israel.

On television this week, the newly-civilian Effie Eitam (Fine) argued that a Palestinian state in Judea, Samaria, and Gaza would be too truncated to fulfill their aspirations, and that both Jordan and Egypt would have to play a role in providing additional political or physical breathing space.

On our side, attracting and absorbing all the immigrants that we need will require a thriving economy that is at least as free and dynamic as the United States. Over the last few years, we've patted ourselves on the back for bringing inflation and government spending in check. But shaking off some of our past vices is not good enough: we cannot rely on Jews fleeing to Israel, and to attract immigrants from the West we need to stop expecting them to make an economic sacrifice.

Having a child in Israel may be considered a great Zionist act – ironically making the haredim the greatest Zionists of us all. But Zionism has never relied primarily on birth rates and it cannot in the future. The next century of Zionism will depend, not on draining swamps, but on scrapping regulations, trimming government and cutting taxes.

◆ ◆ ◆

It is frustrating to write about the Israeli economy, because the unrealized potential is so great and would go so far toward solving so many problems. It is hard to accept that the challenge of increasing growth is barely discussed, and when it is, it is usually dismissed as impossible given the state of the global economy and the security situation.

Interesting Times: Stocks and Bombs
August 17, 2001

Remember a year or two ago when it seemed like the Arab-Israeli conflict was on its way to being wrapped up, the high-tech boom seemed endless, and the cultural war seemed to be the main issue driving Israeli politics? In the 1999 elections, Labor and Likud groped for an agenda, while the battle between Shinui and Shas stole the show.

For a fleeting moment, Israel seemed to be transcending the war-and-peace dominated politics of the previous 50 years. The Palestinian resort to violence did not just crush the hopes of the Oslo era, it also caused Israeli politics to snap back into familiar grooves, and returned all non-security issues to the back burner.

When politicians finally get around to thinking about the economy, this too becomes an asterisk attached to the security situation. Wait for NASDAQ to recover and the tourists to return and then we'll talk – this is what now passes for economic policy.

It is understandable that security trumps economics in the public square.

What is not really appreciated, however, is the power of the economy to contribute to our national safety and survival. Attending to the economy should not be thought of as a luxury to be put aside for better times, but an integral part of our existential challenge.

Economic and military strength are tightly interwoven. Peace is ultimately a function of convincing the Arab world that Israel cannot be destroyed, so the fact that the Israeli economy is larger than those of all of its neighbors is a major contribution to the cause of peace. Now imagine for a moment if, in the next 15 years, the economy were to double in size, and if the fruits of this doubling were spread more fairly among Israelis, Jews and Arabs. Israel's economic growth could play a major, perhaps even decisive, role in ending the Arab-Israeli conflict.

Doubling our GNP is not a matter of miracles, but creating a 'virtuous cycle' between three economic factors: people, participation, and production. Put simply, we have more people, and if more of them work and those who work produce more, than doubling our economy is no dream. Israel has great untapped potential in all three areas.

For the last decade, Israel has experienced roughly zero productivity growth. What economic growth we've had is almost entirely attributable to population growth, not to Israelis working more productively. This means that the productivity gap between us and more advanced Western economies has widened, and that we have considerable untapped potential. Productivity is not a zero sum game: there is nothing stopping us from copying what makes other countries more productive and realizing similar gains.

Instead of constantly fighting over how to allocate the government's budget, politicians should be racing to implement reforms that cost the government nothing and yet could produce radical gains in productivity.

A straightforward way to increase productivity would be a flat tax. A single low income tax rate – say about 30 percent – would obviously be much more simple and efficient, but it could also be designed to be more fair because low income workers could be completely exempt (including the social security and health taxes they are paying now) and numerous loopholes for the wealthy could be closed.

Israel should copy the many Central European countries and England which rapidly privatized dozens of government companies by giving away most of the shares to the public. There is no reason to continue the primitive practice of selling large 'controlling' chunks of companies to individuals or small groups. Giving most of the shares away to the public is not only fair and efficient, but would create unstoppable political momentum for privatization instead of the current stalling.

Israel also has a relatively low rate of workforce participation. The combination of large families and low workforce participation in the Arab and haredi communities creates devastating poverty in those sectors. This situation cannot be blamed on cultural factors alone; government policies should be designed to increase, not decrease the incentives to work generally, and particularly in these sectors.

If the Israeli economy were growing from a combination of greater productivity and participation, the third factor – people – would appear as well. Israelis working abroad would come home and immigration from Western countries would turn from a trickle to a significant flow. Rising prosperity – provided specific efforts are made to include the Arab sector – would turn Israel's supposed demographic time bomb on its head: Israeli Arab birthrates would drop and Jewish immigration would rise.

Falling stocks and bombs are devastating, no doubt, but it is the damage from forgoing economic reform that is self-inflicted, and therefore in some ways the most tragic.

◆ ◆ ◆

This column is a flashback to something I wrote to myself just after the assassination of Prime Minister Yitzhak Rabin. The enormity of this self-inflicted wound hit me harder than anything in the nine years I have lived in Israel, including the darkest days of the terrorist offensive against us.

Interesting Times: Thoughts of Rabin on a Concrete Roof
October 18, 2002

Though I am not usually among those who write as a form of therapy, seven years ago I sat on the concrete roof of a bus stop – the only free spot – opposite the Knesset, and recorded what I saw and thought:

I find it hard to focus on the man. It is 7 a.m. Flowing through the Knesset plaza in front of me is a river of people approaching the casket that contains the body of Yitzhak Rabin. The river has been flowing past this spot since yesterday afternoon and all through the night. Now the line stretches about a mile long. People standing patiently in line, not cutting, barely moving. Most of them probably will not make it to the Knesset plaza in the three hours before the gates close and the casket is taken to Har Herzl for burial.

It's hard to think about Rabin the man because I keep thinking about the people, the whole people of Israel that is here to pay its last respects.

What kind of people are we? Are we really any better than any other country?

Are we even good enough to survive?

I remember one of the strongest feelings of that time was a loss of innocence – the shock of the idea that a prime minister could be assassinated. Just as Americans felt, before September 11, that terrorism was something that happened elsewhere, Israelis never dreamed they would lose a leader by the gun.

It seems too much to expect from a people, any people, to collectively grow, as a person sometimes does, out of a tragedy. That the murderer was an Israeli Jew, a former yeshiva student and law student at Bar-Ilan University, compounds the corrosive nature of the act immensely.

This is a test. A test greater than Israel has ever faced.

I did not contemplate then a third possibility: that Israel would neither 'grow' nor plunge into civil war, but mainly avoid grappling with how the nation came to be so divided over how to achieve peace and security.

One striking thing about the crowd was that, unlike most Israeli crowds, it could not be easily characterized as part of one 'camp' or another.

How will Israel stand up to this test? The first measure will be whether inciting language – such as calling Rabin 'traitor' or 'murderer' – becomes unacceptable, and whether those who used or turned a blind eye toward such language express regret.

The religious Zionist camp as a whole, with some justice, is on trial here. Will those who find halachic authority for anti-democratic acts be confronted by defenders of a Judaism that supports democracy? Which Judaism will dominate?

Again, not much progress here. With some notable exceptions, the leaders of religious Zionism have not gone beyond condemning the murder, and are unwilling to take any responsibility so long as the Left will not admit to its own history of incitement. During the Lebanon War, they note, it was Ariel Sharon who was branded a 'murderer.'

What an irony that Judaism, a religion obsessed with peace and the sacred value of life, with justice and unity of the Jewish people, is now on trial in the Jewish state as an accessory to murder. It will take more than heartfelt condemnations to remove the stain.

The majority of the religious Zionist community, who are by and large model citizens, need to be as vocal in defense of true Jewish behavior as the extremists are in voicing their perversion of Judaism.

A more moderate form of religious Zionism did not obviously emerge, but it is telling that, some years later, Ehud Barak made territorial concessions that even Leah Rabin could not stomach, and yet was not met by protests as wide or as sharp as those of 1995.

The extreme Right must be blamed for creating a climate of hatred and violence that led to this unthinkable murder. Those on the mainstream Right who did not do enough to condemn and isolate the extremists should also admit their grievous sins of omission. At the same time, peace process supporters should not dismiss those who live in the territories as troublemakers who are less than full citizens of Israel and whose fear for their homes, and for the fate of the country, are not legitimate.

It is said that God favored the house of Hillel over the house of Shamai because Hillel would always begin an argument by presenting the case of Shamai. It is hard to conceive of a better model for Israel today.

It is now 9 a.m. I've spent two hours here, but it is very hard to break away. As the sea of people passes in front of the casket, what is happening in their hearts? Are they becoming harder or softer? Closing or opening?

Though at first glance it may seem that almost no change has occurred in the intervening years, the popularity of the unity government must be attributed in part to a strong desire to put traditional rivalries aside, particularly while the nation is under fire.

Now I am sitting by the six-meter-high Menorah across from the Knesset plaza. I never looked at it closely before. Its branches are etched with scenes starting with the Bible at the top and progressing through Jewish history to the founding of the state at the base of the trunk.

At the foot of the Menorah, in the round, fenced-in clearing of Jerusalem stone pavement, is a carpet of lit candles, notes, songs, and flowers. My favorite is a torn paper Israeli flag, taped to the rail, with the word sovlanut (tolerance) written on it in blue.

So is this where the dream ends – on a bright sunny day in November, the birds chirping, the helicopters flying, the cell phones ringing? It is as if all Jewish history was funneled into this young country, only to be diffused into a pool of sorrow on a single fine day. That's the way it looks today, as Israel prepares to bury Yitzhak Rabin.

After 2,500 years, Jews still fast to mourn the assassination of Gedalia ben Ahikam, the Jewish governor of Judah appointed by the Babylonians. Seven years after the murder of Rabin, the elected leader of a Jewish state, we have barely begun the job of removing the tarnish from the dream of Jewish statehood, a job that may never be done.

◆ ◆ ◆

It is nice to find something worthy of praise every once in a while, like the Reform movement's ability to change course and even to admit past mistakes. The contrast with Israeli politicians is, unfortunately, great.

Reform Reforms
October 29, 2002

Today a group of 41 Reform rabbis on a solidarity mission will make an unusual stop. The group will visit Ariel, a city located east of the Green Line. It is unfortunate that such a visit is unusual enough to merit commendation, but so it is, and so it does.

Rabbi Ammiel Hirsch, executive director of ARZA-World Union, North America and leader of the mission, explained its purpose: "This is a non-ideological mission to express our solidarity with the people of Israel during this most difficult time." As to why they are visiting a 'settlement,' Hirsch stated, "We want to go there because we want to identify with the suffering of our people wherever they may live, and refuse to go along with the distinction our enemies make between a baby in Ariel and a baby in Tel Aviv."

These statements and actions are a refreshing contrast to our own politics, in which the Left is often unable to distinguish between its ideological opposition to the settlement enterprise and the need to support those of us who are literally under fire. Opposition leader Yossi Sarid, for example, in Monday's *Ha'aretz*, dismisses all distinctions between the extremists and the settler leadership, and concludes that "we have the right of self- defense from the likes of Effi Eitam, his rabbis and pupils, before they bring down the horrors upon us, before Jewish fascism runs over us all."

In his entire op-ed, Sarid felt no need to show a modicum of the solidarity that the Reform rabbis have decided to show, even though they would no doubt agree with Sarid regarding the dangers of Jewish extremism. Even Labor Party leader Binyamin Ben-Eliezer, in his recent attempt to pander to his party's left wing, has not tried to temper his anti-settler rhetoric. On the contrary, he has upped the ante by saying that he believes 'the gun is cocked' for the next assassination of an Israeli leader, such as himself.

Compare the heating up of the rhetoric here with an admirable evolution and humility displayed by the Reform movement. As early as June 2001, that is before the heightened sensitivity produced by September 11, the Board of Trustees of the Union of American Hebrew Congregations passed a resolution stating plainly: "We must not be reticent to acknowledge our own errors of judgment. We must admit, first and foremost, that we have been wrong about the readiness of the Palestinians for peace."

The resolution of the Reform movement's umbrella organization continues, "We were wrong about something else as well. We did not pay nearly enough attention to the culture of hatred created and nourished by Palestinian leaders... Attempts to justify and explain [Palestinian] actions are still made, often by diplomats and sometimes by well-meaning Jews. But to excuse the Palestinians from the normal standards of moral judgment is to patronize them and to separate them from humanity. The only explanation that makes sense is a deep and profound hatred, among some segments of their population, for Israelis and Jews."

Given the enthusiasm with which this same community had embraced the Oslo process, these statements represent a course correction almost as profound as the Columbus platform of 1937, which reversed the 1885 Pittsburgh platform's opposition to Zionism.

In Pittsburgh, Reform rabbis declared: "We consider ourselves no longer a nation, but a religious community, and therefore expect neither a return to Palestine... nor the restoration of any of the laws concerning the Jewish state.' In Columbus, they proclaimed: 'We affirm the obligation of all Jewry to aid in its upbuilding as a Jewish homeland by endeavoring to make it not only a haven of refuge for the oppressed but also a center of Jewish culture and spiritual life."

Today, the rabbis' visit to Ariel comes on the heels of a petition signed by 120 Reform rabbis that speaks of Palestinian 'self-determination,' without mentioning a state, and flatly opposes an "imposed solution" to the conflict.

Israel has and arguably is still paying a high price for its inability to set aside ideological battles, even when under attack. Though there are certainly exceptions to this positive evolution in positions toward Israel in the Reform movement, would that some of our own political and ideological organizations displayed such an ability to adapt to changing realities, even at the risk of questioning past judgments.

◆ ◆ ◆

At first glance, this column may seem to be obsolete in the wake of the Bush Administration's determination to topple or tame rogue regimes racing to obtain weapons of mass destruction. It is not, because the missile threat of the future may not only be from states, and there is no guarantee that the regime change campaign will be completely and permanently successful. The fact that Saddam Hussein did not succeed in repeating the 1991 missile attacks against Israel and other countries before he fell does not change the nature of the threat.

There remains no justification for the West deliberately leaving itself open to missile attack, in keeping with an ideological remnant left over from the Cold War.

Interesting Times: Brilliant Pebbles Now
November 9, 2001

This week, US President George W. Bush told an anti-terrorism conference in Warsaw, "We will not wait for the authors of mass murder to gain the weapons of mass destruction. We act now, because we must lift this dark threat from our age and save generations to come." Bush was talking about the prospect of a nuclear-armed bin Laden, but his statement is equally valid toward other mass murderers, such as Iraq's Saddam Hussein.

As the West debates whether or not Saddam is a target of the war on terrorism, Saddam himself is wasting no time. Just days ago, Saddam told assembled "warriors" of Iraq's Nuclear Energy Authority that "progress has continued and will accelerate" on Iraq's nuclear program. As the US bombs the Taliban in Afghanistan, Iraq is busy with its own Manhattan Project. Saddam clearly believes that the more dangerous he gets, the less the West will be willing to confront him. September 11 was a break-through for Saddam in this calculus of fear, because now Americans realize that they are vulnerable on their own soil.

The current American campaign in Afghanistan does not frighten Saddam. On the contrary, the repeated American official denials that Saddam is next and refusal to link him to either Osama bin Laden or to anthrax terrorism confirm to him that being fearsome works, and being more fearsome would work better.

To some, September 11 is the ultimate proof that the major threat to the West is not rogue states armed with missiles, but terrorist networks using trains, planes and automobiles – whatever comes to hand. How ridiculous, they say, it is to invest in missile defenses when the real threat is from a nuke in a truck or a boat.

What the anti-missile defense crowd does not get is the iron connection between the terror network and missiles in the hands of Iran or Iraq. Missiles are an integral part of the cycle of fear; missiles allow rogue states to intimidate the West into going after their terrorist surrogates rather than the regimes behind them. And the cycle works both ways – missiles provide cover for terrorism, and terrorism makes the use of missiles more thinkable, therefore making the threat from missiles even more potent. The upshot is that a crash program to develop missile defenses is more urgent than ever.

The shame is the US could have easily had effective global missile defenses in place by now. In 1991, the first Bush administration decided to build a system called Brilliant Pebbles, so named because they were even smarter and smaller than the "smart rocks" that scientists had envisioned could be used to crash into missiles in flight. Putting 1,000 Pebbles in space would have cost $11 billion, less than one-third the cost of a Clinton administration plan for a much less capable ground-based missile defense site in Alaska.

Using actual data from the Gulf War, a detailed simulation showed that if Brilliant Pebbles had been deployed, they could have shot down every Scud missile shot by Iraq against Israel and Saudi Arabia. As the former director of the program, Henry Cooper, laid out in the *Wall Street Journal* (May 7), "all first-generation Pebbles technologies" had been validated in field tests by 1994, despite the cancellation of the program for ideological reasons.

Just as Europe had a "nuclear umbrella" during the Cold War, missiles in the hands of rogue states are the umbrella that protects the global terror network. The war on terror cannot be won without neutralizing the terrorists' "missile umbrella." One way to do this is to topple the rogue regimes themselves, an effort that the West must pursue in any case in its own self-defense.

But going to war should not be the West's only protection against missile threats. Nor should Israel, the only country in the world whose existence could be threatened by missiles, sit idly by waiting for everyone else to wake up. The Arrow program is fine as far as it goes, but Israel should be developing more sophisticated anti-missile technologies on a crash basis with the United States.

In the absence of American urgency, it might make sense for Israel to start building its own Brilliant Pebbles system. The Israeli program would ideally become a contribution to an American-led effort. But if

Iranian and Iraqi missiles are not enough to jumpstart a serious American missile defense program, perhaps the prospect of an independent Israeli space defense would be.

◆ ◆ ◆

Some day Israelis will discover that economics is not a zero-sum game. No one defends socialism anymore, but the veneer of talk about fiscal restraint, privatization, and other free market friendly concepts covers over the same old mentality: if someone benefits, it must be at someone else's expense.

Interesting Times: Tora Bora Blues
December 7, 2001

Osama bin Laden is reportedly holed up (literally) in a nearly impregnable mountain redoubt called Tora Bora. Though the name means 'Black Widow' in Pashtun, it sounds like a yeshiva on overdrive, or perhaps a hassidic Polynesian island. It would be poetic justice if a cave so named were to become his tomb.

The network of caves and tunnels built into a mountain sounds like an architectural wonder, perhaps worthy of preserving or reconstructing for a 'museum of terror' – a must-see on any future Afghan tourist itinerary. I have been thinking in architectural terms lately since my recent visit to Barcelona, a city that revels in the almost surrealistic creations of its favorite son, Antonio Gaudi.

For many, the nearest point of reference to describe Gaudi's buildings would be Dr. Seuss. As almost anyone with children (or who was a child) knows, Dr. Seuss's books are loved not only for their whimsical use of language, but the fantastically shaped creatures, plants, and buildings that trigger the imagination.

It is difficult to find a square corner in any of Gaudi's creations, and every element – from the chimneys on the roof to the grates on the windows – is a work unto itself. As I climbed around the roof of the 'Pedrera' (stone quarry, as it was nicknamed by Barcelonans for its undulating stone facade), I could not help but think about our own little dream – building a modest expansion on the roof of our apartment.

For months we have been plotting this small construction project, and contemplating with dread the bureaucratic hoop-jumping it will take to make it happen. We are told that to build a couple of rooms legally we have to amend the plan of the neighborhood, a process about as simple as amending the Declaration of Independence. Looking at the plans for Gaudi's Pedrera, I could only imagine the reaction of Jerusalem bureaucrats to an addition in the shape of some crouched animal covered with brightly-colored tiles, with some wild chimneys thrown in.

As our plans gelled, we discovered that in addition to bureaucratic hassles, we faced something that may be a uniquely Israeli invention – what I call the 'pleasure tax.' Some countries have high sales taxes, others have high income taxes; Israel is a country blessed with both, plus taxes on anything that moves to boot. But what if something happens that it is not a form of income and is not at anyone's expense, just a gratuitous good thing that befalls someone – wouldn't it be terrible if such a thing were to escape taxation? This is where the 'pleasure tax' comes in.

In our case, we were told that if we somehow succeeded in negotiating the maze of committees and rezoned our airspace, we would be hit with a 50 percent tax on the value of whatever we built. With scientific precision, this tax seems designed to ensure any smidgen of financial benefit that we might enjoy from our exertions would be efficiently sucked away by our beloved government. Other taxes in the works are on sunny days and particularly short checkout lines in the supermarket.

It is more than the government's insatiable need for revenue that is behind such taxes. Despite the veneer of free-market talk and the hi-tech enclave within the Israeli economy, the mentality that prefers dragging everyone down to helping one person up remains distressingly entrenched.

This mentality, which can be traced back to the Bolshevism that was fashionable here half a century ago, can be detected in the four-way talks on the economy that broke down this week. Each of the four players – government, central bank, business, and unions – says it won't do the right thing unless the others do so as well, even though actions demanded of each are independently justifiable. The bank should cut interest rates, the unions should stop striking, the government should cut taxes and spending, and businesses should restructure responsibly. If anything, the package deal being pursued may serve to stave off the structural reforms that are necessary to really boost productivity and revive the economy.

Too often, though, we don't think in terms of how everyone can get ahead, but how to prevent anyone from getting ahead. It's as if we are in a race in which each runner is so busy trying to hold the others back that the goal of winning, either as a society or individually, has been forgotten. The ironic result of this mentality is an economy so government-heavy that it is both stagnant and radically unequal. Our aversion to economic freedom has produced everything that it has sought to avoid - unemployment, radical income gaps, and a lack of social cohesion.

◆ ◆ ◆

If Israel were growing economically as fast as Hong Kong was in its heyday, or even as fast the US was in the 1980s, its social and strategic situations would be much improved. In addition, Israel should grow out of its identity as a place of refuge, which means holding itself to the low standard of being better places that people run away from, and trying to be a place that people from successful countries also find attractive.

As someone who moved to Israel from the US, I know that Israel can attract Jews who are not running from anything. But if Israel really wants another million immigrants, it has to at least reduce the economic sacrifice it effectively demands of them.

Attractive Aliya
December 27, 2001

The news of the tragic economic collapse in Argentina was accompanied here by a macabre form of excitement: Now the Jews of Argentina will move to Israel. The prospect of any boost in aliya is indeed exciting and welcome, but the assumption that persecution or hardship is the normative engine of aliya should be scrapped.

Argentina is home to about 200,000 Jews, who constitute the sixth largest community in the Diaspora. According to the director of an absorption center who spoke to Channel 1, about one-tenth of Argentinian Jews are expected to move to Israel over the next five years. At this rate, the flow of Argentinian Jews would still be a relatively small part of the annual immigration to Israel.

From 1975 until 1990, fewer than 20,000 immigrants arrived in Israel each year. In 1990 the dam that had been holding back Soviet Jewry broke, leading to two years of massive immigration not seen since the founding years of the state: almost 200,000 in 1990 and 180,000 in 1991. Since then aliya has been slowly dropping from about 75,000 per year from 1992 to 1995 to about 60,000 last year. In the first nine months of this year, however, immigration from the former USSR is down one-third from the same period in 2000.

As a result of the last decade of immigration from the former Soviet Union, Israel has increased its share of world Jewry from 29 percent in 1989 to 37 percent in 2000. What has remained remarkably steady over this same period is North America's share of the pie: almost half.

According to a study led by Hebrew University Professor Sergio DellaPergola published in the American Jewish Yearbook 2000, this steadiness is illusory.

Between now and 2080, these demographers predict that Israel's Jewish population will double, while North American Jewry will shrink by about one-third, to 3.8 million. At that time, about 80 percent of Jews under the age of 15 will live in Israel.

These are obviously projections of current trends and do not take into account dramatic political or social changes. But they do suggest that Israel must radically change its traditional thinking on two fronts: both what drives aliya and the role of aliya as a national priority.

The reaction toward events in Argentina indicates that Israel still thinks of aliya more as a function of hardship elsewhere than of Israel's attractiveness. Israel has largely become used to the idea that it can attract Jews almost exclusively from countries that have essentially fallen apart. Half a century after the Holocaust, we still seem to think of ourselves primarily as a refuge, rather than a destination of choice.

Israel should never forget that it is a refuge for Jews, and will even go out of its way to save Jews in distress, as in Ethiopia in 1991. But we should aspire to be more than a safe haven, even though safety may not be Israel's strong suit at the moment. Our goal should be to be attractive even to Jews who are safe, free, and prosperous.

But as difficult as it may seem to attract immigrants from countries that are not collapsing, even this goal is insufficient. Aliya, after all, is moving Jews from one place to another, and does nothing to address the relative shrinkage of the Jewish people as a whole over time.

DellaPergola projects that the world's Jewish population will be only 15 million in 2080, only slightly higher than today and less than 1939. Total world population has almost tripled since 1939, and will rise by roughly a third by 2080.

One might ask why it matters whether the Jewish people becomes a smaller fraction of a percent of the world's population, or whether Israel becomes even more outnumbered by the Arab world. Perhaps it does not. But it turns out that what Israel has to do to attract more Jews is also what must be done to break out of demographers' gloomy predictions for the Jewish people.

Even though American Jewry is in many ways successful and an exemplar of pluralism that we can only envy, it falls on Israel's shoulders to lead a Jewish renaissance. Only an Israel that is thriving economically, culturally, and spiritually will have the power to be a 'light unto the nations' that attracts not only aliya, but reverses the demographic hemorrhaging of the Jewish people. We should consider the possibility that Judaism's unique combination of religion, peoplehood, and way of life has something to offer those searching for a path to meaning in the modern world. There is nothing wrong with being a small people and proud of it, but we cannot afford the pride of being a vanishing breed.

◆ ◆ ◆

Judaism is a religion that reveres the golden mean. It tries to steer clear of hedonism and asceticism, between universalism and parochialism, and between messianism and improving the real world. Yet extremists are to religion what weeds are to a lawn: without constant attention to prevent it, they appear and grow by themselves.

Teach, Don't Burn
December 28, 2001

Our educational system is not having a good month. A few weeks ago, Teacher's Union head Avraham Ben-Shabbat was accused of purchasing a false academic degree. He denied the charge, but admitted to submitting essays he had not written and seemed to see nothing wrong with this. Now this newspaper has revealed that the principal of a Beit Shemesh school approved the public burning of a copy of the New Testament handed out by missionaries.

Eleven-year-old Ariel Lesnick, a witness to the event, told the *Post* that a teacher in the Orot School said, 'God sent it and gave us the privilege, and we'll be able to burn the New Testament.' A spokeswomen for Sha'alei Torah, the organization that administers the school, said the teacher had received permission for the book burning from the principal, Rabbi Yair Bachar.

Following criticism from parents, Bachar had second thoughts about his decision, and appointed Rabbi David Spector, the rabbi of the Givat Sharet neighborhood of Beit Shemesh, as rabbinic decision maker for the school. According to the spokeswoman for Sha'alei Torah, "Everybody knows we made a mistake. We wouldn't do it again and we don't think it's the right thing to do." But the subsequent ruling of Rabbi Spector is not nearly so unequivocal. Spector claims that, "It is appropriate to burn the New Testament in private." The official reactions generated by the Post story have been reassuringly strong, but no final decisions have yet been made.

Education Minister Limor Livnat issued a statement 'utterly condemning' the incident, summoned the teacher and principal to a disciplinary hearing, and temporarily suspended the two men. An official statement noted that the ministry "views with great severity the fact that educators were involved in the action." Deputy Foreign Minister Michael Melchior, a rabbi, called the act a "desecration of God's name." As a people that has suffered from seeing its own books burned, "the Jewish people cannot and will not accept the burnings of books holy to others," said Melchior.

Concluding that book burning should not be tolerated is, however, the easy part. As Spector's ruling indicates, there are rabbis and educators whose only problem with book burning seems to be how it might look, not with the principle of destroying books that are holy to billions of people.

In recent years, valid criticism has been leveled at new Israeli textbooks that seem to downplay and even distort Jewish history in a misguided nod toward 'multiculturalism.' In reality, neither extreme is warranted. Our schools should not be giving Judaism and Jewish history short shrift, but it is just as mistaken not to teach about the other great cultures and currents of the world.

The multiculturalists seem to think that bigotry and jingoism can be prevented by avoiding anything that might give students pride in their own culture. The parochialists act as if badmouthing or ignoring other cultures will help preserve our own. Both are wrong. We should aspire to an educational system that gives students a solid and unapologetic grounding in their own culture, and yet is not afraid to fairly survey the vast majority of the world that is different from our own.

It is therefore not enough to condemn and even to suspend the book burners of Beit Shemesh. Livnat is rightly incensed that a woefully inadequate treatment of Zionism has crept into some of our newer textbooks, and has yanked those textbooks pending revisions. A similar approach should be taken to rooting out the book-burning mindset, which will still exist even if an actual book burning never happens again.

The book-burning in Beit Shemesh should be taken as a warning signal and an opportunity to address the wider problem of excessive narrowmindedness in parts of our school system. There is nothing wrong with an honest appraisal of the roots of anti-Semitism that appear in the New Testament – an appraisal that some brave Christians are themselves carrying out. There is something wrong if our students have no clue what the New Testament or the Koran – let alone Eastern religions – have to say about the world. The desired approach should not be a novel one to educators: Teach, don't burn.

◆ ◆ ◆

The story of Israel's "development towns," some of which are in the Negev, is a sad one. It is the economically weakest of society who pay the highest price for misguided, quasi-socialist policies that are designed to help them. The plight of the Beduin is particularly acute, as they are caught between the loss of their own culture, educational deficit, and the imposition of well-meaning but often wrongheaded Israeli social engineering.

The Negev's Misguided Battle
January 1, 2002

The residents of the Negev leading the struggle on behalf of the frozen Negev Law sound like they will do what it takes to win this political battle. What they do not seem to realize is that the 'benefits' they are fighting for, far from developing the Negev, will perpetuate the record of failure that has characterized 'development towns.'

The Negev Law, which the government wants to freeze as part of proposed budget cuts, has three components: tax breaks, funds for local governments, and support for factories. This concoction has become the standard package for helping areas where the government, for whatever reason, wants to encourage settlement or aid the population. The problem is that none of these measures has the desired effect.

Tax breaks are a standard way for governments to help a certain sector or encourage some activity, and in some cases they make sense. But tax breaks and mortgage assistance linked to specific places are of little benefit to the people living there, and do little to encourage people to move to these places. The reason is that the effect of these 'benefits' is mainly to raise the price of real estate. If the 'benefit' were taken away, real estate prices would drop accordingly and the intended beneficiaries would be no worse off.

Throwing money at notoriously poorly run local authorities is even worse.

Local authorities are chronically short of cash, responsibility, and authority – all of which they must beg from the Interior and Finance ministries. Former interior minister Natan Sharansky was moving in the direction of giving these authorities more decision making power in exchange for holding them fiscally accountable. Until such reforms are enacted, funneling more money into these governments will have little impact on the people who live in distressed areas.

Lastly, there is the standard practice of trying to create jobs by paying businesses to build factories. This method has also been a colossal failure, because it encourages the building of uneconomic, capital-intensive factories that go belly-up the minute the grants run out. Few jobs are created as a result of this form of corporate welfare, and much suffering is caused by trapping people in factory jobs that are not sustainable.

So if the Negev Law is more of what has caused 'development towns' to be anything but, what is a better way to help the Negev? The first part of the answer has to concern those who have been ignored in this whole debate – the Beduin. Over one-third of Negev residents are Beduin, and they are by far the country's poorest and most distressed population. Though there is much talk of poverty, only in Beduin towns is it at truly third-world levels – including the lack of proper plumbing, electricity, and basic health and educational services. Beduin towns are considerably poorer than even other Arab communities.

The courts have ordered the Interior Ministry to somehow integrate the Beduin living in some 45 'unrecognized' villages into regional plans.

Local elected leaders, together with groups such as the Center for Jewish-Arab Economic Development, have been making some progress with plans for mixed urban-rural villages similar to the moshav model. This process should be accelerated to ease the Beduin onto a workable path to development, unlike the crash (and crass) social engineering that has failed in existing 'recognized' Beduin towns.

As to the rest of the Negev, a sensible way to help would be through infrastructure projects that encourage the development of Beersheba as a thriving urban hub that sustains the largely failed towns around it. There is no reason, as the population doubles over the next few decades, to think of Beersheba as a stray satellite of Tel Aviv. Beersheba can be its own urban center, like Jerusalem, Tel Aviv, and Haifa. Upgrading the regional transportation infrastructure can help make this happen.

It is a shame that the protesters trying to help the Negev are so passionately pursuing the continuation of failed policies. If they want to help themselves, they should not only be trying to scrap the Negev Law, but the edifice of misguided programs that have locked them in poverty rather than promoted development. The Negev does not need a further infusion of government resources, it needs to divert the billions of shekels wasted in existing budgets, programs, and subsidies into projects that make economic and national sense.

No one should be under the illusion that the almost 3 percent drop in per capita GDP last year is only a function of external events. The Negev Law is a classic example of business as usual policies that will prolong the current recession for the Negev and the nation.

◆ ◆ ◆

The story of Israel's Beduin population, who comprise about one-fifth of Israel's one million Arabs, is not all negative. Illiteracy among Beduin, for example, has been reduced from 95 percent to 25 percent, and almost all the illiterate are aged over 55. The Beduin do suffer from the culture shock of modernization, from extreme poverty, in Israeli terms, and from being a minority within a minority.

Though the IDF is making some effort to reverse the trend of reduced enlistment described here, not much progress has been made on this front.

Interesting Times: Unbenign Neglect
January 11, 2002

Israeli society has often been called tribal in nature, in that it is broken up into so many distinct groups that stick to themselves. Many of these 'tribes' are within the Jewish majority, so that Israel's true minorities often have trouble being heard over the din of bickering Jewish groups. Of all these minorities, the Beduin represent the most potent combination of societal significance and official neglect.

The Desert Patrol Battalion that lost four of its soldiers before dawn on Wednesday is composed mostly of Beduin, and three of the soldiers who fell were Beduin. The unit, established 15 years ago, operates in the Gaza Strip along the border with Egypt, and has seen some of the fiercest combat of the past year. Chief of General Staff Lt.-Gen. Shaul Mofaz recently awarded the unit a citation for its outstanding work in foiling terrorist attacks.

All Arabs who serve in the IDF, including the Beduin, are volunteers. As such, the Beduin in the IDF represent the exact opposite of the trend toward 'Palestinianization' that is normally associated with Israeli Arabs, particularly since the violent rioting in October 2000. Accordingly, one might think that the Beduin, who have a strong tradition of loyalty to the state, would be encouraged, showered with appreciation, and highlighted as an example to the rest of the Israeli Arab community.

Instead, the word that most often comes to mind with respect to Israeli treatment of the Beduin is neglect. Of all Israel's problems that have been allowed to fester in the shadow of the debate over peace and security, there is little to compare with the plight of thousands of Beduin who are living in villages without the most rudimentary services.

Jafar Farah, director of the Advocacy Center for Arab Citizens of Israel, notes that six of the seven poorest towns in Israel, including Rahat, Kuseifa, and Tel Sheva, are Beduin. "Half of the houses have no sewage, electricity, or running water," he told this newspaper recently. "There is 40 percent unemployment, and there are no factories to attract investments." Over one-third of the Beduin in the Negev live in "unrecognized" villages, meaning that the government officially and deliberately provides them with almost no basic infrastructure.

At the same time as Israel is largely neglecting the Beduin, the Islamic Movement within Israel is not. This group works hard, with both threats and financial incentives, to induce the Beduin not to serve in the IDF. Given these efforts, the rejection those who serve must often contend with in their own communities, and official indifference, it is a wonder that enlistment among Beduin has not dropped further than it already has.

According to Salame Abu Ghanem, the founder of the Organization of Negev Beduin Heroes, who serves as Beduin affairs adviser to Infrastructure Minister Avigdor Lieberman, in another year or two Beduin enlistment will drop to zero. "The youth see that the state doesn't help the veterans. They die for the Jewish state, for the Jews, and the Jews treat them like lepers," he said.

The IDF has reportedly started a new recruiting drive among the Beduin, and is considering a new program, modeled on that created for haredi soldiers, which would combine two years of army service with one year of study toward a high school diploma.

MK and former defense minister Moshe Arens (Likud), who heads the Knesset caucus attempting to help the Beduin, argues for a four-pronged approach to helping this community. First, the army must step up its recruitment efforts, which are not sufficiently institutionalized. Second, the police should institute a policy of not hiring Israeli Arabs who have not served in the IDF. Third, an extensive scholarship program for Beduin veterans should be instituted, along the lines of a program that has already begun at Ben-Gurion University. Last, the government should help Beduin veterans with their housing needs.

Arens points out that, if Israelis are worried about poverty, radicalization, and alienation among Israeli Arabs, the army can be a powerful antidote to all three. The IDF is the most powerful integrative force Israel has for all its communities, and has a similarly positive affect on the Beduin.

Few Israelis realize that about one quarter of all Israeli Arabs are Beduin, and that the Beduin have not just the highest birth rate in Israel, but among the highest in the world. The neglect that all Israeli governments have shown toward the Beduin borders on the criminal, and contradicts any religious or democratic notion of the proper values of a Jewish state. But if this government, like its predecessors, will not take action because it is right or out of loyalty, gratitude, or common sense, the least it should do is act to prevent a bad situation from becoming immeasurably worse.

◆ ◆ ◆

The most dramatic phenomenon in the 2003 Israeli election was the rise of Shinui, which became the third largest party by almost tripling in size, all based on a backlash against the rise of haredi (ultra-orthodox) parties. The fact that this took place while the war with the Palestinians still raged is testimony to the simmering power of the religious-secular divide in Israeli politics and society.

This column is about the Kinneret Compact, an effort to form a new social contract in the area of religion and society.

Interesting Times: Not Just A Bus
January 18, 2002

What really boils the blood of an extremist? Not those on the other side, but those ideological neighbors who break ranks, and who threaten the extremist's monopoly on virtue.

This is true in the religious sphere, in which right-wing Orthodoxy has much less of a problem with secular Jews, who offer no religious alternative, than with other Jewish streams – including liberal Orthodoxy – that challenge their interpretation of Judaism. The reverse is also true: It is more comfortable for secular Jews to contrast themselves with the opposite extreme than it is to consider the possibility that other forms of Jewish observance might have something to offer them in the modern world.

What really warms the heart of a moderate? Seeing the extremists on both sides hopping mad and the broad middle standing up for itself. For me, the recent release of the Kinneret Compact was a moment to bask in, that rare moment when good news is news, because it is so rare that it becomes a man-bites-dog story.

The Kinneret Compact was drafted by prominent Israelis from across the political, religious, and social spectrums (see www.rabincenter.org.il), and reads much like Israel's Declaration of Independence. Indeed, the declaration sent extremists on all sides spinning because it reaffirmed the concept of a Jewish and democratic state set out by Israel's founders.

What is striking, then, about the Kinneret Compact is not its differences with our founding document but its similarity. Israel may be unique in that, after more than 50 years, there is still considerable debate over the essence of the state. The reason is not just the fact that the Arab world still challenges our right to exist – if anything, this external challenge, as much as it has divided our society, has also provided a powerful incentive toward unity. The reason is that Israel's self-definition would be unique, inspiring, and problematic even if the Arab world didn't exist.

Most states just are; they don't need adjectives built into their beings.

Many states, like Israel, define themselves as democracies, but this is just a commitment to a generic type of government, not a statement that is unique to any particular state. Some states, such as Saudi Arabia, Iran, and the late Taliban regime, define themselves in religious terms. The experimental part of Israel from day one, that was happily if controversially reaffirmed by the group meeting by the Kinneret, is the attempt to mix together religion and democracy in the same ball of Play Doh.

To both the secular and religious extremes, combining religion and democracy is a form of blasphemy. To both, it is impossible for Israel to be more than a state with Jews in it. To most haredim, the state is significant as a place were Jewish study can flourish, but the only state rating the adjective "Jewish" would be a theocracy. The view of their secular counterparts was best summed up by author Amos Oz (a critic of the Kinneret effort), who once said that a state can't be Jewish any more than a bus can.

The authors of the Kinneret Compact, whose signatories are a who's who of Israel's mainstream and some brave souls from both the haredi and extreme-secular worlds, beg to disagree.

"There is no contradiction between Israel's character as a Jewish state and its character as a democracy," they say with refreshing clarity. The declaration notes with approval the myriad legal, cultural, educational and symbolic ways that the state's Jewish nature is expressed.

If there is anything that is disturbing about the Kinneret exercise, it is the amount of effort it took to more or less reaffirm the consensus as it stood more than 50 years ago. A Jewish state, as it was conceived by Theodore Herzl and David Ben-Gurion, was to be more than a refuge or a place where Jews live.

The question is whether a state must be something utilitarian – like a bus – or whether it can develop a meaning and sense of purpose of its own. The reaffirmation that Israel is a Jewish state recognizes the possibility of a state that stands for something, the way the United States stands for freedom. The next task, which we have barely begun, is figuring out what Israel stands for and what it could mean to be a "light unto the nations."

◆ ◆ ◆

For all my complaints about how Bush has not yet fully applied the lessons of 9/11 to the Middle East, and particularly the Arab-Israeli conflict, I shudder to think what might have happened if someone else had been president. Some argue that any president would have done the same. Not only do I doubt that Al Gore would have, I do not think that even Bush's father would have defined the war against terrorism, as Bush did in his "axis of evil" speech, to include any rogue regime that was developing weapons of mass destruction.

Bush the Bold
January 31, 2002

When historians sum up the first decade of the 21st century, US President George W. Bush may stand as one whose role in rescuing the free world is best compared with that of Winston Churchill, some six decades before. We take the victory against Nazism for granted now, but as historian John Lukacs points out (*Five Days in London*), in May 1940 the only man standing in the way of Hitler's subjugation of Europe was Churchill.

There is now no single threat to the free world like Adolph Hitler, but the diffusion of the current threat does not make it less deadly. One might think that on May 22, 1940, when 10 German Panzer divisions had invaded France, reached the English Channel, and had surrounded British, French, and Belgian forces, that there would be no doubt in Britain of the need to fight back. But even with such an obvious threat at Britain's doorstep, Churchill had to struggle within his war cabinet with those who wanted to ask Italian leader Benito Mussolini to broker a deal with Hitler.

The British example shows that the temptation of democracies to appease ruthless dictators exists even under the most dire circumstances. All the more so when it is difficult to put a name and a face to the threat, or when the threat is still more potential than actual in form. Even after September 11, another American leader might have been satisfied with pounding the caves of Afghanistan and pretending that the job was done.

Instead, Bush has from the beginning defined America's war aims broadly, and over time has not only stuck to ambitious goals, but broadened them further. In his speech from the Oval Office on September 11, Bush formulated a doctrine from which he has not wavered: "We will make no distinction between the terrorists who committed these acts and those who harbor them." At first, as the State Department pulled together a motley coalition that seemed to include Iran, Syria, and Yasser Arafat, this doctrine was called into question. But Bush quickly righted the policy with a speech to the United Nations that again placed every terrorist-sponsoring nation in America's sites.

Bush's State of the Union address Tuesday continues this trend. There is now an essential corollary to the Bush Doctrine: "The United States of America will not permit the world's most dangerous regimes to threaten us with the world's most destructive weapons." In other words, Bush has just brought the target list to a third level – not just terrorists or the regimes that harbor them, but any rogue regime seeking to arm itself with weapons of mass destruction.

Not satisfied with expanding the war aims, Bush hammered it home by naming names. North Korea, Iran, and Iraq form an "axis of evil," that is "arming to threaten the peace of the world," he proclaimed. Addressing directly those who think America can rest on its Afghan laurels, Bush warned, "We can't stop short. If we stopped now, leaving terror camps intact and terror states unchecked, our sense of security would be false and temporary."

Bush clearly realizes that America's challenge is no less than to create the new world order than many seemed to assume would follow the Cold War, but did not. Instead, the world order that emerged since the 1991 Gulf War has been one of gradually strengthening radical forces, and increasingly cowed and impotent Western powers. No one believed that the West's feckless efforts at 'nonproliferation' would do more than delay the inevitable: rogue regimes with nuclear weapons.

Speaking of the "axis of evil," Bush declared, "By seeking weapons of mass destruction, these regimes pose a grave and growing danger. They could attack our allies or attempt to blackmail the United States. The price of indifference would be catastrophic." Bush could have said that the price of indifference *was* catastrophic, and further apathy would be much worse.

Bush's landmark speech to the Congress finally laid down a marker: The US will not let the nightmare scenario continue to unfold. Now some of those who for years dismissed the possibility of America taking effective action against rogue regimes will oppose the extended Bush Doctrine as dangerous, imperialist, impossible, or all of the above. But it is not Bush who is being overambitious. On the contrary; it is our pre-September 11 world that was characterized by reckless complacency as the threats to the West grew and grew. Bush is being bold, bolder then the world and certainly America's enemies expected, but not bolder than necessary.

The rise of antisemitism in Europe in conjunction with the Palestinian offensive against Israel that began in October 2000 shows that when anti-Israel radicalism is on the rise anywhere it will increase everywhere. Antisemitism and the war against terrorism are intimately linked; success in the latter will produce a marked drop in the former.

Incidently, following Dennis Prager ("Why the Jews?: The Reason for Antisemitism"), I favor the form 'antisemitism' over 'anti-Semitism,' so as not to play into the idea that 'Semites' are the object of the hatred in question. We are speaking of Jew hatred; euphemisms should not be allowed to disguise this hatred for what it is.

Stop Whitewashing Antisemitism
February 28, 2002

For some time now, the country and the world have gotten used to the idea there often is no such thing as the position of the government of Israel. Whose position, observers must ask, Prime Minister Ariel Sharon's or Foreign Minister Shimon Peres's? One might think this split voice would at least come together in the battle against antisemitism. One would be wrong.

Last week, Sharon decried the dangerous wave of antisemitism confronting French Jewry. The French government, illustrating part of the problem, responded by attacking the messenger. "Repulsive and despicable," huffed Foreign Minister Hubert Vedrine. On Tuesday, President Jacques Chirac said he was "shocked and hurt" by Sharon's remarks, and insisted "there was no upsurge in anti-Semitism in France," and France remains "very vigilant – and extremely severe in punishing any manifestations, whatever they may be."

As a feat of denial, these official French remarks are amazing, but nothing in comparison with our own foreign minister, speaking in Paris. "I am certain that France is not anti-Semitic, neither historically nor currently," Peres told reporters after meeting Chirac. Not satisfied with this, he continued, "I am convinced the French leadership is staging a serious and determined battle against antisemitism in France."

Peres's wholesale whitewashing of French history is mind-boggling, to say the least. Theodore Herzl, whose own epiphany concerning the depth of antisemitism against even the most assimilated Jews occurred at the trial of Capt. Alfred Dreyfuss, must be turning in his grave. Even Chirac, who to his credit was one of the first to confront the memory of Vichy-Nazi collaboration in the slaughter of French Jewry, would have to disagree with Peres's blanket exoneration of French history.

Perhaps Peres's comment was colored by the pivotal role France played in providing arms in the first, fragile years of the state and his own experience with French assistance to Israel's nuclear reactor program. But even in this respect, the French record is checkered: The Iraqi nuclear reactor Israel destroyed in the prescient and daring operation in 1981 was also built with intense French involvement.

Even after that experience and the Gulf War, Saddam Hussein has for years counted on France to ally itself with China and Russia against the US and Britain in the UN Security Council, an alliance that succeeded in stripping Iraq of effective UN inspections. Today as well, the constant French quest for an "independent" foreign policy seems to be consistently at Israel's expense – whether opposing President George W. Bush's fingering of the "axis of evil" or launching its own plan to save Yasser Arafat from international isolation.

Regarding the wave of antisemitic attacks within France, it is appalling Peres would sing the praises of the French government while

French Jewry is crying out for help. To Roger Cukierman, president of the Representative Council of the Jewish Organizations of France, government denial of antisemitism is the main problem.

As Cukierman wrote in *Le Monde* (February 1), "The leaders of the country like to play down anti-Jewish acts. They prefer to see these as ordinary violence. We are deluged with statistics designed to show that an attack against a synagogue is an act of violence and not anti-Semitism." According to a report released in January by the Paris office of the Simon Wiesenthal Center, antisemitic attacks in France have gone up about tenfold since October 2000 (see www.wiesenthal.com).

French literature professor Eric Marty summed up the situation in *Le Monde* (January 16), "Every Jewish building in Paris requires protection, every Jewish festival is an occasion for concern and anguish, anyone walking in Paris or its suburbs wearing a kippa is imprudent and any child leaving school may be beaten because he is Jewish, only because he is a Jew."

France, home to the third largest Jewish community in the Diaspora, suffers from the highest level of anti-Jewish violence of any Western nation. Rather than defending the abysmal attempts of the French government to sweep the problem under the carpet, Peres should have urged the French government to do what any civilized society must: condemn, root-out, and punish those who are terrorizing Jews.

◆ ◆ ◆

This was written around Jerusalem Day, the day the city was unified in 1967. I still sometimes pinch myself that I live in Jerusalem. Much of the time it may be a hassle, or humdrum, but it is also a privilege. As much as I often enjoy leaving it, it is hard to imagine living anywhere else.

Interesting Times: Jerusalem of Charisma
May 10, 2002

To leave Jerusalem is to relax – so why is it I don't want to live anywhere else?

Nobody seemed more torn over and yet in love with Jerusalem than its modern poet, Yehuda Amichai. "Jerusalem is a merry-go-round,"

Amichai wrote, "spinning and spinning from the Old City to all the neighborhoods and back to the Old City. And you can't get off it." What is it that is so captivating about Jerusalem?

Tranquility is not exactly our strong suit here. Our city center is infamous for its concentration of horrific bombing attacks. The city has gamely dotted this same area with colorful lions – made of durable concrete and whimsically transformed by dozens of artists (see http://lions.jerusalem.muni.il/).

The lions are a good example of how Jerusalem sometimes tries to be a normal, even hip, city. If Chicago, Toronto, and New York can have cows, then Jerusalem can have its stately mascot, the lion. As in a normal city, this sort of street art is beloved by children, enjoyed by residents, and beaten up over time by vandals.

On Wednesday night, we could hear explosions going off somewhere outside our apartment in Talpiot. Hearing such noises, the mind quickly works through a process of elimination: no sirens (probably not an attack), not to the south (probably not the IDF retaliating for shooting at Gilo), tonight Jerusalem Day begins (probably fireworks!). Sure enough, a glance out the window confirms that colorful blasts are bursting over the city center.

But even in more tranquil times, it is difficult to reconcile Jerusalem's normal face with what makes the city weirdly irresistible. We have traffic jams, drunks, beggars, dirt, concerts, pubs, movies, and even street life - just like other cities. Yet – security aside – the classic Tel Avivian picture of Jerusalem is a very unmelted pot of haredim, secular Jews, and Arabs at constant loggerheads.

I have to admit there is not much mixing among Jerusalem's different worlds. But what outsiders – and even many Jerusalemites – tend to miss is the eternal side of the city.

In his book, *Israel: An Echo of Eternity*, Abraham Joshua Heschel devotes an entire chapter to Jerusalem. "Jerusalem is not the first among cities," he writes, "She is the first among visions.... Jerusalem, the charismatic city, is like a hassidic master, whose sheer presence is a bestowal, whose heart and mind are never disengaged from God." Part of me wants to say that Heschel must never have sat in a traffic jam, or tried to do anything at the Interior Ministry. But charisma is the right word; and all the more apt given the usual tribulations of city life. Charisma is something beyond looks, eloquence, or a sense of humor – it is a mysterious attractive force that can sometimes compensate for the lack of all three.

So what is charismatic about Jerusalem, particularly to someone who is not imbued with the intense religious yearning that drove Heschel? I wish I felt the hand of God in Jerusalem, like Heschel did. I guess I'm not built that way. But I do feel the charisma and I think I know why.

I come from Washington, DC – another town with certain backwater qualities that thinks of itself as center of the universe. The famous Saul Steinberg *New Yorker* cover depicting the world ending at the East River also fit Washington to a tee. Washingtonians divide the world between 'inside the Beltway' and beyond – those poor souls who do not control the reigns of government.

Yet Jerusalem sometimes makes Washington look positively modest. There is actually a stone in the floor of the Church of the Holy Sepulcher that claims to mark the exact center of the world. Washington may act sometimes as if people from all over the world face it in prayer, but this is not boasting in Jerusalem's case. No other city in the world is holy to three major religions.

Jerusalem is not just central, it is deep. "Jerusalem is a see-saw;" writes Amichai, "sometimes I dip down into past generations and sometimes I rise skyward and then yell like a child yelling, his legs swinging way up." As a student, I worked on a dig in Jerusalem on a hill overlooking the Old City, surrounded by normal city streets. At that dig, a tiny scroll was found wound up in a silver amulet, and on it was written a prayer in Hebrew – the same prayer we bless our children with every week. The scroll, now in the Israel Museum, predated the Dead Sea Scrolls by centuries, making it the oldest piece of the Bible ever found. Now that's charisma.

◆ ◆ ◆

I do not permit myself to write about my brother Alex, who fell in battle as an Israeli soldier in Lebanon in 1987, but on the 15th anniversary of his death I did. When I write or speak about Alex, my job is simply to encourage people to read his book, which tells his story far more eloquently than I can.

For excerpts from the book and more about Alex, please visit www.alexsinger.org.

Interesting Times: Reading Alex's Life
August 30, 2002

I just reread a book of writings that were never meant to be public, let alone published as a book. Yet, despite its serendipitous origins, the book probably has more power to affect the reader's life than most self-help texts.

Today I will go to Har Herzl and visit my brother's grave, 15 years after he fell in battle on his 25th birthday, at Har Dov in Lebanon. It is his book, *Alex: Building a Life* (Gefen), that I read, and that has helped me and many others these long years.

Alex's book is a collection of his letters, diaries and drawings, compiled by his family in the days after his death. The reason for its impact is not the ultimate sacrifice that Alex made, though one must admit that the ending is part of what draws people to the story. The reason is that it is an unfiltered, unplanned, unself-conscious window into a way of living life.

For all his angst over being indecisive, what distinguished Alex was the short distance between decision and action. He decided, having returned to Cornell from a trip to the Soviet Union in the early '80s, that synagogues should organize weekly letter writing campaigns to Soviet Jews. So he launched one himself.

He decided to make aliya after graduating and to join the IDF, so he showed up at the draft board within days of moving here. He decided he should visit an Arab country before moving here, so he backpacked around Jordan, alone. But what struck me most was not so much these big decisions, but how this pattern permeated his life at the micro level.

Alex wouldn't think about writing letters, he would just write them from an airplane he was about to jump out of in paratroop training; on a few minutes' break in a grueling hike, while all his colleagues were collapsing with exhaustion; while guarding (when he wasn't supposed to). No window of time was too small to fill with a letter or a drawing.

Reading Alex's letters makes one realize how self-absorbed we all are. Here he was, a "lone soldier" in basic training with "kids" (as he rightly called them) four years his junior, struggling with physical challenges, tormented at times by whether he had made the right choice. Yet he would write to each of us about our lives and problems as if he had not a care in the world.

As a writer and editor, I am particularly impressed by how cleanly he expressed himself in a pre-computer era, with simply a pen and paper. Alex wrote like he drew: fast, naturally, and with a sparing use of lines.

This is a powerful combination not just because anyone reading the book feels like they have lost someone they just got to know, but because it is hard not to take lessons for your own life.

The other striking thing about Alex's thoughts from 15 years ago is how much has happened since then, and yet how we have essentially returned to the starker version of the Arab-Israeli conflict that existed in his day. Alex lived in a world without the Internet, before the first intifada, during the final throes of the Cold War; and, of course, before the Oslo Accords, Camp David, the current war and September 11.

And yet a letter to a friend from Cornell shows the same fundamental dilemma we have today: how to fight a war for survival under the scrutiny of the world and our own values.

As Alex explained, "You see, the officer must think, and do his thinking with a sense of justice far less abstract than that of the law professor or the civil judge... The young men I'm with are learning to think and make decisions harder than any in the civilian world, and they are not abstract or far away."

Alex continued, "We will win the next war, as we've won every war until now, and Israel will not be pushed into the sea."

"But I don't want to lecture anymore about Zionism and decision making. I'd rather tell you about walking through a wadi in the middle of the night with a million stars over my head, and singing as I walk because I'm so content and so enjoying myself, and climbing mountains and looking over the desert, and seeing eagles and a huge waddling porcupine, and the goodness of the rest which always comes after a night of trekking with so much weight on my shoulders... I'm feeling wonderful and very much at peace with my decision to stay on."

I still miss you, Alex.

For more about Alex and his book, see www.alexsinger.org.

This is about an incident in which settlers forcibly resisted attempts by Israeli police to evacuate an illegal outpost called Gilad Farm. Most Israeli towns in the disputed territories were created with the approval of Israeli

governments, including governments led by the Labor party. The outposts were set up illegally, that is, without any governmental approval.

What disturbed me is that those who defend the settlement enterprise as a whole, as I tend to do, were making excuses for ruffians using force against police sent to evacuate them. This editorial refutes those excuses one by one.

Enforce the Law
October 21, 2002

On Saturday night, 12 policemen were injured, and on Sunday eight more, while trying to evacuate a small group of settlers from the illegal outpost Gilad Farm in Samaria. The violence these settlers have used against the security forces is unacceptable, and the multiple excuses proffered for it do not hold water.

Excuse #1: Ben-Eliezer lied. Settler leaders and MKs, such as Shaul Yahalom (National Religious Party) and Gidon Ezra (Likud), claim that Defense Minister Binyamin Ben-Eliezer made a secret deal to provide for the peaceful evacuation of Gilad Farm. The reported deal was that if the residents left of their own accord and did not return to sleep at night, they would be allowed to farm the land during the day, and existing structures would not be removed.

If Ben-Eliezer reneged on a deal, than it is not surprising that the result was the opposite of the purpose of the deal, which was to evacuate the site peacefully. But such duplicity, if it occurred, does not justify violence against security forces that are doing their job and implementing a decision made by defense minister and prime minister.

Excuse #2: It is just some young hotheads. It is true that some 1,000 people who came to Gilad Farm to show solidarity left peacefully of their own accord, leaving a much smaller group of "youth of the hilltops." But such youths are either old enough to be held responsible, or young enough that others must take responsibility for them. Youth does not justify violence.

Excuse #3: What about all the illegal Palestinian building? It is impossible to deny that the law is being implemented selectively. The decision to bar all Jewish access – and the press – from the Temple Mount is a clear violation of a number of basic laws. Our neglect there is also a violation of the Antiquities Law, in which we do not accord the greatest piece of our archeological heritage the care that is lavished on much less ancient sites.

But, while much illegal Palestinian building is ignored, what is not is bulldozed – a rare occurrence on the Jewish side. Even if the law is being unevenly implemented, that is an argument for more enforcement on the Palestinian side – not for ignoring the law on both sides.

Excuse #4: The land was bought, fair and square. The family of Gilad Zar, who was murdered in a terrorist attack and is the namesake of the farm in question, has title to the land it is farming. But owning the land and permission to create a new settlement are two different things. This government, as part of its founding guidelines, committed to not allowing any new settlements. Citizens have the right to oppose this decision and seek its reversal, but not to take the law into their own hands.

Excuse #5: The evacuation desecrated the Shabbat. The evacuation attempt did take place just after Shabbat, which meant that many soldiers and police were kept on duty during Shabbat in order to prepare for the operation. Ben-Eliezer and Prime Minister Ariel Sharon both admit that this was a mistake.

They claim that procedures will be clarified in the future, so as to prevent a recurrence. But again, how does such a mistake justify violence against security forces?

Excuse #6: It's all politics. There is a widespread claim that the only reason these outposts are being evacuated now is to help Ben-Eliezer with his standing in the Labor primaries. The law, in other words, is being manipulated for crass political purposes. The same, however, can be said about the failure to dismantle illegal outposts as quickly as they pop up.

Why is political influence in favor of settlements kosher, while political winds in the other direction are not? Again, this is an argument for implementing the law more quickly and fairly, not for allowing the law to be ignored completely.

Those who attempt to justify the fracas at Gilad Farm make a lot of valid points about a lot of things, but they do not come close to justifying the unjustifiable: violence against security forces who are implementing the law and who risk their lives daily in the fight against terrorism.

Some defenders of the holdouts at Gilad Farm would have us believe, as Mohandas Ghandi once said, "An unjust law is itself a species of violence. Arrest for its breach is more so." Laws can be unjust, and they

THE OTHER ISRAEL

can certainly be unwise. But the way to oppose them is to protest and, if necessary, to be arrested. Let the "youthful hotheads" practice their hands at civil disobedience, and let the police and the IDF do their jobs.

◆ ◆ ◆

The debate over the war in Iraq exposed the immorality of pacifism in the face of extreme evil. It also showed that the extreme left cares more about opposing the United States than it does about the plight of oppressed peoples. The same hypocrisy tends to extend to left-wing attitudes to the Arab-Israeli conflict, as Oriana Fallaci has eloquently pointed out.

Dore Gold, who wrote a best-selling book about Saudi Arabia, "Hatred's Kingdom," told me he was surprised when the Conservative Book Club chose his book as a selection. It is strange that being against the Saudi regime is now considered conservative while defending such regimes against the US is considered liberal.

Interesting Times: The End of Human Rights
November 22, 2002

On the cover of the November 11 issue of *The New Republic*, a generally sensible journal, is the question "Is America's war on terrorism undermining global human rights?"

The question is a teaser for an article by Peter Maass called "Dirty war: How America's friends really fight terrorism." The article, which details the messy ways in which countries like Pakistan 'fight terrorism,' makes the fair point that the human-rights abuses of US allies can backfire. There definitely is a danger of the US getting too close to rotten, unpopular governments who use the war against terror to prop themselves up.

The most egregious example of this syndrome not only predates September 11 but contributed to that attack. The hijackers were not Iranians, Iraqis, or Afghans, but Saudis and Egyptians – two of the Arab countries most closely associated with the US. Remarkably, just after 9/11, Secretary of State Colin Powell continued to see no problem: "Egypt, as all of us know, is really ahead of us [on fighting terrorism]... We have much to learn from them and there is much we can do together."

271

Actually, the Saudi-Egyptian model for 'fighting terror' is to crush internal opponents while allowing the same militant Islamists to vent their hatred of the US and Israel. Clearly this model is not a particularly successful one for Western interests.

But what is striking about the critique by Maass and by human-rights organizations is the strange inversion of the cause of human rights it represents.

Throughout the Cold War, the cause of human rights became identified with opposition to a certain brand of Third World dictators: Nicaragua's Anastasio Somoza, Iran's Shah Reza Pahlavi, the Philippines' Ferdinand Marcos, Chile's Augusto Pinochet, and the apartheid regime in South Africa.

At his inauguration in 1977, US president Jimmy Carter said: "Our commitment to human rights must be absolute... Peoples more numerous and more politically aware are craving and now demanding their place in the sun – not just for the benefit of their own physical condition, but for basic human rights."

Human rights, in other words, meant sympathy for opponents (including insurgencies) of nasty little dictators, some of whom happened to be friends of America. Throughout this period communist dictatorships, such as the Soviet Union itself, North Korea, Cuba, and others did not seem to raise the same passion in the human-rights community.

Let us say that, back then, it was understandable, if not excusable, that the human rights movement allowed itself to be steered into opposing pro-American dictators with much greater venom than the anti-American variety. Let us say that it was necessary to maintain a sort of neutrality in the Cold War, even though that too was a struggle between the freedom that America stood for and the Soviet empire of dictatorships.

Now that the Cold War is over, one might think the human rights community could finally call a spade a spade and go after the world's worst regimes without worrying about which side they were on. One might also think that anyone who cares about human rights would go hoarse cheering the possible removal of a particularly brutal leader such as Saddam Hussein.

Yet this is what Human Rights Watch (HRW) has to say about the pending war in Iraq: "[We] do not make judgments about the decision whether to go to war... We avoid judgments on the legality of war itself because they tend to compromise the *neutrality* needed to monitor most effectively how the war is waged – that is, compliance with international humanitarian law" [emphasis added].

This is a bit like a fire chief saying he is neutral about pyromaniacs. But HRW is not even the fire chief, because unlike the International Red Cross, HRW does not need to enter war zones to do its job, and therefore has no need to maintain strict neutrality in order to stay in the good graces of dictators. HRW's job is not to be neutral, yet it acts as if it is a fire critic trying to be neutral between pyromaniacs and the fire brigade.

What this amounts to is a bastardization of the very concept of human rights. If championing human rights is not about rooting for the fall of tyrants, then what is it?

It would be one thing if the human rights community were saying to the US, "We're for you, just remember, the ends don't justify improper means." But HRW is not just concerned about excesses committed in a good cause, but about American motives.

"Although in making a case for war George Bush has referred to the Iraqi government's severe repression," the statement continues, "this is clearly a subsidiary argument to his call to address Iraq's alleged possession of weapons of mass destruction and to force 'regime change.' There can be little doubt that if Saddam Hussein were overthrown and any weapons of mass destruction reliably surrendered, there would be no war, even if the successor government were just as repressive."

In other words, don't expect HRW to support a war that does not have primarily humanitarian motives. But why should the average oppressed Iraqi care about Bush's motives? Why should a human rights group care more about Bush's motives than about what will promote human rights? Why, for that matter, should people who claim to care about human rights, many of whom seemed very disturbed by US unilateralism, be more concerned about what the French say than what is good for the Iraqi people?

The struggle for human rights must primarily be one for freedom and democracy. Human-rights groups who do not join that struggle might as well be fighting fires with a water pistol. They should cheer, not complain, when the fire brigade finally shows up.

◆ ◆ ◆

The murderer later confessed and said that he had killed his baby daughter to "win a war" he was waging against his ex-wife. Even a society that, to a large degree, had become numbed to terrorism was torn apart by this crime.

Hodaya
December 13, 2002

The murder of 22-month-old Hodaya Kedem-Pimstein by her father may be destined to be remembered as our crime of the century, like the kidnapping and murder of the baby of Charles Lindbergh in the US in 1932. This crime was even more unspeakable, the murder of a baby by her own father.

At a time when it seems there is no lower depth to sink below than the crimes that are being committed against us, we have managed to inflict one even lower still.

The ability of a parent to murder his or her own child is unfathomable. It runs contrary to the deepest bond in nature. It is also the ultimate violation of the core element of society and civilization, the unit that is expected to fight to the death to protect its members, the family.

For most of a week, we have been transfixed by the fate of a baby, just old enough to start becoming conscious about her world, yet young enough to retain the pure trust in the two people she loved most in that world.

But we as a society have been through so much, weren't we supposed to have become numbed to tragedy? Have not the hundreds of lives lost to terrorism and on our roads just become a blur of statistics?

Our obsession with Hodaya's fate may indicate that we are not as numb as we thought.

During the days that she was missing, thousands of volunteers pored into the Jerusalem neighborhood where Hodaya's father lived to help with the search. Some may take this outpouring of public sentiment for granted, but they should not.

As fate would have it, five-year-old Nur Abu Tir went missing at almost the same time as Hodaya, not far away, in Umm Tuba in southeast Jerusalem. The police exerted similar extraordinary efforts to find her, but she has still not been found.

Her family is crying out about the lack of Palestinian interest in the case. The three major Palestinian dailies published short items about Nur based on wire service reports, and refused the family's request to publish a picture.

"It's a disgrace," Muhammad Abu Tir, a relative of the missing girl told this newspaper's Khaled Abu Toameh. "We haven't seen one Palestinian journalist here. On the other hand, some Israeli journalists spent hours in the village. I'm sure that if Nur was the daughter of Yasser Arafat or any other senior Palestinian Authority official, the situation would be different."

But has the Israeli press over-covered the Hodaya story? On one day, for example, the first 13 pages of Yediot Aharonot were devoted to this one story, during a very busy political week.

The irony is that it may have taken a case of ultimate inhumanity to bring out a human side of us that sometimes seems to have been extinguished: the ability of society to take a single human tragedy so personally.

At times like this we see how an entire society can be joined in shock, as if it were one family. It happens during wars, such as the Yom Kippur War. It happened when 73 soldiers died in a helicopter crash near She'ar Yashuv in 1997. It happened when Yitzhak Rabin was assassinated.

Each time it happens, we ask ourselves why we cannot retain the same bonds, the same ability to care, in better times.

The answer is that we cannot care about every tragedy equally, because life would then be unlivable. But a society that is incapable of letting down its collective guard to feel for a single child would also not be a healthy one.

Hodaya lost her life, but she also gave us something: the reassurance that once this war is over, and we have stopped steeling ourselves, that maybe we can regain our ability to be horrified by the loss of a single human life.

For a brief moment, she made us more human. May she rest in peace.

◆ ◆ ◆

This was written as Senator Joseph Lieberman was announcing his candidacy for president in the 2004 elections. I have few illusions that he will ever take the advice I suggest here, but I still think it is correct. Prime Minister Tony Blair's courageous performance leading up to the war in Iraq has since

*demonstrated the power of a liberal who will resist the worst instincts of his own
party and stand on principal.*

Interesting Times: Lieberman Should Battle the Lemmings
December 27, 2002

I wish Joe Lieberman would be himself. So does he. Rumor has it that
he was not happy with having had to veer left once he joined Al Gore's
ticket in the 2000 campaign. Democratic-style class and race warfare did
not befit him, and he knew it.

Joe Lieberman came to the US Senate the same year that my former
boss, Sen. Connie Mack of Florida, did. Just after the 1988 election, the
US opened an official 'dialogue' with the PLO in response to Yasser
Arafat's carefully-scripted pledge to renounce terrorism.

In one of the first of many bipartisan alliances Lieberman formed
over the years, he joined Mack in introducing a bill embodying widespread Congressional skepticism toward Arafat's promise, called the
'PLO Commitments Compliance Act.' Since the proposal, which became law, was known as the Mack-Lieberman bill, Lieberman would joke
that in some circles people thought his first name was Mack.

Lieberman seems to share my problem with Democrats: the policies
they advocate are often at odds with the values they claim to promote.
The discomfort of so many Democrats with President George W. Bush's
plan to liberate Iraq, for example, makes a mockery of that party's
commitment to human rights.

A Lieberman candidacy, then, will be a bracing one for the Demo-
cratic party, one that could revive the long-dormant legacy of Henry
'Scoop' Jackson. The Jackson-Vanik Amendment linking trade with the
Soviet Union to freedom to emigrate was a proud moment both for the
Democratic party and for America.

The first post-September 11 presidential election would seem to be
an ideal time to recreate a Jackson wing of the party, but whether
Lieberman succeeds depends on where the Democrats are in the lemming cycle.

The lemming cycle, for want of a better name, is the tendency of left-
wing parties to choose unelectable left-wing candidates when they are
not hungry enough for power. After 12 long years of wandering the

political wilderness courtesy of Ronald Reagan and George Bush the father, the Democrats were ready to nominate a relative centrist like Bill Clinton.

The theory among Democrats is that they did poorly in 2002 because they were not true to themselves, as if being more anti-tax cut and anti-war would have helped. This suggests they are itching to shed eight years of Clinton-Gore discipline and follow their hearts leftward.

So like lemmings – and like the Labor party here – they will nominate someone who will be trounced in the general election, as Walter Mondale (1984) and Michael Dukakis (1988) were.

Lieberman may be the only Democrat who can compete with Bush on the 'moral clarity' playing field, and not just because of his passionate support for regime change in Iraq. He has gone against the Democratic grain on some social and economic issues as well.

His being Jewish, far from being a liability, is one of his greatest assets, since it allows him to be overtly religious without being right-wing. Americans are very religious people, or at least like it when their politicians are, in the correct measure.

But if the Democrats are in lemming mode, it will not matter that Lieberman is their most viable candidate. Trying to out-pander his party rivals certainly will not help. If he tries to be just another Democrat, he will not only not get the nomination, but will also harm his chances of building something within the party for the future.

This is also true regarding Lieberman's stance toward the Middle East, which will be particularly closely watched. On this week's swing through Israel and the Gulf states, Lieberman did not stake out any new policy territory.

At some point, however, Lieberman will have to make a fundamental choice: Does he continue to take the standard Democratic line of pressing Bush to be 'more engaged in pursuing peace,' or does he come at Bush from a completely different direction?

In his conduct of the war on terror, Bush had brilliantly coaxed the battle into the enemy's home turf, slowly cutting through the proxies to confront the terror masters themselves. There is, however, a major hole in the moral clarity Bush has shown, which he only partially closed with his June 24 demand for Palestinian democracy.

Though Bush has applied a lite-version of his regime change doctrine to Yasser Arafat, he has not taken the step that moral clarity demands: treating the Arab-Israeli conflict as a branch of the Islamist war against the West.

Bush still plays along with the Arab idea that the fight with Israel is about justice for the Palestinians, not a fight against what in Arab eyes is simply an American proxy. The effect is to create a dichotomy: On the one hand, there are terrorists who fight America and are an unmitigated evil, and on the other, there are terrorists who use unacceptable means but have a valid cause.

Bush may be Mr. Clear, but Lieberman could be even clearer. He could say that Palestinian terrorists do not want a state next to Israel – they want one instead of Israel. He could say the enmity behind the suicide attacks of September 11 has the same ideological source and ultimate goal as the enmity behind suicide bombings in Israel.

The Arab-Israeli conflict is simply a microcosm of the Islamist-Western conflict. Peace in both cases depends not on deals, terms, and negotiations, but on Western determination to win. And the hope for any brave Muslim moderates who believe in living with Israel or America lies not in America or Israel restraining themselves, but in fighting their common enemies more effectively.

But how can a Jewish candidate for president, of all people, say these things? He can say it because accusing an American of being too pro-Israel in this global war is like accusing him of being too pro-British or too pro-free-French in WWII. Lieberman can't win on this issue by pretending he is not pro-Israel; he can by embracing the truth: The most pro-American, pro-peace, and pro-freedom thing to do is to unequivocally support Israel.

◆ ◆ ◆

A friend, who is also a rabbi and a passionate Jewish educator, told me that this piece, which is still among the most important to me that I have ever written, should not be included in this book. He said so because he thought it was so wildly divorced from reality that it would embarrass me.

Perhaps this is an impossible vision. From where we stand, it certainly seems impossible, like Theodore Herzl's vision of Jewish state. It is hard for me to believe, however, that it is only my vision. It is a vision in search of a Herzl to make it come true.

Interesting Times: What Good are Jews?
January 3, 2003

In an editorial last week, the *Wall Street Journal* noted that, "contrary to perceived wisdom, Christianity is booming." At around 2 billion adherents, Christianity is not only the largest world religion, but growing by leaps and bounds.

In Africa, for example, there were 10 million Christians in 1900. Today that number has jumped to 360 million, which is almost half the population of the continent. In Latin America and Asia, Christianity is also growing rapidly. Writing in the *Atlantic Monthly*, Philip Jenkins, author of *The Next Christendom*, claims that "it is Christianity that will leave the deepest mark on the twenty-first century." As Jews, we tend to pretend that we do not have a horse in this race. In numbers terms, the Jewish people clocks between Sikhism (19 million) and Bahaiism (6 million). We are the progenitors of monotheism, and therefore of Christianity and Islam, so what does it matter that we are tiny?

We even revel in the notion that we are tiny and indestructible, and subconsciously connect the two attributes. We have trained ourselves to believe that to be small is a good, perhaps elevated condition.

Let's stop kidding ourselves. It is one thing to make a virtue out of necessity, another out of decline. We are not only tiny, but outside of Israel, we are a shrinking people.

A decade ago, the National Jewish Population Survey shocked American Jewry by revealing that intermarriage rates had reached 52 percent. The latest NJPS has not yet been fully released, but it is not expected to show a substantial improvement in this figure.

In a nice attempt at spin, a UJC press release called the American Jewish population 'fairly stable,' based on a drop from 5.5 million to 5.2 million over the last decade. But the US population as a whole grew by 11 percent during this same period.

Does it matter that we are moving from tiny to tinier? Yes, if it means we are abandoning precisely what makes many of us proud to be Jews.

Divorced from seeking a real influence on the world, the concepts of being a 'light unto the nations,' a 'chosen people,' and of tikun olam (mending the world) become elitist conceits that border on racism. Rather than being embarrassed by these notions, as many Jews are, we should be trying to live up them.

In historic terms, we could argue our job is done. Jewish monotheism and values are the basis of Western civilization, which is increasingly dominant on earth. We can take pride in the success of Christianity, which is mainly growing among the billions of people who still aspire to modernity and belong to none of the world's major organized religions. We sparked the transformation of a ruthless, pagan, and backward world into one in which freedom and prosperity still have far to go, but have made tremendous strides and are ascendant.

But is that it? At the very moment that we have, after two millennia, regained our sovereignty and the fundamentals of our moral code – one God, one ethic – are taken for granted, do we have nothing to offer, nothing to say?

At the risk of sounding like Osama bin Laden and his dreams of past Islamic glory, I would point out that Jews once numbered 10 percent of the population of the Roman empire – the modern world of that time. If the modern world today numbers 2 billion people, perhaps it is too ambitious to aim for 200 million Jews. But why shouldn't we aspire to a population of 50 or 100 million, particularly at a time when the modern world is itself growing rapidly?

Obviously, it is impossible to make such gains through natural growth alone. Luckily, the current negative attitude many Jews have toward proselytizing – almost a dirty word – is an historic aberration.

According to Lawrence J. Epstein, author of a history of Jewish attitudes toward conversion (see www.convert.org), it was Judaism that invented missionizing. "Christianity used the Jewish missionary zeal and methods," Epstein writes, "ultimately transforming the Jewish concept of conversion from an ideal into a requirement and transforming the means of effecting conversion from offering into intrusive missionary work."

Strong rabbinical support for conversion continued well beyond the loss of Jewish sovereignty, but it has also extended into modern times. The founders of the Reform movement in America took Jewish universalism for granted. As Leo Baeck wrote in his famous book, *The Essence of Judaism*, "the Jewish religion is intended to become the religion of the whole world...Every presupposition and every aim of Judaism is directed towards the conversion of the world to itself."

Either we have something to offer the world or we don't. If not, we might as well dwindle into nothingness. But if so, we should be looking beyond shifting Jews around, from the Diaspora to Israel, and sifting among the small pools of people with lost ties to Judaism from bygone ages (though those with Jewish roots should surely be welcome as well).

The question is whether Judaism can, for one out of 10 people, be the religion that best fulfills the needs of the modern world. Islam is far behind, in that it first has to stop being at war with modernity. Christianity is doing well, and this may well be the 'Christian century.' But the relative Christian emphasis on faith, rather than reason and ethics, is not for everyone.

The vacuum that exists between Jewish secularism and fundamentalism in Israel is very disturbing in this respect. Judaism may well not succeed in thawing out Jewish law and practice and return it to the living, evolving, adaptable organism it once was. The centuries of being turned inward may have shriveled our halachic muscles beyond the point of rejuvenation. But if we fail to even try, we should not delude ourselves into thinking that our population is "fairly stable" or our future as a people is fairly secure.

Some people die from bee stings. What happens to these people is that their immune system overreacts, lowering blood pressure to prevent the venom from circulating, but also causing the body to go into shock. When stung by national defeat and exile, the Jewish people went into survival mode, setting aside a revolutionary tradition that changed the world. But the tragedy is not just that the instincts that kept us alive could be our ruin, but that we are missing the moment of our greatest opportunity.

◆ ◆ ◆

I must admit to some simplification here. I did not mean to suggest that all tax cuts or any sort of economic growth will automatically lead to greater equity. My point is one that applies throughout the West, but particularly in Israel, where people who care most about reducing poverty often care least about fostering economic growth, and that this disconnect is harmful to their cause.

In a way, it's similar to the problem of pacifists and peace: the people who care most about peace sometimes contribute most to the necessity of war, or to encouraging the aggression of others.

Interesting Times: More Envy Than Compassion
January 17, 2003

Let's say the world is divided between people who care about poverty and those who don't. Wouldn't it be a shame if most of the people who cared about poverty advocated policies that increase it?

This, unfortunately, is not an imaginary situation, particularly in Israel. Think 'social lobby' and what comes to mind is people fighting budget cuts, privatization, and anything that smacks of free-market reform.

What drives me nuts about this is the waste of precious human caring. While almost everyone cares in theory about the poor, few devote their energies to doing something to help them. Those who work hard to collect and distribute charity are doing God's work and there is no question they are helping. But what about those fighting on the macro level for policy change?

A new Israeli magazine, for example, which is generally an oasis of creative thinking in the largely parched local realm of opinion journals, devoted most of an issue to criticizing privatization. In her introduction to the issue, *Eretz Aheret* editor Bambi Sheleg writes that the pro-privatization consensus is a result of the collapse of "the centralized economy that existed from the nation's founding, in an effort to maximize equality in society." While admitting the "deep sicknesses' that led to socialism's failure both here and internationally, she mourns the "entrenched feeling that the social solidarity that characterized the state's founding is not needed."

Sheleg represents a strong strain of thinking that responds to free-market philosophy by saying, "We are not America." It is the ethos of America versus the socialist ethos, which is seen as, perhaps, flawed but morally superior.

The problem with this thinking is that it ignores evidence that economic freedom and the growth it produces are the best way to help the poor and even to reduce inequality.

There is an overwhelming connection between economic freedom and prosperity. Israel is in the 'mostly free' category in a recent study, and could clearly benefit from joining the 'free' column.

The critics tend to admit that free markets produce growth, but argue that the price comes in terms of inequality and social disintegration. But this is not necessarily true either. A 1992 book by economist Gerald Scully found that "the share of national income going to the middle classes is 30 to 50 percent higher in most-free nations compared to least-free nations."

It is certainly intuitive that inequality is rampant in corrupt despotisms. It is also true, as *New York Times* economist Paul Krugman noted, that the mansions of the "Gilded Age" that he remembers visiting as a youth, which had "belonged to a bygone social era," were replaced by an America dominated by the middle class. But does growth really ameliorate inequality in already developed nations?

In Israel's case, the answers are yes, no, and why care? Yes, because the greatest source of inequality here is not capitalism but our socialist legacy. It is this legacy that has concentrated much of the economy in the hands of government and a small group of interlocking families and companies that have access to government.

What Israel really has now is islands of capitalism in a socialist sea. Those islands – the hi-tech sector – were the engine of the economy, but most people had little access to it. The rest of the economy remained mired in high taxes and lack of credit, and dependent on government connections and largess.

Krugman complains that America has returned to a new Gilded Age, in which the super-rich have left the middle class way behind. If so, Israel is doubly unequal, because we have both the old, connected rich and the nouveau riche of the New Economy.

But this brings us to 'why care?' The question remains: what matters more, battling inequality or helping the poor?

The idea that wealth 'trickles down' is much derided, but it is undeniable that the poor in richer countries are much richer than the majority in poor countries. The worst kind of poverty is unemployment, and growth is the only engine that can create jobs. The next worst kind of poverty is that of the working poor, who have little opportunity for entrepreneurship and for whom advancement means joining the 60 percent tax bracket.

Jewish and Western ethics demand that a society be measured by the prospects of its weakest members. In that case, the social lobby should be at the forefront of freeing up our economy.

Economics is not a zero-sum game. If redistributionist schemes kill growth, they hurt the poor. If growth can be made more equitable, that is a worthy goal, but not at the expense of growth itself. Those who claim to care about the poor while having no interest in what produces growth are doing more harm than good, and evidencing more envy than compassion.

◆ ◆ ◆

The greatest thing about Yehuda Amichai is that his poetry could be appreciated even by people who normally find poetry inaccessible. Nor was it necessary to be an Israeli or know anything about Israel to connect with his art. His poetry was somehow both universally human and quintessentially Israeli.

Yehuda Amichai
September 25, 2000

The missing of poet Yehuda Amichai began with his funeral yesterday, at which we needed him to express what we have lost. We needed Amichai, because he would have been able to, in a quirky line or two, convey what it means to lose someone who has so unpretentiously shaped and reflected the national character.

The poet Natan Zach tells how Amichai's first and most famous book of poetry was born. At age 24, after serving in the Palmach during the War of Independence, Amichai showed Zach a collection of poems written in a plain notebook of the sort children use for mathematics classes, with grid squares on the pages. Zach decided to publish them as a book, and chose the title *Now and in Other Days*. The book, with its fresh, colloquial use of language, created a new school of modern Israeli poetry. But no one matched Amichai's own ability to combine the modern and the ancient, the lofty and the mundane, and the Jewish, Israeli, and universal.

Amichai was Israel's national poet, but not in the sense of a Walt Whitman, who exuded American patriotism, or the poets who have been catalysts for nationalist passions within the Arab world. He was national in that his intensely personal expressions of pain, loss, protest, love, and beauty somehow spoke for a people that often suppressed such emotions in a flurry of nation-building.

In another country, his poetry might have been called 'anti-war.' In Israel, however, Amichai was simply able to put into words the pain that most stoically endured. He wrote of the site of a famous battle, "Yad Mordechai. Those who fell here still look out the windows like sick children who are not allowed outside to play." A poem titled 'Memorial Day' describes "A man whose son died in the war walks in the street like a woman with a dead embryo in her womb."

Just as he was able to bring matters of war and peace to a more human level, his poems were shot through with irreverent Biblical imagery. According to Amichai, "The real hero of the Isaac story was the ram/ who didn't know about the conspiracy between the others/As if he had volunteered to die instead of Isaac./ I want to sing a song in his memory/ about his curly wool and his human eyes/...." Rather than be bound by the uniquely Israeli gulf between religious and secular, Amichai would mix the two incessantly, as they were mixed in his own background and temperament.

Yet what made Amichai so widely beloved was probably less his ability to so personally express national pain, or infuse secularism with religious imagery, but the vibrant normality that exuded from his poems.

Amichai wrote of his mother that she was "like an old windmill/ Two hands always raised to scream to the sky,/And two descending to make sandwiches." He wrote about tourists, schoolchildren, mayors, and the streets of Jerusalem – the city he loved and could not abide.

Zach rejected the description of Amichai as a "national" poet, saying he would be more aptly identified with Jerusalem, his home. Here, too, Amichai was able to look at the city not just as a capital or focal point for three world religions, but as a hometown. In a 1997 interview, Amichai said, "Every year I say I'm going to leave Jerusalem. The problem is not only between Arabs and Jews, but Arabs and Arabs and Jews and Jews. There is so much infighting. I love rivers and lakes, and Jerusalem has none of them."

Yet in this same interview he reminded us why so much of his poetry is about his home city: "The most wonderful thing about Jerusalem is that I always find little corners that I don't know. It is the biggest small city in the world." Yesterday, Amichai's coffin lay in the square of Jerusalem's City Hall, as the prime minister and other notables eulogized him. The presence of hundreds of Israelis from all walks of life said more than the official speeches.

Walt Whitman once wrote that, "The proof of a poet is that his country absorbs him as affectionately as he has absorbed it." Though he did not live long enough to receive a well-deserved Nobel Prize for

Literature, Amichai passed Whitman's test with flying colors. If we are lucky, his poetry will help define what it means to be Israeli for generations to come.

◆ ◆ ◆

One of the interesting cultural contrasts for an American who moves to Israel is the radically different approaches to the separation of church and state. As different as each country is in this respect, the case can be made that separation works for America, while it is very important that Israel remain a consciously Jewish state. That said, Israel has much to learn from the religious pluralism that America enjoys, which has actually contributed to making the United States a more religious country.

Interesting Times: Who's Afraid of the Ten Commandments?
July 4, 2003

Alabama Supreme Court Justice Roy Moore is probably about as close as you can get to a Shas-style politician in America. He campaigned for his job as the 'Ten Commandments Judge.' And indeed, when he took office he erected a two-and-a-half ton stone rendering of the Ten Commandments in the rotunda of his courthouse.

On Tuesday, a federal appeals court (11th Circuit, Atlanta) found that the monument violated the Constitution's First Amendment prohibition of the establishment of religion. In April, the US Supreme Court took the same position, striking down a resolution passed by the Kentucky legislature that would have allowed a large plaque of the Ten Commandments to be displayed in front of the state capitol.

Decalogue fans, however, need not lose heart. Last week another federal court (3rd Circuit, Philadelphia) decided that a plaque of the Ten Commandments hung on the facade of the Chester County Courthouse for the past 83 years need not be removed.

"We cannot ignore the inherently religious message of the Ten Commandments," Judge Edward R. Becker explained. "However, we do not believe... that there can never be a secular purpose for posting the

Ten Commandments, or that they are so overwhelmingly religious in nature that they will always be seen only as an endorsement of religion."

It was a bit of a stretch for Judge Becker to pretend that the Ten Commandments can be taken out of a religious context. But this just shows how ridiculous things have become; the only way to save the Ten Commandments is under the rubric of 'historic preservation' and by downplaying their religious nature.

Yet the spirit of Becker's decision seems eminently correct. In the American context, most would agree that neither extreme makes sense – banning all mention of religion or overtly associating the state with a particular religion. The question is how to reach a proper balance. From an Israeli perspective, what is striking is the intensity of American religiosity. The spate of court cases reflects how very common the symbol of the Ten Commandments is in American life, and how strong the popular impulse is to celebrate and honor the core values these commandments represent.

Israel, by contrast, is an overtly Jewish state. Here separating 'church' and state is as much an anathema as mixing them is to Americans. Yet it is inconceivable that a modern Israeli courthouse would prominently display the Ten Commandments, or any sign of religious influence.

It is true that in some areas, such as marital affairs, Israel does largely follow Jewish law. But in general, supposedly secular America is more religious than Israel, despite our decided lack of separation of synagogue and state.

It is perhaps not surprising, given the separation in the US and its lack here, that religion is banging on the door of American officialdom to get in, while here the clamor tends to be more about keeping religion out.

This contrast, however, should be instructive to anyone who cares about a healthy relationship between religion and society.

Separation of church and state does not necessarily make society more religious. Europe shows that this separation does not automatically produce a society as religious as America, which turns out to be more the exception than the rule.

It is clear, though, that the association of religion with politics, and the use of the law in some areas to "enforce" religion, has produced a hyper-secular majority.

In America, Jews are often at the forefront of those seeking to purge religious symbolism, such as the Ten Commandments. When I lived there and had a right to be, I was embarrassed by this. There could hardly be a more inclusive form of religiosity for Jews than pride in the Ten Commandments, which emphasizes Christianity's Jewish roots. How could modern day Jews explain to Moses that those tablets were threatening to Jews, of all people?

In the end, though, American Jews tend to have a healthier attitude toward religion than their secular Israeli counterparts. American Jewry is threatened by assimilation. But American Jewish pluralism keeps the boundaries between religious and secular open and blurred, while Israeli secularism has almost become a religion of its own. In our tribalized society, it is difficult to dabble across religious boundaries without threatening one's societal identity.

American Jews have more to learn than to fear from their Christian neighbors. From a survival perspective, pride works better than paranoia. As a community, American Jewry is more threatened by assimilation into a secular sea than by a Christian religiosity that is sometimes more respectful of what Judaism has to offer than Jews themselves.

In Israel, it is the supposed guardians of religion who need to examine whether their success at blocking religious pluralism and maintaining influence on law and government has made our society more Jewish or less.

On both sides of the Atlantic, we should remember that striking the right balance among religion, society, and government is not a luxury any more.

Before September 11, we were under the illusion that Judeo-Christian civilization had no competition. It does, and the strength of our response depends in part on navigating between the shoals of excessive clericalism or secularism, each of which can weaken us.

We need the moral convictions that come from religious values, and we need the unity and dynamism that, ironically, only a pluralistic society can produce. Based on Israel's experience of political assertions of religion in the public square, monuments to the Ten Commandments may well backfire. The goal, however, of reminding increasingly secular societies of the roots of the values they hold dear is a worthy one, which secular zealots ought to pay more attention to, rather than reflexively resist.

Chronology

❧

December 1988

At the very end of the Reagan Administration, outgoing Secretary of State George Shultz opens a "dialogue" with the PLO, thereby ending the legal ban on contacts in place for 13 years. The ban was lifted because Yasser Arafat accepted Israel's right to exist, UN Security Council resolutions 242 and 338, and renounced terrorism. This dialogue was cut off two years later, after the PLO attempted a terrorist attack on a Tel Aviv beach.

August 2, 1990

Iraq invades and occupies Kuwait. Yasser Arafat's support for Saddam Hussein leads Persian Gulf states to cut off funds to the PLO. Hundreds of thousands of Palestinians are forced out of the Gulf states.

March 1991

President George H. W. Bush says that Gulf War victory opens a "window of opportunity" for resolution of Arab-Israeli conflict. Secretary of State Baker travels to Middle East on first of eight peace missions.

October 31, 1991

Madrid Conference. Palestinians, in a joint delegation with Jordan, attend talks between Jordan, Syria, Israel, and Lebanon. Multilateral negotiations begin on arms control, security, water, refugees, the environment and economic development. The Arab states eventually back out of the multilateral talks, despite efforts by the US and Israel to revive them.

September 9-10, 1993

After months of secret negotiations in Oslo, Norway, Yasser Arafat and Yitzhak Rabin exchange letters of mutual recognition of Israel and the PLO. Arafat's letter states, "The PLO commits itself to the Middle East peace process, and to a peaceful resolution of the conflict between the two sides and declares that all outstanding issues relating to permanent status will be resolved through negotiations."

September 13, 1993

Oslo Accords. President Bill Clinton, Israeli Prime Minister Yitzhak Rabin, and PLO, Chairman Yasser Arafat meet and watch Israeli Foreign Minister Shimon Peres and PLO official Mahmoud Abbas sign the agreement on the White House lawn.

October 26, 1994

The Treaty of Peace between Israel and Jordan is signed at the White House.

November 4, 1995

Israeli Prime Minister Yitzhak Rabin is assassinated following a peace rally in Tel Aviv by an Israeli university student, Yigal Amir. Shimon Peres becomes prime minister.

February-March 1996

Four suicide bombings in Jerusalem, Tel Aviv, and Ashkelon kill 67 Israelis over seven days.

May 31, 1996

Likud Party leader Benjamin Netanyahu becomes prime minister of Israel, defeating Labor's Shimon Peres in early elections called after the assassination of Yitzhak Rabin.

September 1996
Government opens a new exit to an ancient Hasmonean tunnel running alongside the Temple Mount in Jerusalem. Palestinians riot and Palestinian police open fire, killing 15 Israeli soldiers. 61 Palestinians are killed in fighting with Israeli forces.

January 17, 1997
Hebron Accord (Wye Agreement) is signed between Israel and the PLO. According to the "Note for the Record" prepared by the U.S., Palestinians commit to "combat systematically and effectively terrorist organizations and infrastructure [and to] confiscation of illegal firearms."

February 7, 1999
Jordan's King Hussein dies of cancer.

May 17, 1999
Labor Party leader and former IDF Chief of Staff Ehud Barak defeats Netanyahu in elections. During the campaign, Barak promised to withdraw Israeli forces from the security zone in southern Lebanon within one year.

January 3, 2000
Barak and Syrian Foreign Minister Al-Shara meet in Shepherdstown, West Virginia for a week of talks. In March, President Clinton meets with Syrian President Hafez Assad in Geneva, but fails to close Israeli-Syrian peace deal. In June, Assad dies of a heart attack and his 34-year-old son, Bashar, takes over.

May 24, 2000
Barak keeps promise to withdraw from Lebanon, but Palestinians take the lesson that Israel will withdraw unilaterally from territory rather than accept relatively small numbers of military, let alone civilian, casualties.

July 11-25, 2000
Barak, Clinton, and Arafat meet at Camp David in attempt to reach comprehensive Israeli-Palestinian peace agreement that would establish

a Palestinian state. Barak surprises Clinton with major concessions on Jerusalem and borders. American negotiators later report that Clinton told Arafat, "If the Israelis can make compromises and you can't, I should go home. You have been here fourteen days and said no to everything."

August-September 2000

Monitors of Palestinian media report that "Palestinian Authority (PA) television broadcasting of violence and hate has reached unprecedented levels this summer and has created an atmosphere of the eve of outbreak of war.... [The broadcasts include] Israeli soldiers depicted as rapists and murderers, calls for eternal war against the Jews, military marches, denial of Israel's right to exist, and education of Palestinian children to see all of Israel as stolen." In December, a Palestinian minister told journalists that the PA began to prepare for the use of violence immediately after the failure of the Camp David summit.

September 28, 2000

Opposition leader Ariel Sharon visits the Temple Mount, just before the Rosh Hashana holiday. Sharon is heavily guarded and the visit itself passes quietly. The next day and over the following weeks, deadly rioting breaks out among Palestinians and Israeli Arabs.

October 17, 2000

Summit in Sharm el-Sheikh, Egypt, with Clinton, Barak, and Arafat to bring an end to the fighting. Appointment of international committee to investigate the sources of the conflict, chaired by Senator George Mitchell.

December 23, 2000

Clinton verbally conveys to Israeli and Palestinian delegations what became known as the "Clinton Parameters" – an outline of the remaining differences between the parties and how they might be bridged. The parameters were presented as a take-it-or-leave-it proposal that would expire when Clinton left office just a few weeks later.

December 28, 2000

Israel reports to the Mitchell Committee that over the past three months there have been "around 9,000 attacks by Palestinians against

Israelis – civilians, police and military – virtually all life threatening. Of these, some 2,700 involved the use of automatic weapons, rifles, hand guns, grenades, explosives of other kinds. Some 500 Israelis have been injured in these attacks and 39 killed. Around 292 Palestinians have been killed and around 9,000 injured."

January 2001

Terror attacks continue. Barak calls elections and is expected to lose. Negotiations continue between the left-wing remnants of Barak's government and the Palestinians at the Egyptian resort at Taba. The talks are inconclusive.

February 6, 2001

Likud leader Ariel Sharon wins election by a landslide.

April 30, 2001

Mitchell Committee issues its report calling for an immediate and unconditional cease-fire, a renunciation of terrorism, and a resumption of peace talks, as well as a freeze on construction of Jewish settlements in the West Bank and Gaza.

September 11, 2001

Four aircraft are hijacked by 19 terrorists bearing Saudi and Egyptian passports: two planes ram into and destroy the World Trade Center towers, one crashes into the Pentagon, the last crashes in Pennsylvania when the hijackers are overwhelmed by passengers. About 3000 died, including more than 200 who were not US citizens from over 50 countries.

October 7, 2001

Joint American-British operations begin in Afghanistan against al-Qaida and the Taliban regime, following large protests in Egypt, Pakistan, and Gaza.

January 3, 2002

Israel seizes the Karine-A smuggling ship en route from Iran to the Palestinian Authority carrying tons of weapons and explosives.

January 29, 2002

President George Bush makes his "axis of evil" speech to Congress, proclaiming that the US "will not permit the world's most dangerous regimes to threaten us with the world's most destructive weapons."

March 27, 2002

"Passover Massacre" – a suicide bomber blows himself up in the middle of a Passover seder in the Park Hotel in Netanya, killing 30. Two days later Israel launches Operation Defensive Shield, in which the IDF enters the heart of all seven Palestinian towns in the West Bank to kill and capture terrorists. A week later President Bush declares "enough is enough" and sends Colin Powell to the region, but the IDF operation continues for a few more weeks. Following the operation, terror attacks are greatly reduced for months. Palestinians claim Israel committed a massacre in Jenin, but a UN report later found that about 50 Palestinians were killed there, most of them armed, while Israel lost 23 soldiers in the fighting.

June 24, 2002

President Bush calls on "the Palestinian people to elect new leaders, leaders not compromised by terror. I call upon them to build a practicing democracy, based on tolerance and liberty."

January 28, 2003

Sharon wins reelection, the first prime minister to do so in decades. He easily beats Labor party nominee Amram Mitzna, who pressed for opening talks with Arafat despite ongoing terrorist attacks. Likud goes up to 40 Knesset seats, Labor down to 19.

March 19, 2003

War in Iraq begins with attempt to kill Saddam Hussein. Baghdad falls on April 9, later declared by Iraq's provisional Governing Council to be a national holiday.

April 29, 2003

Palestinian cabinet approves Arafat choice of Mahmoud Abbas (Abu Mazen) as prime minister, US releases text of "road map" days later. Road map begins with mutual Israeli-Palestinian declarations at Aqaba summit with President Bush on June 6, 2003.

About the Author

SAUL SINGER is a columnist for and the Editorial Page Editor of the *Jerusalem Post*. Before moving to Israel in 1994, he served for ten years as a foreign policy specialist on staffs of the United States Congress, including those of the House Foreign Affairs Committee, Senate Banking Committee, and Senator Connie Mack. In addition to the *Jerusalem Post*, his writings have appeared in the *Wall Street Journal*, *Middle East Quarterly*, *New Leader*, and *Moment*. He lives in Jerusalem with his wife and three daughters.